ACADEMIC LICENSE:
The War on
Academic Freedom

ACADEMIC LICENSE:
The War on Academic Freedom

edited by Les Csorba, III.

UCA Books

EVANSTON   MIAMI   NEW YORK

ACADEMIC LICENSE: The War on Academic Freedom
Copyright © 1988 by Accuracy in Academia, Inc.

Published by
UCA Books, 1620 Central Street, Evanston, IL 60201

Distributed to the trade by
Kampmann & Company, Inc., New York, NY

Manufactured in the United States of America

Text design by Promac Solutions, Inc., Miami, FL

Jacket design by
Jacques Auger Design Associates, Coral Gables, FL

ISBN 0-937047-11-2

Dedicated to the indomitable pioneers and faithful alumni of *The Dartmouth Review* who have dared to do mighty things and win great triumphs, rather than live in the gray twilight that knows neither victory nor defeat.

ACKNOWLEDGEMENTS

This collection could not have been possible without the direction and support of the staff of Accuracy in Media and Accuracy in Academia, most notably Cliff Kincaid, Reed Irvine, Deborah Lambert, Brian Fitzpatrick, Donald Irvine and Sung Kang. I would also like to acknowledge the encouragement and support of Ambassador Shelby Cullom Davis, whose serious concern for the impact of higher learning on the vitality of the American republic is equal to his commitment to those striving to end the crisis of the closing of the American mind. I am grateful to *The San Diego Union, The Washington Times, Crisis, Commentary* and the Heritage Features Syndicate for allowing the inclusion of certain valuable columns and essays which appeared first in their publications. I am especially grateful to the twenty-four contributors who worked so hard to meet deadlines and who generously committed an enormous amount of time reworking and rewriting drafts. I have enjoyed the experience. And finally, I would like to acknowledge the virtuous patience of my bride Anne who, shortly after pledging "I do, for better (and for worse)," had to endure my frequent absences while I prepared the finishing touches on the book.

Contents

PART THREE:
THE ASSAULT ON ACADEMIC FREEDOM AND FREE SPEECH

FOREWORD

THIS BOOK COULD not be more timely. Only yesterday, as I write this, Professor Julius Lester, a black, has been purged by the Black Studies faculty of the University of Massachusetts in Amherst. Professor Lester, who is very well respected and has published numerous books and articles, and who has received several awards for teaching excellence — he is said to be a rivetting classroom lecturer — has also had a mercurial spiritual and intellectual career. He first came to general attention as a fiery black-power orator during the turbulent 1960s. He has been interested in Eastern religion and is a convert to Catholicism. Today he is a convert to Judaism. I have followed his career from a distance, and judge these various shifts not to be a sign of frivolousness but of seriousness. He goes where his serious thinking leads him.

Professor Lester's problem with the Black Studies faculty was that, while himself black, he had the temerity to criticize James Baldwin, who had castigated a black newspaper reporter for revealing Jesse Jackson's 1984 "Hymietown" remark. Baldwin said the black reporter should not have tattled on Jackson, another black. Professor Lester said that the reporter was right to report on Jackson. The purge vote of the Black Studies faculty against Professor Lester was unanimous, but not binding. The university took a hands-off position.

Professor Lester is all right. He has shifted to the Judaic Studies Department. But the Black Studies faculty is not all right; and neither, so far in this incident, is the University of Massachusetts.

Again, even as I write, Stanford University has been escalating its long-standing war against the Hoover Institution, which a liberal faculty and administration regards as too conservative and independent. One of the finest research institutions in the country, Hoover stands in peril of losing its cherished independence for ideological reasons. The dust is far from settled on this one.

The same Stanford has been much in the news for abolishing its course in some of the great books of Western civilization and replacing it with a new course in which "race" and "gender" will affect the choice of books to be read. It is surely an intellectual abomination that such factors as skin complexion and reproductive equipment should, at least in part, determine the literary and philosophical material assigned in a required course.

Among our leading universities, Harvard, interestingly, is notable for having held out against this sort of thing, more or less, while so many others have caved in. Several leading institutions have gone so far as to establish quotas for hiring minority — this usually means black, sometimes hispanic — faculty members. But as a friendly academic economist remarked despairingly to me recently, "There just are hardly any blacks taking Ph.D.s in economics these days." He went on to say that he might be able to find some African black Ph.D.s at the London School of Economics, but that these would not "count" in the quota.

The widespread academic behavior, for which all of this can stand as a synechdoche, is of course thuggish and institutionally self-destructive. A much more complicated attack upon civilized values, however, is going forward under the aegis of "literary theory." In the various modes of literary theory, Marxists, feminists and other champions of the allegedly oppressed read works of literature from the particular point of view being applied. I have Marxist readings of Shakespeare's *The Tempest* as a work about "imperialism," or as a work about male oppression of females. Poor Miranda. Poor *Tempest*.

At the same time, extreme epistemological skeptics of various kinds are busily denying that we can really know what "great" literature really is. What they have in mind is a retirement plan for Homer and Dante, and the substitution of something or other.

At bottom what all this amounts to is a concentrated assault on literature itself as a transmitter of the great and extended conversation that lies at the heart of Western culture. In other words, the not so hidden agenda of the assault consists of a will to undermine Western culture itself — and substitute an entirely new culture with a new set of assumptions. These assumptions are usually as utopian as they are destructive. Coercion is beginning to be used on many campuses in an attempt to impose them.

The timeliness of Mr. Csorba's collection thus is shown by the fact that its themes are re-illustrated almost daily in our newspapers and news magazines, a fact which may explain the extraordinary readership gained by Allan Bloom's *Closing of the American Mind*. The educated American is worried, and rightly so, about what is transpiring in our colleges and universities.

There seems little doubt that at the top of a civilized agenda stand twin tasks that have almost nothing to do with the federal government. We must somehow reclaim 1) our colleges and universities, and 2) our mainline churches — reclaim them for civilization and even sanity. Both sorts of institutions have been occupied, quietly, by people who have no interest at all in transmitting the essence of their academic and religious traditions. Far from it. Regarding those essences as oppressive, they are actively hostile to them and mean to destroy them.

Such recovery will be a slow process, inch by inch and block by block. If it shows significant signs of success by the year 2000, we should count ourselves fortunate. But the job must be done because, in Yeats' famous phrase, our civilization is half dead at the top. The present book, *Academic License*, represents a fine step in the right direction.

Professor Jeffrey Hart
Hanover, New Hampshire

INTRODUCTION

IT WAS JANUARY 1986 at a quaint, delightful college outside Detroit, Michigan. Heavily clothed students were hurrying to classes and I was running late for a noontime speaking engagement to answer whether academic freedom is threatened on college campuses by "right-wing McCarthyites."

As I approached the head table where two university representatives sat preparing to grill me, students and faculty members swiftly moved away, causing me some embarrassment. It was like the Biblical account of the parting of the Red Sea, I thought. I hurried along trying to appear unshaken. I sat down and listened to the pointed questions, innuendoes and harsh denunciations. "Campus Spies" and "Thought Police" were the loudest cries I heard from audience participants.

I was invited to Oakland University because I had taken issue with a professor who had reportedly told her students in class that the 3,000 or so Cubans in Nicaragua are part of the "Cuban Peace Corps." Two of her students told me that the professor, who taught a introductory Latin American course, claimed that the Cubans in Nicaragua are "predominately part of medical teams and teachers." The story and her teachings obviously stirred my interest.

Take for example an examination in her class. One of her questions read:

Nicaragua suspended civil rights in October of 1985 because of:

a: a "personal" whim of the dictator, Jose Napoleon Duarte.

b: the "brutal" aggression by North America and its allies.

c: the attempt of the Communist Party to overthrow the government.

d: the fear of a rightist coup that would overthrow President Mejia Victores.

The only answer that could conceivably have been correct, we pointed out, was "b". But, is "b" itself correct? We do know that answer "b" is the reason given by the Sandinista regime, but as I pointed out to the professor, even *The New York Times* wrote, "there is no reason to swallow President Ortega's claim that the crackdown is the fault of 'the brutal aggression by North America and its internal allies.' A more likely explanation is an eruption of discontent over a crumbling economy and military conscription."

So I listened patiently to the professor in a private meeting with her before I entered what my campus host dubbed the "Lion's Den." She passionately argued that the criticism she received from Accuracy in Academia was much like the torturous treatment intellectuals received in Brazil years ago where she once studied. And this was precisely the tone at the gathering of students and professors where I spoke. I was an academic torturer. And AIA was responsible for heinous human rights violations.

During the forum, I tried to respond to the slanderous and misguided charges leveled with a measured, calm and scholarly approach. Unlike my intoxicated critics, I tried to be sober in my treatment of the subject of academic irresponsibility. I suggested that instead of reading and believing unbalanced and inaccurate newsclips and editorials, critics should focus in on the organization's publications and its publicly stated purposes.

How could students who are regularly enrolled and duly registered for their classes be "spies", I asked softly, but rhetorically. And how can an organization which had only one staffmember at the time and no enforcement powers, be described as "thought police?" Fair questions, I figured. But the hysterics continued to fly. I tried to conclude the forum by pointing out that teaching is "oral publication" and academics should not be immune from criticism of their teachings, just as they are not immune from the criticism they receive of their books and articles.

It was over and I was relieved. A group of scruffy-looking radicals ran up to me, their verbal assaults unrelentless. "This is the first thing the Nazis did to dissidents," I heard. Some of our newspapers, *Campus Report*, were destroyed, and so, I thought it was time to leave.

It should be noted that prior to my visit, the local campus paper, *The Oakland Sail*, and certain professors had universally condemned me and the organization I served. Professors had a sign-up table in the student union where they could sign a petition "turning their names into AIA." Funny stuff. But the day following the forum, the same campus paper that vilified me had this to say about the event.

...Thursday's panel discussion of academic freedom turned into a rhetorical dart game, with Les Csorba of Accuracy in Academia the target. The target won in this scholarly game, however, and successfully deflected the verbal missiles thrown at him.

Of course, his task wasn't that difficult. Both faculty and congressmembers were worked up for an eight syllable word for "hate."

Disguised under lofty phrasing and deca-syllable words, their message boiled down to: We don't like AIA...

Unfortunately, they have forgotten how to speak like real people. Trapped in bureaucracy, the university representatives spoke like a reel of red tape, traveling in wordy circles and getting nowhere. Their message was lost in their haste to impress everyone with how many big words they know.

And in the middle of their so-called 'brief statement', which sounded like a lead-in to 'War and Peace, Part Two,' the audience fell asleep, tired of waiting for the gist of these ramblings and sick of having to sift through unnecessary garbage to get to it.

Csorba, whether you like the 22-year-old man or not, handled himself with poise, confidence and brevity most of the OU reps lacked. He was direct, to the point, and best of all, he was refreshingly succinct...a faculty word for brief. What was amazing about Csorba was that he could even begin to respond after a faculty member finished reciting. Most audience members were either asleep or whispering. 'Hey, out of 4,684 words he said 3,987 had more than 20 letters.'

If we had to decide whether or not to allow AIA an office on campus based on that "discussion", AIA would be moving in today.

And that's really sad. This panel discussion was an excellent chance for the university population to express exactly why AIA is so offensive, but they became so caught up in showing their outrage that they failed to use reason and facts to back up their statements.

Instead, we ended up with a rambling muddle of emotional statements that led to nowhere: These statements could have been very powerful if only they had been backed up with solid research and facts, but they were not...

Rehashing such a laudatory editorial may seem self-serving, but its point is compelling since it came from a publication ideologically and publicly opposed to Accuracy in Academia. It re-invigorated me and encouraged the organization to press on. You could say it was a turning point.

The message I shared at this forum is a message that is becoming more universally accepted in an academy frequently battered with heavy criticism. The university is in exile, as neoconservative philosopher Irving Kristol coined it. The academy lives in a time warp. Never before in the history of the United States, wrote Kristol, "have universities so militantly divorced themselves from the sentiments and opinions of the overwhelming majority of the people." The student radicals of the sixties and early seventies, who made a name for themselves by igniting American flags in flames and burning down ROTC buildings on campus, became the teaching assistants and professors in the seventies. In the eighties, they have become increasingly fortified by tenure. Some occupy key positions as deans or administrators or department chairman or chairpersons. They are firmly entrenched. They control academia with intense determination.

The obvious result has been an assault on what we've traditionally called a "liberal education." The classical or "great" books of Western Civilization which teach virtue, order, and civility, and which lie as the political foundation of our constitutional republic, have been attacked by academic disciples fostering new trendy quasi-academic disciplines, such as "Peace Studies", "Women's Studies," "Black Studies" and so on. Caldicott, Sagan, Dewey, Keynes, Galbraith are frequently required authors on reading lists while Shakespeare, Aristotle, Adam Smith, Max Weber, James Madison, Cicero and the Bible receive modern day intellectual punishment. They had the unfortunate appearance of being white, male and even "elitist." So they are ignored or sit on dusty shelves.

Conservatives, the various assortments that exist, have particularly felt the jolt of this significant shift; a shift that reflects the country's movement rightward philosophically and electorally and the academy's movement massively to the left, away from the overseers who support them and away from the students who are required to listen to them.

In his book, *The Rise of the Right*, William Rusher noted that there is one remaining battle that movement conservatives must fight and must win. "As the media will be the battleground of the first," he wrote, "the academy will be the arena of the second." The publisher of *National Review*, Rusher prophesied "it will be the most important and most difficult battle of them all." As professors Herbert London and Stephen Balch conclude in these pages, "the future of higher education hinges on how the internal crisis of American liberalism is eventually resolved."

Assorted conservatives have been prevented from speaking on some campuses. Conservative alternative campus newspapers have been harassed and denied distribution rights. Conservative students, bold enough to defend their views in class, have been penalized academically. And conservative academics interested in salary hikes, promotions, or tenure, have met real discrimination - the kind that affirmative action programs are designed to prevent.

In a speech to the Education Writers Association in New Orleans on April 17, 1988, Education Secretary William Bennett charged that there is a "rising tide of left-wing intolerance" on American college campuses. "Some places are becoming increasingly closed, increasingly conformist, increasingly insular and in certain instances even repressive of the spirit of the free marketplace of ideas," said Bennett. In a telephone survey conducted by the *Detroit Free Press* on April 18, 1988, 76% agreed with Secretary Bennett that "conservative views" are "being stifled on campus."

As Joseph Epstein of *The American Scholar* notes: "University academic departments nowadays seek out feminists, Marxists, and others in whom the political impulse runs stronger than any other, to teach their bias — and to do so in the name of intellectual diversity." Yet that "diversity" which has translated into a faculty departmental groupthink, has produced a chilling effect that discourages conservative professors from challenging their colleagues on the left, lest they be condemned as "McCarthyites," charged with "violating academic freedom" or accused of being "intolerant of intellectual diversity."

Yet one of the greatest and underpublicized threats to the integrity and quality of higher education, which has prided itself on being free and open, is the erosion of what some academics frequently employ as their defense from accountability or scrutiny — "academic freedom." As Professor Allan Bloom discusses in *The Closing of the American Mind*, academic freedom during the fifties "had for that last moment more than an abstract meaning, a content with respect to research and publication about which there is general agreement." Professor Bloom observes that academic freedom has become nothing more than the rhetoric about the protection of unpopular ideas. "Today there are many more things unthinkable and unspeakable in universities than there were then, and *little disposition to protect those who have earned the ire of the radical movements,*" he writes (emphasis added). This is where much of the great intellectual crisis lies in the academy in the eighties, around the ambigous right we call "academic freedom."

Now if we were to judge by the number of times we hear the phrase "academic freedom" used, then we would have to assume that the right of academic freedom flourishes all across the land. At colleges everywhere, professors speak of their "academic freedom." Unfortunately, we all know what talk is worth. To speak reverently of a right is one thing. To practice that right responsibly and extend it to others is something a little different, something a little more difficult. And to see whether this right flourishes, we have to consider how it is practiced, never mind how often we hear the phrase spoken, or how passionately. This book, a chronicle of academic freedom cases, attempts to do just that.

Most professors, I think, recognize the responsibilities which accompany this right of academic freedom. Yet many claim that there is simply no evidence that professors are violating these professional ethics on a scale as to warrant criticism or publication. Again, this book documents the evidence and the truth - the good, the bad, and the ugly. It demonstrates that while the country has moved rightward, the academy has become a stronghold or bastion of the modern cultural left. In essence, the academy in recent years has frequently become a launching pad for assaults against the rise of rightward or conservative thinking — a traditional mode of thought that intellectual believers in secular or moral relativism hold in passionate contempt. Students are going one way, while their professors are desperately trying to pull them back the other way.

This book is about academic freedom, or the lack or deterioration of academic freedom on college campuses today. It is about the function of academic freedom, its proper use, its definition, and how it is occasionally abused, and misused, or what we might call *academic license*. The contributors in the pages to follow discuss how the use of academic freedom has related to their various academic experiences, how it has assisted them or, more frequently, how it has been used to punish them for unorthodox views - how there has been "little disposition to protect those who have earned the ire of the radical movements." Most of the edited papers and speeches were presented and delivered at Accuracy in Academia's first annual conference titled "Academic Freedom or Academic License?" in Washington, D.C. on June 26 and June 27, 1987. Others were included here because of their obvious significance in this debate over academic freedom.

The distinguished authors in the following pages range from a former college president, a former congressman, a former senator, both former and currently active campus Marxists, conservative professors, a pacifist syndicated columnist, an internationally noted scientist and physicist, best-selling authors and college students. Their experiences in the academy in the eighties are fascinating, in some cases, incredible. Their views are forceful and diverse. They have different remedies for the many illnesses that hurt the academy today.

Most of them concur, however, that academic freedom on college campuses is nothing more than a useful device which gives license to some people and silences others.

Les Csorba
Washington, D.C.
May 1, 1988

PART ONE

The Academy in Exile

CHAPTER ONE

THE EDUCATION OF TOMORROW'S MEDIA ELITE
by REED IRVINE

The social sciences...were supposed to be in possession of the facts about social life and had a certain scientific conscience and integrity about reporting them. The social sciences were of interest to everyone who had a [political] program. This interest could be to get to the facts — or to make the facts fit their agenda and influence the public.

- Allan Bloom,
The Closing of the American Mind

A harmful truth is better than a useful lie.

- Thomas Mann

I AM HAPPY to report that Accuracy in Academia has survived the slings and arrows of outraged academics and media who declared war on us when we first announced that we were launching an organization to combat the spread of misinformation on college campuses.

I had a premonition that this organization was not going to be welcomed by all with open arms. I had become used to being the target of criticism and abuse since I started Accuracy in Media in 1969.

It was my experience with Accuracy in Media that convinced me that something had to be done and could be done on the college campuses. As I traveled around the country lecturing about the news media, I was asked why our journalists are so frequently more critical of the United States than our enemies. Why, people asked, do they so often show hostility to our free enterprise system and to business? Why

3

are they so naive about Communist countries such as Cuba, Nicaragua and Vietnam, and even the Soviet Union itself? Why, I have been asked, do the journalists who staff our large media organizations appear to be out of tune with the ideas and values of most Americans?

The validity of these questions and observations have been demonstrated by the Lichter-Rothman survey of 240 of the so-called media elite and by a Times-Mirror survey of 3000 reporters and editors employed by daily newspapers throughout the country.

Both of these surveys revealed that two-thirds of the journalists could be classified as liberal. The Lichter-Rothman survey showed that in every presidential election from 1964 through 1976, at least 81% of the journalists voted for the Democratic candidate.

At this same time, the Harris survey showed that fewer than 20% of the general public classified themselves as liberal. In the 1972 election, when 81% of the media elite were voting for George McGovern, 60% of the voters cast their ballots for Richard Nixon.

The 1985 Times-Mirror survey found that journalists were twice as likely as newspaper readers to favor American companies withdrawing investments from South Africa, and to oppose prayer in schools and increases in defense spending. This survey found that journalists were overwhelmingly supportive of legalized abortion and were overwhelmingly opposed to capital punishment. Their readers were overwhelmingly supportive of capital punishment and only a bare majority, 51% supported legalized abortion.

As one who for many years specialized in the economics of development, I was particularly troubled by the Lichter-Rothman finding that nearly three-fifths of the media elite believe that the United States exploits Third World countries and causes their poverty. This is a belief in mind-boggling contradiction to all the known facts, but it is in perfect harmony with the propaganda line of the Soviet Union. One has to ask why it is that men and women clever enough to get good jobs with our most prestigious media organizations — *The New York Times, The Washington Post*, ABC, CBS, NBC, *Time* and *Newsweek* — should succumb to such obvious Marxist propaganda as the line that we are the cause of the poverty of the backward countries of the world. Why are they at such odds with most Americans in their political preferences and their views on social issues?

The answer, I have concluded, lies in their *education*. Most journalists today are the products of our liberal arts colleges, where our youth are being indoctrinated with views and values radically different from those of mainstream America. This is based in part on my own experience — on the fact that I was thoroughly impregnated with liberal-leftist ideas during my impressionable high school and college years. The over-whelming liberal-leftist domination of our liberal arts faculties has increased since I graduated 45 years ago, and there is no reason to believe that the professors have become less proficient in the art of converting students to their own viewpoints since that time. I look at my own alma mater, the University of Utah, and I see today an economics faculty that is acknowledged to be dominated by Marxists, headed by a professor who openly links arms with the head of the Communist Party in the state.

Marxist ideas had a strong appeal to a minority of the students in my class in 1942, but in the ensuing years, I observed that one of the basic Marxist tenets came to be almost universally accepted among our intelligentsia. This is the principle of "economic determinism," the simplistic notion that all human activity, all history, can be explained in terms of economic forces.

The great appeal of this doctrine was alluded to in a tribute that Alexander Cockburn, who was then writing for the *Village Voice*, paid to Laurence Stern. Stern was an immensely influential editor at *The Washington Post* who died in 1979. Cockburn, a far leftist himself, noted that Stern had been a Trotskyite "in his hot youth." He didn't say what Stern was at the time of his death, but he asserted that Larry Stern's "heart and head lay on the left side of the political spectrum" and that he was not one of those who was "incapable of making up his mind until all the facts are in."

The magic key that enabled Larry Stern to know what the facts were going to tell him before he even knew the facts was Karl Marx's theory of economic determinism. This was impressed upon me several years ago when Ralph McGill, one of our most prestigious journalists, devoted a column to an attack on a sugar mill in Peru by guerrillas. McGill said that without knowing the details it was clear that the problem was exploitation of the peasants by the greedy capitalists and landlords, who refused to pay decent wages and provide education and medical care for the workers and their families. The facts were actually quite different. The workers were unionized, well paid, and had excellent benefits. The attack was the work of a band of political extremists. Proof that the Marxian magic key is not a reliable substitute for the facts is abundant.

Editorial writers and reporters are very fond of this solution to all the turmoil in the Third World. It spares them the need to undertake the tiresome task of learning the facts about scores of small countries that no one is eager to visit. They are generally hot, humid and boring. The notion that capitalist exploitation, or colonialism, was the cause of poverty in the Third World and that poverty would breed communism was virtually the official creed in this country throughout the 1950s and 1960s.

The fact that communism in this hemisphere came first in Cuba, one of the richest countries, not the poorest, was only a minor inconvenience to the true believers. They just ignored the facts or altered them to fit their own theory.

It is not necessary to experience a liberal arts education to master the theory of economic determinism. It can be picked up easily just by reading *The New York Times* or *The Washington Post*. But there is evidence that our colleges remain its chief breeding ground.

Lichter and Rothman surveyed one-sixth of the class of 1982 of the Graduate School of Journalism of Columbia University. They found that student journalists being groomed to take over the nation's leading media organizations admire Communist dictators more than leaders of the free world.

They found that 78% of students disapprove of President Reagan, and by margins of 3 to 1, they reject Jeane Kirkpatrick and Margaret Thatcher. As Lichter and Rothman point out, Columbia's journalism students rate Communist dictator Fidel Castro as high as Thatcher and place Castro well above their own president. The Communist Sandinistas in Nicaragua are viewed more favorably than any of the conservatives listed, with 41% of the students approving of dictator Ortega and his military junta, and only 26% disapproving.

Lichter and Rothman found that 89% believed that the goal of U.S. foreign policy was to protect U.S. business and that 75% believed that we exploit Third World countries and cause their poverty. These students showed considerably more vulnerability to these Soviet propaganda themes than did the journalists working for the elite media organizations. If the teachers at Columbia weren't indoctrinating the students with these ideas, they at least were not effectively exposing them as false. Where these ideas are prevalent, belief in economic determinism is bound to be strong.

In his essay in *The God that Failed*, Arthur Koestler tells how he publicly announced his departure from the Communist Party. He gave a speech in the spring of 1938 before the

German Emigre Writers Association in Paris. About half the members of the audience were Communists. Koestler said his speech contained no word of criticism of the Communist Party of the Soviet Union.

But it contained three carefully chosen sentences which he knew would be taken by the non-Communists in the audience as platitudes but which the Communists would recognize as a declaration of war.

They were:

1. No movement, party or person can claim the privilege of infallibility.
2. Appeasing the enemy is as foolish as persecuting the friend who pursues your own aim by a different road.
3. A harmful truth is better than a useful lie.

Koestler relates that at the conclusion of his speech, the non-Communists applauded while the Communists sat in heavy silence, most of them with folded arms. This, he says, was their spontaneous reaction to those commonplace statements. He commented: "You might as well have told a Nazi audience that all men are born equal, regardless of race and creed."

Those words of Arthur Koestler's had a profound effect on me when I read them 35 years ago, particularly the third statement: *"A harmful truth is better than a useful lie,"* which was a quotation from Thomas Mann.

The proper attitudes, the right ideas that I learned in my college years were more important than the facts, more important than the truth, centered around the belief that the control of the means of production by individuals was wrong. The pursuit of profit by individuals was supposed to be responsible for all the evil in the world, ranging from crime in the streets to world wars. Peace, prosperity and social justice were all to be found in a revolutionary change that would produce the social ownership of the means of production and the elimination of the profit motive.

If the facts got in the way of this glorious vision, then the facts, not the vision, would have to give way.

In any case, factual information was really irrelevant. To one who had mastered the Marxian theory of economic determinism, all history, past and yet to come, was easily explained. If the facts didn't fit the theory, they should be brushed aside.

The useful lies that were tolerated, even eagerly embraced, by those who thought as I did in those days led to some horrible consequences. The Gulag, now made famous by Solzhenitsyn, was no secret even then. But those who believed in useful lies preferred to avert their eyes, while denouncing those who insisted on telling the truth.

Koestler described the embarrassing reality. Of his Communist or fellow-travelling intellectual colleagues, he said:

> "At no time and in no country have more revolutionaries been killed or reduced to slavery than in Soviet Russia. To one who himself for seven years found excuses for every stupidity and crime committed under the Marxist banner, the spectacle of these dialectical tight-rope acts of self-deception, performed by men of goodwill and intelligence, is more disheartening than the barbarities committed by the simple in spirit."

The leftist intellectuals may have known these things, but beguiled by the concept of the "useful lie," they became co-conspirators in the crimes that were taking place on an unprecedented scale.

In my lifetime, the world has made enormous progress in technology and the physical sciences — physics, chemistry, medicine and all the rest. At the same time, we have seen an enormous erosion of human freedom as more and more of the world's population has fallen under the control of totalitarian dictators.

If we live in fear of nuclear war today, it is not simply because our physicists have learned how to tap the power of the atom. It is because one of the countries that has both nuclear weapons and the power to use them to attack any country in the world is a totalitarian dictatorship whose conduct is not guided by any moral considerations nor by any concern for public opinion, domestic or foreign.

The growing gap between the world's scientific and technological progress and its political and social retrogression may be explained to a significant degree by the fact that the physical sciences quickly reject "useful lies." When the empirical evidence undermines a beloved theory, it is the theory that is abandoned, not the empirical evidence that is covered up.

The reverse is often true in the political and social sciences.

Joseph Epstein, editor of *The American Scholar*, recently wrote that, "Marxism, a doctrine discredited among economists around the world and one that has brought more misery to mankind than perhaps any other modern body of ideas, is very much a going concern in American universities." He added, "Marxist academic intellectuals..., rattling away about their dead doctrine, seem in a position akin to that of Galileo's returning to life to put forth the doctrine that the earth is flat, when everyone now knows better..."

Those who know and respect empirical evidence know that Epstein speaks the truth when he says that Marxism is a discredited doctrine that has inflicted a great deal of unnecessary misery on the world. One need only compare the economic progress of countries such as North Korea and South Korea, East Germany and West Germany, Taiwan, Hong Kong and Singapore and Communist China to see that the rigid system of state planning and control that characterizes the Marxist regimes has been no match for the free market economies.

It is safe to say that there are fewer true believers in any country that has been under a Marxist regime for any length of time than are on the college campuses of the United States. Jean Francois Revel, in a speech at a small mid-western college in the United States, recently complained that when Europeans host a conference and wish to invite a Marxist to participate, they have to look to America to find one.

This is easy to explain. In the Communist countries, the facts that contradict the theory are the stuff of daily life — long lines, shoddy goods, poor service, inefficient use of all the factors of production, and in a pervasive compulsory irrationality. Because the flaws in the system are so obvious and well-known to the people in these countries, they can never be permitted to enjoy such elementary human rights as freedom of speech and freedom to emigrate, not to mention the freedom to elect their rulers. A Communist country that was not a police state would not remain Communist long.

But it is easy for professors in comfortable democratic countries to overlook the harsh realities of the Marxist failure. As Lin Yutang pointed out in his excellent but little known book, *The Secret Name*, many western intellectuals are enamored of the romantic 19th century revolutionary rhetoric. They know the vocabulary, but they know little about the revolutionary reality.

Howard Zinn, professor of government at Boston University, has written that "communism as a set of ideals has attracted good people — not racists, or bullies, or militarists — all over the world." He said Marxian ideals include "peace, brotherhood, racial equality, the classless society, the withering away of the state." And he promised that Communist regimes would do an effective job of bringing about the swift economic progress needed by new nations. In 1967, Zinn predicted that the Vietnamese would probably be no worse off under the Communists and that the lower classes would probably be better off.

It would be interesting to see Professor Zinn trying to convince the Vietnamese, the Cambodians and Laotians of the great benefits brought by communism. It would be interesting to see how he would fare in trying to convince the Afghans, the Soviet Jews, the Tatars, the Tibetans and the Miskito Indians that Communists are not racists or bullies.

It is little wonder that when I debated Bertell Ollman, a Marxist professor of political science at New York University in 1985, that he could not be induced to name a single Marxist government in the world today that he would hold up as an ideal. Ollman wanted to talk only about poverty and injustice in the United States, not about Marxist failures.

It is amusing to see how far these people will go in trying to find fault with the United States and its highly successful free market system. Nobel Laureate George Wald, for example, thought that he had found a serious flaw in the free market system. He said that poor people in this country were suffering from disease because iodized salt cost more than non-iodized salt and the poor couldn't afford to buy it. When Dr. Thomas Jukes pointed out to him that the cost of iodizing salt was minuscule and that the salt companies charged the same price for both iodized and non-iodized products, Dr. Wald lapsed into silence.

In correcting George Wald's misinformation about the price of salt, Dr. Jukes was reminding this famous scientist that he should derive his theories from facts, not vice versa. He was doing what Accuracy in Academia wants to see done on college campuses throughout the country. He was correcting an academic's error.

All of us can and will make mistakes now and then. That can be excused. What is inexcusable is deliberate distortion and refusal to correct errors when they are pointed out.

We have seen significant improvement in the willingness of the media to acknowledge and correct errors over the past 18 years, though they are still far from perfect. But in the two years Accuracy in Academia was been operating, we have found the situation in the colleges to be much worse than the media.

We found a history professor at Princeton who loaded a scholarly book he authored with numerous footnoted refer-ences that proved to be invalid. We learned to our amazement that the historians who discovered and exposed this scholarly fraud were attacked by radical historians who accused them of being excessively concerned with "factual accuracy."

We found a professor in Miami who regaled his students with vicious lies about such great Americans as George Washington, Abraham Lincoln and Theodore Roosevelt. His stories were taped by one of his students. When we asked him if he had told his students that Washington died of pneumonia contracted when he dived out a window into a snowbank to escape an irate husband whose wife he had been visiting, the professor denied having said it. Furthermore, he said he didn't know the circumstances of Washington's death. When we said we had him on tape, he abruptly hung up the phone.

We discovered that a freshman class in American history at Virginia Tech was using as its principal text a book by a Marxist who ignored our heroes and great achievers and focused on the losers. He devoted nearly a full page to an antinuclear kook who in 1982 threatened to blow up the Washington Monument but mentioned General Douglas MacArthur only as the commander of the troops who drove the bonus marchers out of Washington in 1932. The teacher, the history department and the college refused to acknowledge that this was an inappropriate text for a freshman history course.

We have learned that colleges, unused to having their practices scrutinized and criticized by outsiders, are even more reluctant than the media to admit error or to take corrective action.

We have also discovered that our universities, while theoretically devoted to a scholarly willingness to hear and entertain a diversity of ideas, are often closed to teachers and lecturers who espouse views that are not approved by the dominant liberal culture.

I don't want to leave the impression that all of academia is working in unison to close the American mind. We are fortunate to have many honest, brilliant scholars who are interested in accuracy, in fairness, who are open to criticism, and who welcome disagreement and debate.

But the reaction to the establishment of Accuracy in Academia has ranged from great enthusiasm on the part of many students, parents and some professors to wild hysteria on the part of some professors and journalists.

The greatest tribute was paid by *Izvestia* — the Soviet daily paper in which, it is said, you fill find no *pravda* (truth) — which carried a page-one article about Accuracy in Academia on October 22, 1985. It said: "Teachers at universities are quivering with fear. They tremble at the utterance of each word. For who knows? Are the students taking notes on their lectures for their own purposes, or are they listening for the purposes of reporting what the teacher says to the ultra-right organization, Accuracy in Academia?"

Accuracy in Academia has confounded its most virulent critics by doing what it said it was going to do, not what they feared it was going to do. We have exposed serious abuses in academia, and I believe that what we have done has encouraged others to fight those abuses. We have been accurate and fair. By our prodding and by our example, we hope to elevate respect for facts and accuracy in academia.

Our dream is that by exposing the intolerance so prevalent today on college campuses we can shame our liberal academics into adopting a policy that is on everyone's lips today — "glasnost."

The screams of *Izvestia* and *Izvestia's* spiritual brothers in this country indicate that Accuracy in Academia is regarded as a serious threat, even though at the present time it consists of myself and two young men recently out of college.

But it has not been a threat to academic freedom. It has broadened the debate on campus, making it possible for voices that have been too long silenced or muffled to be heard loud and clear. It has risen to the defense of those in the academic community who have been persecuted and discriminated against because they dared to speak out in defense of their country and its values.

Accuracy in Academia does pose a threat — and I hope it will continue to be a serious one — to those who today are doing to their students what some of my professors did to me in my college years; exploiting the natural and commendable idealism of their young students and imbuing them with the principle that has led both to the gas chambers at Auschwitz and the Gulags of Siberia — the principle that the ideals they believe to be noble can be served by useful lies and covering up or ignoring the painful truth. As Shakespeare said: "Thrice is he armed that hath his quarrel just/And he but naked whose conscience with injustice is corrupted."

Reed Irvine is the founder and chairman of Accuracy in Academia and Accuracy in Media. He graduated Phi Beta Kappa from the University of Utah and was a Fulbright Scholar at Oxford. Mr. Irvine was an economist with the Federal Reserve Board for 26 years until he retired in 1977 to devote full time to AIM, which he founded in 1969. Mr. Irvine also edits Campus Report, *the monthly publication of Accuracy in Academia, which he founded in 1985.*

CHAPTER TWO

THE TENURED LEFT

by STEPHEN BALCH and HERBERT LONDON

Academic freedom, which is the foundation on which teaching and learning prosper, has been transformed. As a principle, it was meant to shield the academy from external pressure and manipulation, but, like most other freedoms, it simultaneously conferred a responsibility, involving a willingness to uphold basic standards of inquiry and to render judgment on the quality of colleagues' ideas.

LIKE IONIZED PARTICLES transiting a cloud chamber, two quite different campus projects involving tiny fractions of the collegiate population have recently succeeded in precipitating reactions of surprising scope and visibility. While the resulting trails move in very different directions, their vectors reveal much about the dubious atmosphere of American higher education in the 1980s.

The first of these two passages has been that of the divestiture movement, with its demand for the liquidation of university investments in firms with holdings in South Africa. An effort under way for several years, the movement accelerated greatly with the spreading violence in South Africa during 1985. At one level it sought to free the academy of any taint of involvement with apartheid; at another, to intensify economic pressures to further that government's progressive delegitimization. Finally, many of its organizers, through an exercise in guerrilla theater, hoped to recover some measure of that radical consciousness which prevailed on campuses during the late 1960s.

In a variety of ways the divestiture movement is a classic embodiment of the ethos of campus protest born during that decade. For one thing, it assumes that students (or at least an activist fringe) are equipped with the moral and political perception necessary to judge the policies of the institutions entrusted with their education. For another, it understands the imperatives of its cause as conferring a license willfully to disregard university regulations, to seize or obstruct university property, and to be sharply uncivil toward university officials offering resistance. The tactics of the movement have in fact created confrontations and threats of disorder not experienced on most American campuses since the Vietnam war.

Though it might wish to disavow the honor, Accuracy in Academia, the second recent campus "movement," also bears the stamp of the 60s in its assumptions and *modus operandi.*

Fathered by Reed Irvine at the beginning of the 1985 fall semester as a counterpart to Accuracy in Media, Accuracy in Academia is essentially a "Naderite" enterprise with a conservative twist. Instead of criticizing the corporate world for deceptive advertising and shoddy merchandise, it levels similar charges at the intellectual products of the academy, which it sees as tainted by a tendentious radicalism. Its informants are not dissatisfied automobile owners or disgruntled nuclear engineers but unhappy academic consumers (that is to say, students).

In both its virtues and shortcomings Accuracy in Academia has much in common with other contemporary ventures in grassroots muckracking. Among its virtues is a flare for in-stant controversy, designed to draw attention to the chosen target; among its shortcomings, a certain surreptitiousness invariably associated with "whistle-blowing" enterprises. But whatever may be said of its tact, the efforts of Accuracy in Academia, unlike those of the divestiture campaign, have been wholly confined to the realm of public criticism, neither fomenting disruption, nor toying with the possibilities of violent confrontation, nor obliging university administrators or faculty members to adopt an institutional stand.

In light of this rather fundamental difference, the response of the educational establishment to each of these two projects might strike an observer unfamiliar with the vagaries of academic life as somewhat surprising. For while the divestiture protests have often encountered an embarrassed resistance on the part of presidents and trustees worried about the value of institutional portfolios, or doubtful about the most effective way of combatting apartheid, almost nowhere they have been seen (for the record, at least) as seriously threatening those norms of reasoned discourse, or that climate of intellectual tolerance, so often cited as constituting the university's special claim to grace. Quite the contrary; on

14

campus after campus they have been accorded the indulgence reserved for activities whose transcendent moral status immunizes them against the ordinary quibbles of law.

Thus, at Harvard, eleven students who conducted an all-day sit-in at the offices of the university's board of governors received only a "formal admonition," the mildest penalty possible and one mitigated still further by a statement complimenting them for having maintained a "constructive level of civility." (Another group of Harvard students, who had physically blockaded a South African diplomat on his way to address a conservative campus group, had their more severe penalties suspended.) At Cornell, the university dropped charges pending as a result of 1,200 arrests between April and December 1985, on the ostensible ground that the installation of a new disciplinary code required that the old slate be swept clean. At Yale, a decision to remove demonstrators blocking campus buildings produced an anguished petition signed by 156 faculty members deploring the university's "Use of Force." This was shortly followed by a ruling from a faculty disciplinary committee, slapping the defendants on the wrist and allowing the reconstruction of their shanties.

By contrast, there has been very little uncertainty about the menace to the climate of freedom posed by Accuracy in Academia, and no hesitancy at all in denouncing it in the strongest possible terms. The Committee on Academic Freedom and Tenure of the American Association of University Professors (AAUP), for example, predicted that "the proposed program of AIA, if undertaken and accepted seriously, [would] lead toward the deadening of discourse and the stultification of learning." Dr. Bruce Mason, chairman of the faculty senate of Arizona State University (one of whose professors had been an early object of AIA criticism), declared that the organization had "poisoned the faculty-student relationship," making "students' innocent questions" seem like "devious attempts to make trouble." Chancellor Joseph S. Murphy of the City University of New York likened AIA's methods to those of a "corps of thought police," and characterized the group as posing a "grave...menace to the free exchange of ideas." And falling back on the inevitable comparison, Dr. John W. Chandler, president of the Association of American Colleges, opined that while "two generations of college professors (had) escaped the battles of McCarthyism," the academy would now have to "gird (itself) to resist another round."

Perhaps the greatest irony in the reaction to AIA has to do with the strong defense it has provoked of established procedures of university self-governance. Such a defense stood at the center of a statement issued by the AAUP and eight other higher education associations in November 1985, intended to constitute their definitive rejoinder to AIA. "We believe," the statement ran, that "the quality of academic performance is best judged through peer evaluation by skilled professionals. Chief executive officers and governing boards are responsible for ensuring both accountability and academic integrity while safeguarding the university from undue outside influence. We encourage colleges and universities to resist this assault on institutional integrity by reaffirming established practices for insuring professional responsibility and academic freedom..."

Brave words, no doubt, but one may wonder where this determination to protect the prerogatives of "executive officers and governing boards" and to resist assaults on "institutional integrity" 'fled when it came to dealing with the disruption and intimidation practiced by proponents of divestiture.

The disparity in the reception accorded anti-apartheid demonstrators and the minions of AIA has much less to do with the respective threat each poses to the life of the academic mind than with that mind's most seasoned prejudices. As an enterprise of the Left, the divestiture movement is guaranteed the automatic sympathy of the vast majority of politically conscious faculty and administrators. As an organization of self-confessed conservatives, AIA provokes the instant wrath of this very same group. To be sure, a decent case can be made for the goals, and against the methods, of each of these ventures, but with some honorable exceptions (largely among conservative intellectuals outside the academy) few observers have seemed able to get beyond a fixation on ideological provenance.

The moral of this tale is not that the academy is a bastion of liberalism, a fact which most would take to be indisputable, but that the liberalism of the academy, like much of that beyond its walls, is now hard pressed to recognize its own principles, and even less capable of defending them when they come under attack from the Left. "No enemies on the Left," once the rallying cry of the Popular Front, has become a veritable shibboleth for the majority of the American professoriate, at least when dealing with campus radicalism.

As a pervasive intellectual reflex, this attitude is between twenty and thirty years old. Its origins may be found in the backlash against McCarthyism, its consolidation in the "cultural revolution" of the 60s. Historically, the development of this reflex coincided with an era of unprecedented institu-

16

tional expansion within the world of higher education, in which the number of jobs, and the influence of the university on American life, greatly increased. This conjunction created a peculiar opportunity for American radicalism, partially compensating for its failure to establish any sizable foothold within the general population. Deprived of a strong institutional base among elected officials or in the labor movement comparable to that of radical movements elsewhere, the Left in America sought sanctuary in the academy. Given the skewed sensibilities of its liberal guardians, and given, too, the intellectual proclivities and gentrified tastes of many 60s radicals, the academy provided a safe, even pleasant, haven for ideological rest, recuperation and regrouping.

Thus it has come about that, despite the sincere desire of most university people to see themselves as exemplars of democratic idealism, the American campus is now the nesting place for a significant population of political extremes. Indeed, with the waning of the more traditional forms of racist and nativist ideologies, the campus has probably become American extremism's principal address.

It is difficult to measure with precision the magnitude of the radical presence within the academy, though enough data exist to allow estimates. In 1984, for example, the Carnegie Foundation for the Advancement of Teaching conducted a survey of the entire professoriate, sampling 5,000 faculty members at 310 2-year, 4-year, and graduate institutions. Respondents were asked to choose which of the five labels best described their political orientation, with designations ranging from "Left," "liberal," and "middle-of-the-road" to "moderately conservative" and "strongly conservative." Reading from "Left" to "Right," the aggregated results disclosed percentages of 5.8, 33.8, 26.6, 29.6, and 4.2 in each of the categories. If "Left" is taken as a synonym for "radical," then the first percentage would translate into something in the neighborhood of 35,000 radical faculty, out of a total academic population thought to number about 600,000. (The inevitable rejoinder that the 5.8 percent on the "Left" is almost balanced by the 4.2 percent calling themselves "strongly conservative" will impress only those who equate the outlook of Herbert Stein with that of Herbert Marcuse.) As with most similar polls, the Carnegie study found the proportion of leftist faculty to be higher at institutions of greater prestige and influence. Thus, while only 3.9 percent of the respondents at 2-year colleges designated themselves as on the "Left," the figure rose to 6.3 percent for the faculty at "research universities" and to 6.7 percent for those at 4-year liberal-arts colleges.

The Carnegie survey covers all segments of the professoriate, including faculties teaching in business and professional programs, mathematics and the natural sciences, physical, home economics, and other fields generally distant from political controversy. When consideration is limited to only those disciplines which set out to analyze and evaluate social and political phenomena, even the semblance of ideological balance vanishes. Needless to say, the largest block of academics within nearly all these disciplines describe themselves as "liberal" rather than "leftist," but with the exception of economics, every field within the humanities and social sciences contains a substantial cohort of radicals, dwarfing anything found at the opposite end of the scale. For example, among the philosophy faculty surveyed at 4-year institutions, a full 21.7 percent designated themselves as "Left" and none at all as "strongly conservative;" for the sociologists, the percentages were 37.0 percent versus 0.9 percent; for the political scientists, 19.8 percent to 4.8 percent; for the historians, 12.8 percent to 3.0 percent; and for professors of English literature, 10.2 percent to 2.4 percent.

Except among sociologists, where the Left has grown substantially, these patterns have remained fairly constant since the late 1960's. What has changed decidedly over the last two decades is the extent to which leftist radicalism has managed to institutionalize itself within the academic world. Whereas twenty years ago the campus Left was largely confined to registering its presence through vocal demonstrations and protest, today it is more comfortably ensconced within a network of journals and professional organizations, university departments and academic programs.

Take journals, for example. Before the 1960s one would have been hard pressed to find more than two or three leftist journals with any claim to scholarly standing. Since then, over thirty such journals have appeared (a few to fall by the wayside) in areas as diverse as anthropology (*Dialectical Anthropology*), art criticism (*Praxis*), criminology (*Crime and Social Justice*), economics (*Review of Radical Economics*), geography (*Anti-pode*), history (*Radical History Review*), and literary criticism (*Diacritics*). And one could easily add to these about a dozen feminist journals (most operating out of a specific discipline) which share the same insurgent perspective.

The journals vary a good deal in style, intellectual quality, and activist commitment, from the sedate, almost antiquarian *New German Critique*, which devotes considerable space to

18

publishing the translated texts to deceased theorists of the Frankfurt School, through more gritty and polemical publications like *New Political Science,* with its topical preoccupations and discussions of movement strategy, to such outlandish periodicals as *Trivia,* a feminist "journal of ideas" whose overall tone of lesbian mysticism is best conveyed in the explanation of its title, a derivation of "trivium (crossroads) ...one of the names of the Triple Goddess..."describing "the matrix of our creative power, the gathering of wise women in which our ideas originate and continue to live."

Were it not that they are accompanied by a measure of academic respectability, the mere existence of these journals would mean little. None has become a major organ in its discipline, but many have achieved respectable circulations and, symbolically more important, institutional affiliation and support. *Praxis,* for example, is published with the assistance of the College of Fine Arts, the Graduate Student Association, the Division of Graduate Studies, and the College of Letters and Sciences of UCLA. The *Insurgent Sociologist* is produced by an "editorial collective" housed in the department of sociology of the University of Oregon. *Trivia* has been regularly funded from the proceeds of a feminist lecture series co-sponsored by the Women's Resource Center at Smith College. (The Winter 1986 issue, which features articles on lesbian economics, the spiritual legacy of the ancient Amazons, and the five-billion-year long racial memory of womankind, broke with this pattern of feminist support. It was subsidized by a grant from the National Endowment for the Arts.)

These journals play an important role in facilitating communication among the constituencies they serve. But anyone familiar with the nature of contemporary college life will also quickly recognize their practical significance in sustaining the careers of radical professors. In the increasingly bureaucratized process by which academic personnel decisions are made, tenure or promotion frequently turns on rather crude and readily quantifiable measures of achievement. Paramount among these are the number of a candidate's scholarly publications, with each citation representing another point on the scoreboard. By providing respectable scholarly venues for articles too pointedly political, or fantastic, for most mainstream publications, the radical journals help contributors to advance their careers without abandoning their activist vocations.

This is not to say that articles of a radical bent find any particular difficulty getting into mainstream publications. Marxist and feminist scholarship is quite commonplace in most established journals, particularly in fields like sociology, anthropology, and history. Of course, some of these articles, despite their ideological orientation, have real merit and deserve publication. Nonetheless, occasions arise which call into question the capacity of mainstream academics to maintain even an elementary standard to critical judgment when evaluating the work of the Left.

A case in point is the lead article in the December 1985 issue of the *American Sociological Review*, the official journal of the American Sociological Association. Entitled "Mythologies of Work: A Comparison of Firms in State Socialism and Advanced Capitalism," the article seeks to assess the reliability of eight widely-held Western "stereotypes" concerning the relative inefficiency of firms of socialist economies. The method employed is that of the case study, in which the researchers immerse themselves in the lives of two comparable manufacturing firms, one in the United States and one in Hungary, and then describe their impressions. The result, as it turns out, stands in sharp contradiction to the conventional wisdom. Whether one is looking at the motivational level of the workforce, the capacity for innovation, the influence of workers in organizing production, the degree of bureaucratic rigidity, or at any of the other operational characteristics analyzed, the Hungarian firm emerges as at least the equal, and often the superior, of the American one. This finding leads the investigators to conclude that a socialist firm can indeed be more efficient than a capitalist one, provided it is shielded from direct state control by an intervening level of corporate structure. They also take pains to indicate that it is just in this direction that the Hungarian economy has recently been evolving.

Food for thought, certainly, and all the more so since the premier publication in sociology attests to the authors' credentials. But who are they? One is Michael Burawoy, a widely publicized Marxist sociologist from the University of California at Berkeley, and parenthetically, an associate editor of the review. Nothing indefensible here; everyone has biases, and it is appropriate for academic editors to credit a scholar of established reputation with the ability to keep his under control, assuming he is in a position to do so. Unfortunately, however, not all the world's social scientists are in this position. One who may well not be is Burawoy's collaborator, Janos Lukacs, research fellow of the Institute of

20

Sociology, Hungarian Academy of Sciences, and the person largely responsible for the case study of the socialist firm.

Now, the credibility of any piece of purportedly scientific research requires that the investigator be free either to substantiate or to falsify the hypotheses he is exploring, as the evidence dictates. Therefore, to accept "Mythologies of Work" as a serious scientific study, the editors of the *American Sociological Review* had to believe that a Hungarian academician could put his name to a study of a Hungarian firm, for publication in a prestigious foreign journal, which would confirm eight negative Western stereotypes about efficiency of socialism. To say the least, this is rather doubtful. Ironically, in recent years the social sciences have experienced several acrimonious controversies about the extent to which the sponsorship of research by agencies of the American government taints the work of those who participate in it, or damages the reputation of entire disciplines. Judging from "Mythologies of Work," involvement with a Communist regime may not be as troubling.

Max Weber once wrote that the teacher "will beware of imposing from the platform any political positions upon the student, whether it is expressed or suggested... [T]he prophet and the demagogue do not belong on the academic platform." While this caution may be honored more in the breach than in the practice, it expresses the standard by which most professors would be willing to be judged. What distinguishes the majority of radical academics from their colleagues is the view that scholarship and teaching are preeminently, and unavoidably, extensions of politics. For the most extreme, the distinction between teaching and indoctrination altogether evaporates.

When pressed as to whether the purpose of his teaching is to convert students to socialism, Bertell Ollman, the doyen of Marxist scholars at New York University, answers that a "correct understanding of Marxism (or any body of scientific truth) leads automatically to its acceptance." (One wonders about the fate of the dull or intransigent student who cannot grasp the "scientific truth.") Michael Parenti, a Marxist political scientist who until recently taught at Brooklyn College, and a former fellow of the Institute for Policy Studies, defines the mission of the radical academic even more boldly. "Our job in academia," he states, "is not only to reach out to working people but also to remind our students that they're workers... that their struggle is also a labor struggle, (and) that labor struggle is the most profound democratic struggle in our society."

21

Such statements imply that the university, and the values traditionally associated with it, are regarded as adversaries, albeit adversaries that provide the radical academic with influence, status, and income. And so, to the question, "What does Marxism have to offer the bourgeois university?," Harvard biologist Richard Lewontin replies, in a paper published in *New Political Science*, "preferably, nothing." He explains:

> That is, Marxism can do nothing for the university; the real question is what can Marxists do to and in the university...*For the natural and social scientist the answer is very clear. The university is a factory that makes weapons — ideological weapons — for class struggle, for class warfare, and trains people in their use. It has no other leading and important function in the social organization.* (Emphasis in original.)

Lewontin specifies three separate ways in which the expertise and academic status of the revolutionary scholar can be used; first, "to demystify and destroy the obfuscation which is part of the ruling-class ideological weaponry;" second, "to create weapons that can be used on our side;" third, to bring about the "delegitimation of the authority of bourgeois ideologues," an activity which must involve "writing, speaking on radio, on television, in schools, in newspapers and magazines." Finally, Lewontin observes, the Marxist professor must create in his workplace "a situation that intensifies contradiction...that intensifies the class struggles, and...must engage in revolutionizing practice in the day-to-day relations on the job."

Recognizing that present circumstances are not those most propitious for overt revolutionary struggle, many radical academics see their function as laying the intellectual groundwork for that time when, in the words of Frederic Jameson (then a professor of French Literature at Yale), "merely abstract doctrine will come back into (students') minds as a solution to urgent problems." Jameson continues:

> At that point, retrospectively, the things we all taught them, in apparently imperceptible accretions that left no trace, will come back and be activated for the first time. That is, it seems to me, no negligible function for us to play, even if it offers very little immediate personal satisfaction. But I think I have to give an even broader historical characterization of the movement in which American Marxists find themselves and in which our pedagogical work takes its significance. Lenin said that the two necessary (but not sufficient) preconditions for social revolution are a class-conscious proletariat and a revolutionary intelligentsia. If, as intellectuals, we can necessarily play only a marginal role in the development of the former, the task of creating the latter is clearly our fundamental one. To create a Marxist culture in this country, to

make Marxism an unavoidable presence and a distinct, original, and unmistakable voice in American social, cultural, and intellectual life, in short to form a Marxist intellegentsia for the struggles of the future — this seems to me the supreme mission of a Marxist pedagogy and a radical intellectual life today.

While these Marxist professors do not dominate opinion in their disciplines, it would be a mistake to underestimate their influence or the influence of Marxist studies. According to Bertell Ollman and Edward Vernoff, the editors of *The Left Academy* (1983), four Marxist-inspired textbooks in American government were published between 1970 and 1982. Before this period three of the most prestigious university publishers, Cambridge, Oxford, and Princeton, issued books on Marx and Marxism, "almost all of them quite sympathetic." Whereas in the 1960s only a handful of courses in Marxist philosophy were being taught, today there are well over 400 such courses offered on American campuses.

When Secretary of Education William J. Bennett recently expressed the belief that a "significant body of opinion" has developed on college campuses which "openly rejects the democratic ethic," his comment was greeted with mocking skepticism. One academic, John Chandler, replied that "The situation (Bennett) describes was a much more pronounced problem in the late 60s and early 70s than it is today." Chandler was thinking of revolutionary displays by students. What he ignored was the extent to which the practitioners of academic agitprop have vacated the quadrangles for more decorous and strategic roosts behind the lectern. In this sense, Secretary Bennett's concern over radicals at war with society is more pertinent now than it would have been in the turbulent 60s.

The decentralized character of academic governance offers numerous opportunities for faculty intent on politicizing teaching and scholarship. What goes on in the classroom is almost totally under the control of the professor in charge. Faculty members with a special sense of intellectual purpose can usually have a disproportionate impact on course and program development. Even the policies of professional academic associations can be strongly influenced by determined and organized minorities. Consequently, in many institutions, while radicals have not become the dominant force, they have made a deeper mark than their numbers alone would suggest. Their principal effect has been to introduce into academic life a shrill and persistent tendentiousness which frequently succeeds in structuring the agenda of academic discourse while simultaneously cheapening it.

One measure of this effect is the increase in the number of one-sided, question-begging, or highly partisan course descriptions now to be found in college catalogues. Take, for instance, the description of Black Studies 145: Capitalism and Colonialism in Contemporary America found in the catalogue of the City College of New York:

> White America is described as capitalist and colonialist. Efforts will be made to comprehend the relative importance of the two phenomena for strategies of liberation depending upon who and what is the American and America.

Or take the following account of Economics 380a. Comparative Economic Systems: The Third World drawn from the Vassar College catalogue:

> The course will compare capitalism and socialism as alternative strategies of development of Third World countries. The first part of the course will address the central theoretical issues in the literature on the possibilities of capitalist development, socialist development, and autarky. In the second part, we will discuss how different socialist countries in the Third World have dealt with a variety of problems, including government ownership of productive enterprises, agrarian transformations, technological development, population growth, and the status of women. Depending on student interest the course will cover the following countries: China, Cuba, Nicaragua, Chile under Allende, Jamaica under Manley, Tanzania, Angola, Zimbabwe, North Korea, and Cambodia.

Lest it be thought that these examples are uniquely egregious, one might contemplate the lecture series, "America After 1984," organized last year at Bard College by Stanley Diamond, then the occupant of its Alger Hiss Chair in Culture, Society, and the Humanities. Topics in this series have included: "The Underside of Justice in the United States;" "American Cultural Imperialism;" "Anti-Communism in America: Its History and Functions": "The Origins and Continuity of the American Crisis: A Native American view;" "Radical Ecologists: The Environmental Crisis Heats Up;" "The Gathering Crisis in Public Education;" "Private Education in Crisis;" "The Media Crisis in America;" and "Race and Gender in America."

At the University of Massachusetts in Boston, a Marxist Studies program offers twenty-six courses, including "Food: Politics and Policy," about which the catalogue states, *inter alia:* "The development of a world network of food trade, aid and finance has created a world food system in which the U.S.'s farm policies, and federal deficits and bank interest rates, fundamentally affect whether Indian farmers will grow more wheat or African peasants will starve."

24

Descriptions like these tend to parody themselves. More commonplace is the gratuitous introduction of political material into conventionally designed courses or, worse yet, the use of the vocabulary and apparatus of scholarship to mask an appropriation of a broad swath of the curriculum by a political movement.

The rapid growth of black-studies programs in the late 60s and early 70s was the first manifestation of this phenomenon. The essentially political character of black studies, which was regarded by its champions as a means of consciousness-raising and by most college administrators as a way of avoiding trouble, has always been an open secret on the campus. While black studies seems to have undergone a contraction from its heyday in the 70's, it is still represented by some 350 college programs, including 141 leading to a baccaulaureate, and it is imitated by smaller clusters of programs in areas like Chicano and "Native American" studies.

Women's studies comprised the second wave, sweeping through the already breached ramparts of academic integrity. As Michael Levin has written, "At a time when black militants were developing black studies, it was possible for other groups to demand a 'study' of their own on grounds of equality... The women's studies course introduced during the 1960s and 1970s did not originate in significant discoveries as did courses in molecular biology or the 'higher criticism' of biblical texts...Nor did women's studies undergo the scrutiny that normally attends even the most modest academic innovation. The very speed with which these courses proliferated suggests that they were perceived as entitled, by historical and political necessity, to a place in academe." As of 1984, there were 476 women's-studies programs, of which 125 led to baccalaureates, and the number continues to grow.

The latest variation on this theme has been the rapid diffusion of "peace-studies" programs, what at last count had a place in the curriculum at well over 200 institutions of higher learning. The emotionally loaded and propagandistic qualities of similiar programs at the primary and secondary school level have already been explored in the pages of *Commentary*; needless to say, they are often duplicated at the college level. What has received less attention is that in many of these college programs, the study of conflict is but the camel's nose of a comprehensive effort at radical indoctrination, justified by the purported power of sweeping social change to eliminate the scourge of war. What is more, many of the leaders in this "field" do not view their programs

25

as merely one more academic major but as the kernel of a new type of professional school, designed to train and accredit a new generation of movement activists.

The Peace and Social Justice Program established at Tufts University in 1983, and often referred to as a model for others, provides a case in point. Upon opening its bulletin one does, to be sure, encounter a few perfunctory nods toward the ideal of "open intellectual inquiry" and the need to avoid "predetermined ideological perspectives" when dealing with a subject that requires "considerable effort and reflection." But one has hardly read two pages before it becomes clear that peace-and-justice theorists have already made some remarkable scientific strides toward firm and final conclusions. Indeed, within the space of a single paragraph they are able to lay to rest what might be regarded as the most intractable issue of their discipline, namely, the causes of war. Citing the best of all possible authorities, they confidently inform us that "history shows" that war arises from "greed, competition, and profit...[from] underdevelopment and economic deprivation, from institutional violence, from in-equalities and powerlessness, and the denial of human rights...[as well as from] unchecked growth and resource depletion, particularly at the initiation of the developed world."

Perhaps the reason for so quickly stripping away the veil of mystery is to spare the curious student the inconvenience of paying any further attention to the program. Alas, no. Its sponsors wish not only to lure students in, but also to visit their desperately needed wisdom on those obdurately remaining without. In fact, as the faculty members describe their objectives, it becomes clear that the inauguration of a Peace and Social Justice Program is meant to be nothing less than the occasion for a reconstruction of the aims of higher education all across the curriculum. As they write:

> The university is not only well equipped to consider and solve hu-man problems, it has a historical imperative to do so. And few of its activities are as intrinsically important as pursuing the specific goals of peace and justice. That the traditions of liberal-arts education im-ply these objectives is, however, rarely discussed... For example, universities traditionally consider their major responsibility to be providing information and theories about the world. We would fur-ther ask how our education can prepare students to change condi-tions in that world rather than merely accept it as it is. Further, how can our education instill in students the desire to act, the antidotes for personal despair, and a sense of personal responsibility for improving our world?...If we desire peace we must teach peace and do it now. This will necessitate a new set of priorities and educational aims.

With such broad ambitions it is not surprising that the program's coordinators imagine themselves spending as much time lobbying colleagues as teaching students. They will seek to build a new sense of "purpose, cooperation, community, and social responsibility that will revitalize the university." Because the goals of peace and social justice require challenging "competitiveness and individualism" and promoting "cooperation and interdependence," this effort will necessarily focus on "personal as well as global change." More specifically, each department at Tufts is to be invited to develop several of the forty-five proposed courses (mostly pulled from the catalogues of other universities) which the peace theorists consider necessary for their grand design. The engineering department, for instance, can offer "Appropriate Technology and Community Control;" mathematics, "The Ethics of Mathematic Modeling for Military Use;" American studies, "Racism and Sexism in American Society;" economics, "Introduction to Third World Poverty;" music, "singing the Blues, Music and Social Injustice;" and so on. Yet even this will not suffice, for peace education should be integrated "as a process, and not merely as a discrete subject...throughout the curricula and into university life generally." Consequently, "every Tufts professor" will be challenged "to interject, if they have not already done so, some peace and justice component into all their courses." Finally, to ensure that the mind will never have a moment to wander, the whole campus is to be immersed in a swirl of films, conferences, lectures, seminars and teach-ins, all sponsored by the program.

Here, then is a plan for turning Tufts into a new, radical bastion of orthodoxy. Appropriately enough, there are also companion projects designed to use the program as an active center for the support of missionary training and proselytism. Thus, the program bills itself as providing skills "that will specifically attract a variety of governmental and non-governmental employers, including organizations in law, peace, education, human services and rights, dispute resolution, community development, international relations." Among its special features are an internship, bestowing college credit for student work with organizations in "broad areas of peace and justice, both on the local and global levels," and an "Alternative Careers Conference" fashioned to "stimulate further ideas for peace and justice careers." Departing from normal academic practise, the Peace and Social Justice Program also throws its core courses open to members of the general public, and conducts off-campus ventures which include "community training projects on peace, justice, and non-violence."

Most peace-studies programs are not so hellbent on intellectual hegemony as the one at Tufts (though quite a few in women's studies could probably match it in this respect). Nor are most quite so intent on explicitly linking the pursuit of peace to the total realization of the Left's agenda. (Most leave the word "justice" out of their formal titles.) Nonetheless, the great majority share in its basic assumptions about the roots of war, the requirements of social justice, classroom advocacy, and the propriety of academic subsidies for political activism.

Scholarly associations, like universities, have usually been conceived of as forums for the exchange of ideas or debate on the merit of rival theories. Their ability to perform these intellectual services has been predicated on an understanding that as institutions they themselves take no position on the matters being discussed. Among those fields regarded as "sciences" there has been the further notion that knowledge is always tentative, subject to falsification through the acquisition of new evidence, and never to be cloaked in the garb of definitive pronouncements. As a result, within many academic associations an ongoing struggle has taken place between those committed to these liberal conceptions and those desirous of turning the organizations into platforms for agitation.

It is one thing ideologically to capture a department, program or even an entire college, but quite another to leave one's impress on a national association with many thousands of members. Still, politics is rich in examples of relatively small groups controlling large organizations by virtue of their energy, discipline, and sense of purpose. Accordingly, while some scholarly associations in the humanities and the social sciences have successfully defended their traditional roles, each has witnessed its struggles, and a few have been seriously compromised.

Almost invariably the attempts to politicize the associations have come from the Left. The size of the leftist component, its organizational base, and the nature of its efforts have, however, varied from discipline to discipline. In the case of economics, for instance, the Left is relatively small and somewhat intellectually isolated. On the other hand, it is fairly well organized, possessing its own association, the Union for Radical Political Economics, which operates both within and alongside the American Economic Association (AEA), and a journal, *The Review of Radical Economics*, which reaches an audience about a tenth that of the *American*

Economic Review. While the radical economists have managed to achieve a certain respectability, and have seen a few of their leading lights gain AEA office, their room for overt political maneuver has been comparatively limited. One factor in this is a provision in the AEA constitution which forbids the association from taking positions on public issues. Nonetheless the Union did manage a small "break-through" at the 1985 AEA business meeting by helping to push through a divestiture resolution, over the opposition of the AEA executive committee.

Among political scientists the fortunes of the radicals, organized in the Caucus for a New Political Science, have waxed and waned. In 1972 when the Caucus still contained members of both the "soft" and "hard" left, it missed by a hairsbreadth electing one of its leaders, Peter Bachrach, president of the American Political Science Association (APSA). Two years later, James MacGregor Burns, another of the Caucus's members, was elected president with the endorsement of the APSA nominating committee. Simultaneously, Caucus-endorsed candidates won nine out of the fourteen seats at stake on the APSA's governing council. These events, followed by an annual convention whose scholarly agenda was strongly colored by Marxism, prompted counter-organization on the part of centrist political scientists, and a split within the Caucus over the importance of winning APSA elections. The resulting victory of the Marxist faction of the Caucus led to a partial withdrawal from APSA politics, the launching of a journal, and a renewed emphasis on organizing local chapters, recruiting graduate students, and working with "community groups." At present the internal life of the APSA has something of a Center-Right tilt, despite the continued presence of a sizable radical cohort. In fact, prominent centrists or neoconservatives such as Seymour Martin Lipset and Aaron Wildavsky have recently served as APSA presidents.

A very different situation prevails among historians, sociologists, and anthropologists. The Organization of American Historians has elected several leftists to its presidency in recent years, including Eugene Genovese in 1978, William Appleman Williams in 1980, Gerda Lerner in 1981, and Leo Litwack in 1986. This year the American Historical Association elected its first woman president, Natalie Zemon Davis, editorial associate for *Radical History Review.* Writing in the *Nation* (May 24, 1986), the historian Jon Wiener has approvingly described the growing gap between the political sensibilities of the Reagan era and the intellectual life of his field. Wiener reports that at the last meeting of the Organization of American Historians in April of 1986, "fourteen past and present officers drew up a petition opposing aid to the contras. The signers included the current president and two past presidents..." Straining to provide some scholarly justification for this naked excursion into politics, the petition pretended to deplore "President Reagan's distortion of history for political purposes in describing the Nicaraguan contras, whose systematic abuse of human rights has been documented by independent observers, as the 'moral equivalent' of the founding fathers..."

Both the American Sociological Association (ASA) and the American Anthropological Association (AAA) also regularly elect radical scholars to top leadership posts, habitually endorse leftist political positions, and in a variety of other ways consistently display radicalized ideological sensibilities. Recent business meetings of the American Sociological Association, for example, have approved the passage of resolutions submitted by the association's Marxist section condemning American foreign policy and endorsing the "sanctuary" movement. Somewhat more officially, the ASA's elected council has, over the past several years, endorsed motions supporting "gay-rights" legislation, defending Roe v. Wade, and calling upon the United States government to respect the "civil liberties and sovereignty" of the people of Central America. (The council did manage briefly to break stride and condemn the "violations of academic rights" in the Soviet Union as well.) Worse yet was the decision in 1984 of the criminology section of the ASA to present its first Latin American Scholar Award to Vilma Nunez de Escoria, vice-president of the Nicaraguan Supreme Court and a former member of the Sandinista National Liberation Front, who was then traveling through the United States on a speaking tour organized by a group named United States Out of Central America. Following the awards presentation, which singled out her work in human rights, she was feted as a guest of honor at a reception hosted by then-ASA president Kai Erikson.

Yet this pales in comparison with what can go on when anthropologists assemble in national convention. Then, in the words of one participant, "late at night, after the reactionaries [have gone] off exhausted," an atmosphere can develop that would be hard to duplicate at any major gathering in North America outside the bounds of Turtle Bay. A typical cascade of denunciation, the product of the December 5, 1982 meeting, included adoption of the following: a motion urging anthropologists not to undertake work for the CIA or the U.S. military, both described as supporting regimes "engaged in overt

30

repression of indigenious peoples...[and] genocidal policies;" a motion condemning U.S. immigration policy for "excluding people from capitalist regimes and nonwhite peoples in general;" a motion condemning a video game called "Custer's Revenge" for its celebration of "the historical oppression of Native Americans by the U.S. government;" and a motion calling upon the U.S. government to "freeze the development, production, and deployment of nuclear weapons" and "dismantle its existing arsenal" (an amendment to include the Soviet Union, and urging a bilateral and verifiable freeze, was defeated). To make this ideological *Walpurgisnacht* complete there were two resolutions denouncing Israel, the first for "the systematic and deliberate destruction of Palestinian and Lebanese peoples and cultures" (passed after an hour of debate and the defeat of several amendments to broaden the focus of the resolution); and the second for restricting research and suppressing academic freedom in the occupied West Bank (passed without debate).

In reaction to such excesses, a resolution approved in 1984 required motions passed at business meetings to be submitted to the AAA's membership via a mailed ballot. Given the apparent proclivities of most anthropologists, this has proved only a partial remedy. When the 1984 business meeting passed a resolution declaring that "mass opposition and resistance to war preparations must achieve new heights," and calling upon "all its members to take part in diverse events across the country expressing this opposition and resistance," it was approved by 82 percent of the membership bothering to vote. (This year, the referendum procedure is itself under challenge in a referendum.)

It is tempting to dismiss all this as meaningless bombast that simply discredits those associated with it. (The same thing has been said about the resolution passed by the UN.) But while most sociologists or anthropologists may keep their distance from such antics, it would be unwise to assume that they are unaffected by them. At the very least these maneuvers represent a continuous endorsement of the advocacy style in social science, and, by lending legitimacy to extreme postures, gradually shift the spectrum of respectable opinion further and further to the Left. They also confer some scholarly respectability on the use of vituperative and emotional language, and, even worse, on hack formulations lifted from Soviet propaganda. Finally, they discomfort those who disagree, as constant reiteration works symbolically to redefine membership in the social-science community along ideological rather than professional lines, threatening dissenters with the status of moral pariahs. Thus, though these

31

motions may heat up the deliberations of a good many conferences, their approval inevitably has a chilling effect.

Ortega y Gasset remarked more than fifty years ago that "the simple process of preserving our present civilization is supremely complex and demands incalculably subtle powers." There is nothing subtle, however, in the intent of the zealots now so amply represented within the ranks of academe, nor much in their doings that would work to strengthen the foundations of civilized life.

In its traditional liberal vision the university perpetuated the ideals of Western Civilization in two separate but related ways. First, it imparted a sense of intellectual method which rejected dogmatic, monistic, and conspiratorial formulations in favor of a broadminded empiricism and a regard for the world's complexity. Second, it conveyed an appreciation for the underlying values of free societies, most notably a respect for the moral worth of the individual and for the ideals of personal liberty and constitutional democracy which emanated from it. As a result the university experience had a dual character, in part a process of intellectual training and in part a process of socialization.

At a deeper level, however, method and values reflected and reinforced one another. Operating within such a system, academics were able to illustrate what was just and admirable about Western civilization simply by adhering to the canons of their own fields of scholarship. Or, taking the other tack, they could promote intellectual openness and tolerance through an honest reading of the West's achievements. A study of ancient Greece was a study of life, not a preachment or conversion; but the highest ideals of that civilization carry their own persuasiveness, and are the precursors of our own.

All this is quite alien to the spirit of what aspires to become the new, radicalized academy. Armed with a variety of totalistic visions and millennial expectations, its partisans have little sympathy either with open discourse or with analytic procedures that fail to guarentee desired conclusions. It is not a coincidence that the epistemological relativism prominent in the early writings of Marx is also a common feature of the theories of contemporary academic radicals, be they feminists, deconstructionists, or Marxists. After all, if one wishes to reach a rather improbable goal without undue let or hindrance, the fewer the methodological constraints the better. As Howard Zinn, professor of history at Boston University, once put it, "In a world where justice is maldistributed, there is no such thing as a 'neutral' or representative recapitulations of the facts." In such a view, objective truth is only what the present dictates or what the future requires.

The organizing principles of radical scholarship inheres in its purpose rather than in its methods or theories. And its purposes is unremitting attack on existing cultural traditions and political and economic institutions. Thus, Paul Attewell, in a friendly survey of the work of radical economists, can locate " a major goal of most Left theorizing" in *"the dual accomplishment of a political-economic analysis and a moral critique in which the economic analysis shows that an 'evil' is systematically and necessarily produced by capitalism"* (emphasis in the original). Of course, a scholarship which sets out to prove that which it already knows, and whose underlying conviction is the necessary and systematic relation of the universe of evils to the structure of a free society, is no scholarship at all. What this statement describes is something quite different: a campaign of defamation.

Perhaps the most ominous aspect of this campaign is the use of the classroom for the cultivation of ethnic and class resentments, particularly among minority students entering into higher education for the first time. Until recently the university served as an important means of integrating the future leadership of American society and assimilating the upwardly mobile. A significant part of it now strives to do precisely the reverse, by fostering political estrangement and cultural segmentation. And even where, as is generally the case, the result falls short of instilling hatred, the atmosphere so created sours the country's image for many of those emerging into active citizenship.

At the very least, the rise of adversarial education has deprived many students of an adequate opportunity to be exposed to what is best in their own cultural tradition. (And given the decline of American secondary instruction, colleges are frequently the only place where such material can be absorbed.) In its search for opportunities to investigate the underside of American life, the Left has littered college catalogues with all sorts of marginalia. Some of these novel courses may have limited academic relevance. Unfortunately, however, time spent studying "Chicago Theater" or "Sex and Violence in the American Family" is time lost from the study of classics of political theory or world literature. The result is often a college graduate with as little sense of the deposited wisdom of the civilization as that of a troglodyte who never opened a book.

To an astonishing degree the relative acceptance of radical ideas at our universities has been accompanied by changed ground rules for teaching, scholarship, and peer review. In the process, *academic freedom*, which is the foundation on which teaching and learning prosper, has been *transformed*. As a principle it was meant to shield the academy from external pressure and manipulation, but, like most other freedoms, it simulateously conferred a responsibility, involving a willingness to uphold basic standards of inquiry and to render judgment on the quality of colleagues' ideas.

The zealots who now threaten the academy do so out of the certainty and urgency with which they embrace their favored truths. But milder men also threaten it when they cease to believe in any truths at all, or lack the courage to bring their beliefs to bear on professional decisions. What follows is a careless latitudinairianism that parcels out portions of the academic terrain among every group too large, too vocal, or too assertive to be comfortably ignored, whatever the intellectual merit of its positions. The *reductio ad absurdum* of this appeasing attitude, a kind of ideological affirmative action, is nicely captured in Professor William Van Alstyne's recent complaint at an AAUP meeting that Marxists are underrepresented in college classrooms since, in contrast to the academy, "two-thirds of the globe is persuaded by Marxism writ large."

In the last analysis, it is less the academy's radical minority and more its liberal majority that is at the heart of the problem. Since the mid-60s a diminished belief in American society has left that majority unable effectively to counter the genuinely impassioned forces of the Left. Accordingly, it is a revival of that robust and clear-sighted liberalism, once so cognizant of extremist dangers in all their forms, which constitutes the essential condition for restoring a healthier campus climate. The future of higher education hinges on how the internal crisis of American liberalism is eventually resolved.

Stephen Balch is associate professor of government at John Jay College of Criminal Justice of the City University of New York, and president of Campus Coalition of Democracy, an organization of college faculty concerned about ideological extremism within the academy.

Herbert London is dean of the Gallatin Division of New York University, a senior fellow of the Hudson Institute, and a member of the board of directors of Campus Coalition for Democracy.

This article is reprinted with permission from Commentary.

CHAPTER THREE

HARVARD STILL HATES AMERICA
by JOHN LEBOUTILLIER

---

*Harvard, I am distressed to say, has become a
frequent arena for tolerating intolerance. In
the year of its 350th anniversary — a
celebration of freedom, diversity and tolerance
that has been the envy of the world — freedom,
diversity and tolerance suffered a major
setback.*

IN THE FAMOUS ancient Yard at Harvard, an inscription in
the gate reads, "Enter to grow in wisdom, depart to serve thy
country better." Consider this noble ideal in the face of certain
realities at this higher education giant. Until recently,
Harvard's chairman of its history department had been a
bonafide Communist; a faithful believer in a political system
that declares itself the enemy of that country Harvard exhorts
its students to serve better.

In his 25th anniversary autobiographical sketch, former
Harvard history chairman John Womack wrote, "In politics,
as I was 10 years ago, so I remain a Communist. This keeps
me busy." I am sure it has. During the past ten years, as
William F. Buckley, Jr. wrote, Professor Womack must
surely have kept busy justifying such Communist enterprises
as the cultural revolution, genocide in Cambodia, boat people
in Vietnam, the invasion in Afghanistan, martial law in
Poland, the illegalization of Solidarity, and the shooting down
of Flight 007.

At a Harvard rally protesting the United States' liberation of
the island of Grenada and the successful rescue of over 600
American medical students, Professor Womack candidly remarked, "The Reagan Administration is looking to kick
brown and black butt for the sheer fun of it." Even Walter
Mondale supported the President's efforts in Grenada, along

with over 90% of the Grenadan people. But not this Harvard professor. He hates America.

When I arrived at Harvard as an undergraduate in 1972, the first class I enrolled in was taught by a history professor who boldly announced: "I am a Marxist and I'm going to teach this American history course from a Marxist perspective." And true to form, every class was filled with Marxist dogma and a Marxist interpretation of American history.

The first paper he assigned was on slavery in the 19th century South. I decided to challenge the opinions of the teacher. But a friend of mine decided to regurgitate what the teacher had said. When I received my graded paper, I was sincerely shocked. I first experienced academic discrimination in its purest form. I received a grade of "B" along with a note from the teacher saying: "You have the potential to be a great revolutionary, but your analysis and your thoughts need a lot of work." My friend, who had spouted Marxism in his paper, received an "A" along with sparkling comments from the professor.

This was my introduction to what really goes on in major universities like Harvard. Over the next four years, I learned that teachers often indoctrinate students with their peculiar philosophies. Students who agreed with the teachers were, more often than not, rewarded with higher grades than those who challenged the teachers' views.

In 1978, I wrote *Harvard Hates America*, which described some of my experiences — ranging from classroom stories like the one above to incidents where teaching assistants sold drugs to students. "I may have mellowed," commented Jerry Rubin, "but not so much as to like this book." Indeed, the book provoked controversy. Like the founding of Accuracy in Academia, it sparked debate. It raised some embarrassing questions for Harvard.

"I guess no one single thing at Harvard bothered me more than the failure on the part of so many students and teachers to realize the rich history and tradition of Harvard," I wrote in *Harvard Hates America*. I added:

> Harvard has produced more presidents, Nobel Prize laureates, and social leaders than any other university in the world. Famous writers, doctors, scientists, lawyers and business leaders have come in profusion from Harvard — and have played important roles in the improvement of life in our country. Yet, despite this legacy, many people at Harvard disavow this tradition and see the destruction of our country as desirable.

> I remember well an incident during my sophomore year that clearly exemplified this inverted sense of idealism. I was in a course called English 70 — English Literature 1660-1960. It was a basic

37

survey course of great American writers dating from the time of the Puritans from Poe, Emerson, Melville, all the way to Miller.

On a Thursday afternoon, my section of twelve students was meeting for our regularly scheduled weekly meeting. We had been reading Perry Miller's *The Puritans,* a collection of writings by the earliest settlers...Not long into the class, we picked up two key subjects: the Puritan work ethic and the Puritans' belief that God had a special relationship with America. One student, a Southerner named Mike, raised his hand, seeking permission to speak. He was a short, thin senior from Georgia.

Finally, he spoke. "Y'all know that I come from the South. And we don't take too kindly to some of this Puritan...crap." ...(A) pert little blond girl named Claire jerked up in her chair (and) said, "...you're so right. So much of this stuff is so corny, so predictable...so...uh...ah...it's damn Middle America, its a joke. Imagine saying that God has a special relationship with this country..."

The irony of it all is, of course, that the founders of Harvard, themselves puritans and among the most educated people of their day, established this famous institution in the hope that "every one shall consider the main end of his life and studies to know God..." The Rules and Precepts of Harvard College adopted in 1646 include this passage: "Seeing the Lord giveth wisdom, every one shall seriously by prayer in secret seek wisdom by Him."

Jerry Falwell, seemingly counting on the tradition of spiritual freedom at Harvard, may have thought his fundamentalist (or puritan) views would be tolerated. Not so. When Dr. Falwell traveled to Harvard in 1983 to deliver a lecture, audience members burst into chants drowning out his words. A number of hecklers made a determined effort to shout Falwell down. *The Harvard Salient* reported that "despite the fact that two protesters physically assaulted police officers, and despite the fact that they and many of their fellows prevented Falwell from effectively expressing their views, neither one was arrested. The administration did nothing to discipline them."

Harvard, I am distressed to say, has become a frequent arena for tolerating intolerance. In the year of its 350th anniversary, a celebration of freedom, diversity and tolerance suffered a major setback. In April of 1986, a spokesman for the Nicaraguan freedom fighters or "contras" was hustled out of a Harvard hall as disrupters stormed the podium shouting, "Death, death, death to fascists." The spokesman was hit in the eye by an egg and knocked to the ground. In May, attorney General Edwin Meese was scheduled to deliver a speech at Harvard University, but students and faculty members threatened to present the administration with petitions signed by over half the student body who disapproved of Meese's invitation and planned award. The university canceled the original date, but finally rescheduled the speech without the presentation of the award.

Embarrassed Harvard alumni will grudgingly remember the 1983 incident when Harvard graduate Casper Weinberger visited his alma mater to discuss U.S. defense policy. Members of the violent Spartacus Youth League yelled and screamed, filled water ballons with red dye, and hurled them at the Secretary of Defense.

At Harvard, it has been the university officials and faculty members who have been tolerant of such abuses. When Adolfo Calero wanted to continue his speech, Harvard's law school said no. His speech was cancelled by a Harvard dean on the inexplicable ground that the audience was dominated by conservatives. The same dean admitted that, prior to the speech, she orchestrated a protest against Mr. Calero.

But the obscene attitudes of Harvard faculty members about controversial speech are most troubling. Randall Kennedy, a professor of law at Harvard, gave a lecture advertised as "Hey, Hey, Ho, Ho, Free Speech has Got to Go!" Kennedy forcefully defended the position of prevention of speech on the grounds that "toleration has its limits." When asked if the protester could abridge the rights of President Ronald Reagan or a Republican Secretary of Defense, Kennedy argued that he would not condemn the silencing of their views. A bright student then asked the $164,000 question. What if a lecturer were beaten or killed during the protest? Kennedy answered, "It's close call, something I'd have to think deeply about."

After a South African diplomat was prevented from speaking at Harvard in 1987, a mathematics professor on campus wrote, "..there is no provision under U.S. law that guarantees uninterrupted free speech...[the South African's] privilege to air his views from a Harvard podium is hardly a 'right.'"

These statements and incidents represent the closed minds of the scholarly community. I encountered them while at Harvard, and I'm afraid they persist in a burgeoning way in the eighties. Professor Allan Bloom's tome, *The Closing of the American Mind*, was surprisingly popular and provocative, precisely because a cancerous problem exists on the college campuses, and the officials responsible for its growth are increasingly reluctant to confront it.

In 1986, Education Secretary William J. Bennett traveled to Harvard to speak, as he put it, "truth to power." Secretary

Bennett, out of deep affection for his alma mater and concern for the state of higher education, boldly took issue with the way those in power at this mighty institution were treating these academic problems. He reminded his Harvard audience that our students "deserve a good education — at minimum, a systematic familiarization with our own Western tradition of learning; with the classical and Judeo-Christian heritage, the facts of American and European history, the political organization of Western societies, the great works of Western art and literature, the major achievements of the scientific disciplines."

Bennett was essentially asking if there is *real* education at Harvard and universities nationwide, a commodity that our students deserve and our nation requires, namely, a real and sustained attention to the students' intellectual and moral well-being. Secretary Bennett was loudly denounced by Harvard President Derek Bok for trying to "hype the media." But Secretary Bennett had anticipated this negative reaction when he said in his speech that the academy in recent days had reacted to his hard-hitting criticisms as though he had "hurled a rock through the stained glass window of a cathedral."

Take the rise of the left-wing Marxist oriented Critical Legal Studies movement at Harvard during the eighties and its assault on traditional legal thought. This "movement" represents the activist agenda that has so politicized the American academy today. Critical Legal Studies adherents adopt a Marxian outlook toward the British-American legal tradition which they claim is socially and economically oppressive. While "Crits" are active at many law schools around the country, the movement has been centered at Harvard. The "Crits" professors have been reported to be "aggressive and forceful" advocates of the radical view of law in their classes. After all, university students are the potential exploited subjects of a legal system that discriminates against the average American worker.

The following is a typical teaching method of a Critical Legal Studies professor and his effort to encourage students to examine what he sees as the unstated assumptions of American law.

Near the beginning of my course on labor law, I engage my students in the following dialogue: Picture an employee who works for a company that produces widgets. One working day, this employee builds four widgets and, at the end of the day, tenders to her boss an amount in cash equal to the cost of the necessary materials and tools, and the apportioned cost of other managerial expenses. She then leaves the shop and takes the widgets with her, planning to sell them and keep the profits. What, I ask, will happen? My students stir restlessly until someone volunteers that the employer will sue the employee, or have her arrested. On what theories, I respond. Someone hazards the guess that the conversion is the crime of theft. I then ask why the employer is not guilty of the same misconduct when he pays the employee a reasonable "rent" for her labor, keeps the widgets for himself, and sells them for his own profit. There is more stirring and murmuring, until someone finally says, "Because the widgets belong to the employer — the law says that they're his property." Why should that be, I ask. After all, there is nothing "necessary" about permitting the employer to "rent" the worker and keep the widgets: why not structure the relationship the other way around? When someone objects that, if we did that "then we wouldn't have capitalism," and enforces a core assumption about the relationship between employer and employee in a market economy...assumptions that should not be immune to re-examination and critique. We might want to consider the current arrangement in light of our democratic and egalitarian aspirations and ask whether it exacts too great a cost in terms of the self-determination and the bargaining power of working people...

Critical Legal Studies is an assault on our successful free market economic system — an economic system that has provided more opportunity, economic growth, prosperity and economic liberty in the United States than anywhere in the world. Yet such an avowedly anti-freedom market philosophy is promoted as if it were revealed truth. If students cannot overcome certain "assumptions" of American law, they, in essence, suffer from a learning deficiency — one that can only be corrected by idealistic academicians raising their low level of consciousness. There is a distinct disdain for our economic system amongst such legal activists. They hate-America too.

The ideological agenda of the Marxist legal scholars, the harassment of conservative speakers, and the obscene attitudes regarding free speech at Harvard of some professors, abound in Cambridge precisely because of a anti-Americanism that has reacted negatively to the relative popularity and success of the Reagan presidency. Many academics and students have sacrificed scholarship for a polemical assault against the rise of the right in the eighties. On March 5, 1987, *The Harvard Crimson* called for President Reagan's impeachment. On what grounds? The conservative *Harvard Salient* reported that in order to justify its call for impeachment, *The Crimson* used the grounds that "our democratic ideals, which — as every schoolchild knows — force us to try every twenty years to impeach whomever happens to be President at the time." *The Crimson* added:

"The tree of liberty," Thomas Jefferson wrote, "must be refreshed with the blood of patriots and tyrants every twenty years."

Jefferson did not make the remarks because tyrants are born in batches. He made them because he thought it necessary that each generation renew its commitment to the values on which its society is based. And Jefferson knew the sacrifice that would entail.

This from a campus publication that will produce, no doubt, and provide us at some point, with many of our future media stars and commentators.

Because of the left-wing philosophy of the campus daily, conservatives organized to found the *Harvard Salient,* a thoughtful, witty, and formidable critic of the radical ethos that pervades the Cambridge community. In a revealing expose of the views of a number of prominent Harvard scholars in March of 1987, the *Salient* noted that President Reagan has proved Harvard intellectuals wrong time and time again.

Three prominent Harvard professors who predicted that Reagan's presidency would be more inflationary than the Carter presidency; that the likelihood of nuclear war would be increased; that the likelihood of arms control agreements impossible; that U.S. support of Jose Napoleon Duarte in El Salvador would be that of injustice and repression, have, as we now know, been proved wrong by history.

Tom Firestone, a recent graduate of Harvard and a former editor of the *Salient* wrote that "a review of Harvard professors' predictions during the Reagan presidency shows that Reagan is more intelligent than Harvard's most distinguished faculty members." Firestone wrote that "several of my professors used lecture time to make jokes about Reagan," including John Womack who publicly called Reagan a "fascist warmonger," who is nonetheless a "cowardly dummy."

Stanley Hoffman, Harvard's leading "expert" on international relations, claimed to be full of "horror" at the prospects of American foreign policy after learning that Reagan was elected in 1980. He predicted a "whole series of disasters" which would heighten the possibility of a nuclear war. Hoffman argued that a military buildup would threaten peace and destroy relations with the Soviets making arms control agreements almost impossible. Yet it was precisely the Reagan defense build-up, the announcement of the Pershing missiles in Germany, that induced the Soviets to come back to the bargaining table and to eventually sign a sweeping arms reduction (not arms control) agreement known as the INF treaty.

In January of 1984, Terry Karl, a supposed expert on U.S. foreign policy of Latin America was doubtful "that there will be a democratic outcome in El Salvador." Again, Reagan proved a Harvard scholar wrong.

"But the issue that aroused the ire within the Harvard faculty," writes Firestone, "was the invasion of Grenada." At a rally condemning this "heinous act," Professor Ruth Hubbard screeched, "Unless we get the U.S. out now, Grenada will become — to put it bluntly — a brothel with the U.S. as its pimp." Firestone reported that the most thorough denunciation came when a Harvard "expert" on the Caribbean, Orlando Patterson, explained that the invasion was "counterproductive" because the overthrown Grenadan dictator Maurice Bishop "really wasn't ever a Communist, but was pressured from the left." As captured documents revealed later, Bishop was in fact a militant Marxist.

One of Reagan's foremost critics at Harvard is John Kenneth Galbraith. In the early eighties Galbraith ventured to predict that "there is little likelihood of a substantial increase occuring in domestic production of oil and gas to meet anticipated demand. In fact, the United States will be fortunate if it finds enough new oil and gas to keep production at current levels..." As we know, Reagan's faith in the free market has proven Professor Galbraith's predictions to be so much natural gas, as Mr. Firestone so aptly coined it. "U.S. Daily output of crude oil has increased from 8.5 million barrels in 1981 to 8.9 million barrels in 1985, the highest level since 1973," wrote Firestone. Finally, Professor Galbraith predicted that "Reagan's fiscal policy will be more inflationary than [Carter's]." The inflation rate under the Reagan presidency has been at historic low levels, in the 3% to 5% range, far below the double digit rates under the Carter years.

In 1986, a group of Harvard professors who feared that the university would offer Reagan a traditional honorary degree to lure him to the university's 350th anniversary celebration, distributed a letter urging the university to consider someone more acceptable. Their argument was, in essence, that Reagan is not intellectually worthy of a Harvard degree. Reagan's invitation was not withdrawn, but his honorary degree was. So the President returned the favor by not participating in the festivities. Prince Charles spoke instead.

I wrote *Harvard Hates America* in 1978, not to embarrass individuals or the institution, but to show how far a great institution has fallen. My concern then is my concern today. Harvard is not producing leaders dedicated to bettering and perpetuating this great experiment we call America. In 1978, I wrote that Harvard should recognize its special role in

America — that of being charged with the responsibility for educating leaders capable of solving problems, leaders dedicated to improving the welfare of the entire country, not followers devoted simply to "making money." It should question, challenge and lead the way rather than following the liberal ethos that has poisoned much of the intellectual climate on campuses today.

Frankly, it's embarrassing to know that Harvard, the school of the best and brightest for centuries, has tolerated the silencing of unpopular speakers; hired professors whose purpose is not intellectual inquiry and scholarship, but passionate political activism; and insulated itself from responsible criticism when such criticism is directed its way. But I love this institution and am still hopeful that it will one day again fulfill Henry Adams' observation that "Harvard College, as far as it educated at all, was a mild and liberal school, which sent young men into the world with all they needed to make respectable citizens."

John LeBoutillier, a former member of Congress, is President of Accuracy in Academia. He graduated magna cum laude *from Harvard in 1976 and received an M.B.A. from Harvard in 1979. He is the author of* Harvard Hates America. *He is also the founder and president of Skyhook II Project, an organization devoted to the rescue efforts of American POWs still believed to be alive in Indochina. He writes and lectures extensively and makes frequent appearences on radio and television.*

CHAPTER FOUR

THE ILLIBERAL LIBERAL ENVIRONMENT AT STANFORD
by GEORGE MAROTTA

What is lacking at Stanford is the leadership to temper the one-sided nature of vocal partisan professors in order to maintain an environment of academic freedom where diversity of views are not only tolerated, but indeed welcomed.

IT IS A widely known and accepted fact that professors in social science departments of our colleges and universities are generally on the liberal side of the ideological spectrum. The authoritative studies on this subject have been done by Seymour Martin Lipset, a professor of political science and sociology at Stanford University and senior fellow at Stanford's Hoover Institution.

One study by Lipsett and Everett Ladd reveals that the more elite the university, the more liberal the faculty. Stanford University is certainly recognized as being one of America's most elite universities. From my general observation over the twelve years I have been associated with Stanford, I have concluded it has one of the most liberal faculties. Now, based on recent specific studies, I can attest to the fact that it does indeed have one of the most liberal social science faculties in the U.S.

Let me state at the outset that there is nothing wrong with being a liberal professor at a liberal institution of higher learning. Nearly everyone is liberal at some point in his or her life. However, I always thought that one's liberal tendencies made one more tolerant of different points of view. Recent events at Stanford have shaken my belief regarding the latter point.

Being on a liberal campus means being subjected to frequent visits by members of the Democratic party. Former president Jimmy Carter visited recently, New York Governor Mario Cuomo was graduation speaker two years ago where he again delivered "The Speech." The June 1987 speaker was former House Speaker Tip O'Neill.

Stanford is so busy looking to placate competing factions on the ideological left that they completely ignore the center and the right. For example, the latest student group on campus demanding attention is the Rainbow Agenda. President Donald Kennedy has bent over backwards listening to their charges. Members of the gay, Jewish, and women's communities have appealed for inclusion. The purposes of the coalition is to articulate the concerns of all minority groups on campus.

Stanford President Kennedy made some interesting remarks at graduation. Referring to the Rainbow Agenda's charges of racism at Stanford, he said that the university "...is well past the point at which it actively rejects people because of differences. But, we still need to ask ourselves about the choices we are making. Are we actively seeking out differences, or welcoming new and sometimes hostile views?"

I know the President was looking to the "left" when he made that statement but I can confidently answer, "No, No, No, Mr. President. Remove the timbers from your eyes and look to the left, center, and right when you ask that question."

The recent loss of the Reagan presidential library at Stanford University turned my disgust with Stanford's intolerance to one of outright anger. And so I would like to describe how the liberal environment at Stanford has deteriorated in recent years to one of outright illiberality and intolerance, especially toward the Hoover Institution, its director and scholars.

There are several sources of friction between the Hoover Institution and Stanford University. One is the liberal ideological preferences of Stanford faculty versus the ideological balance of Hoover fellows.

The major source of friction between the Hoover Institution and the rest of the university is structural. Some have theorized that personality conflicts between Stanford President Kennedy and Hoover Director Glenn Campbell is the major problem, and that changes in leadership would bring lasting improvements. I strongly disagree. Herbert Hoover, with his keen understanding of the nature of academia, knew what he was doing in the late 1950s when he designed the relationships between the university and the institution he founded in 1919. The institution was made part of the "frame" of Stanford University, but he made certain that the appointment of the

46

director, the administration of the institution and the appointment of the fellows would not be under the control of the faculty. The Institution was not subject to "normal academic governance."

The Stanford faculty has shown its dislike for the Hoover director from day one of his arrival — 27 years ago. Faculty members disliked him because he was not like themselves, being a conservative Republican (strike one). Campbell also came to Stanford from being a Harvard economist by way of the U.S. Chamber of Commerce and the American Enterprise Institute, two institutions known to tolerate free enterprise (strike two), and he had been "handpicked" by Republican Herbert Hoover (strike three — he's not welcome).

Actually, the appointment process also involved being approved by the Stanford Board of Trustees and the Stanford president, but some faculty officials like to maintain the myth that Campbell was forced on Stanford by "the Chief."

When he took over in 1960, the Hoover Institution was a sleepy-eyed library/archive that was in poor financial condition. Today, it boasts of a large number of academic superstars who collectively hold 44 memberships in the nation's honorary societies, a half dozen Nobel prize winners, holders of the Congressional Medal of Honor, the Presidential Medal of Freedom, the National Medal of Science, etc., etc.

Campbell has expanded Hoover's endowment from only $250,000 in 1960 to over $100 million today. In contrast, the Hutchins Center for the Study of Democratic Institutions, which at one time had an endowment similar to Hoover's, is now bankrupt.

The Hoover archives are second to none in the world in quality and depth of collections. The physical plant of the Institution is without parallel. The environment for research, both physical and psychological, is first-rate. Over the years, many attempts have been made by Stanford administration and faculty to try to change the original Hoover terms of reference and to harass or change the Hoover leadership.

I have witnessed or heard about the following anti-Hoover actions. Stanford committees have tried to get the Hoover libraries placed under university library control. Financial support by the university for the Hoover library and archival operations have often been reduced beyond the level of cuts in non-Hoover university operations. The Hoover director has been discriminated against in salary levels — compared to other research administrators. A former Stanford president even admitted such and promised rectification, which has not yet been made. Also, University harassment even extended to several crude attempts to fire the director of the Hoover Institution.

I have often wondered if the university's attitude toward the Hoover director might have been based on the director's refusal to concur in altering the basic agreements regarding the semi-independent nature of the Hoover Institution. The present (and future) director has a fiduciary responsibility to maintain the charters and understandings regarding the Institution. I can understand how the director's positions might be interpreted by University presidents as non-cooperation and even insubordination — especially if they held contrasting personal ideological views.

Over the past four years, the Hoover Institution has been subjected to a steady barrage of attacks which, in toto, has created an environment which is not in consonant with the great reputation achieved by Stanford.

In 1983, Stanford professors John Manley (Political Science) and Ronald Rebholz (English) led an attack charging the Hoover Institution with being partisan and circulating a petition requesting the Board of Trustees to conduct an investigation. They cited as evidence the many ties between Hoover fellows and the Reagan administration.

In rebuttal, I pointed out academe's long and legitimate connection with public life. Much of FDR's "brain trust" included scholars from Columbia and Harvard Universities. One of the biggest migrations to the nation's capital occurred during the Kennedy administration while I was serving on the staff of the National Security Council and the Peace Corps.

The Harvard migration following JFK's election was so extensive that the list of faculty and alumni took up almost two pages in the February 1961 *Harvard Alumni Bulletin*. I could find no record of criticism by the faculty of Harvard that their colleagues were somehow playing an improper "partisan" role in serving their country. On the contrary, the record was replete with boasting as Harvard basked in national media attention.

When Jimmy Carter was elected, there was a small migration from Stanford University to serve in the Democratic administration, including then Professor Donald Kennedy as commissioner of the U.S. Food and Drug Administration. Many other Stanford faculty have served under both Democratic and Republican administrations. I do not recall any criticism of improper "partisan" behavior having been made at that time. Isn't it fair to conclude that there seems to be a double standard operating here: It's O.K. for liberal professors to serve in government, but not for scholars from alleged conservative institutes!

It is perfectly natural that there would be so many Hoover scholars performing service. The nature of much of the research at the Institution involves public policy issues with relevance to today's problems. If our nation did not utilize the services of such a distinguished group, our society would surely be the loser.

Since we at the Hoover Institution were being charged in the press with some kind of improper behavior, I was naturally interested in knowing who was attacking us. When the Hoover Institution formally requested from the Stanford administration a copy of the petition with signatures, our request was denied.

We were appalled that the Stanford administration would acknowledge the existence of a "no-name" petition, protecting the accusers for weeks while we, the accused, were smeared by the partisan attack of the ostensibly neutral *Stanford Daily* (student newspaper) journalists, which incredibly included a graduate student assistant to Professor Manley who was a former Nader-raider and an avowed Reagan-hater.

One of the excuses given by the administration was that the persons signing the petition did not know that their names were going to be made public, therefore they would have to be polled to grant permission to release their names. Following the polling, eight faculty members preferred not to have their names made public and were dropped from the petition.

It seems incredible that, in a university environment, the Stanford leadership was preparing to consider a public position making an unfounded (indeed absurd) charge and planned to keep secret the names of the accusers who were more partisan than the accused!

Stanford University's leadership during this period did little to squash what we felt was an improper charge. Indeed by their statements they encouraged the attackers. In response to press queries, Kennedy and Trustee Chairman Kimball commented that while they did not think that the Hoover Institution was partisan, they did reveal that they were planning all along to initiate an inquiry into the "governance" relationships between the University and the Institution.

The student newspaper on May 16, 1983 reported that "Kimball, said...that although the idea of an 'inquiry' probing the 'political partisanship' of Hoover is unlikely, he and University President Donald Kennedy discussed conducting a 'study' of the institution long before any of the current debate began. 'Don and I thought of doing this before any of the petitions,' Kimball said."

By allowing the question to be raised in the Faculty Senate, it seemed to some of us that the University administration was using the Manley-Rebholz attack to serve some of its purposes, i.e. "to build support among the faculty and trustees to alter the semi-independent status of the Institution within the frame (sic) of Stanford University."

Since the Institution had been so successful, we wondered why it was necessary to make any changes at all. In other words, it looked as if we were being attacked first by the liberal professoriate and then by the liberal administration for the same reasons — to deny academic freedom to scholars of the Institution — but with different methodology!

After the Manley-Rebholz petition had been accepted by the University Administration and scheduled for the Faculty Senate, some other Stanford professors became concerned about the precedent being set. If there could be an ideological investigation of the Hoover Institution, what other institute or department within Stanford would be next? Therefore, a counter-petition was organized which gained twice as many signatures, including twenty professors holding endowed chairs at Stanford. It condemned the Manley-Rebholz proposed witch-hunt as a grave threat to academic freedom. Petition organizer, French and Italian department chairman Professor Alphonse Juilland, stated that "Stanford's investigation of Hoover's politics could trigger similar investigations (elsewhere) — resulting in a generalized witch-hunt with liberals trying to track down conservative bias while conservatives would strive to oppose liberal prejudice."

Following the initial charges in 1983 that the Hoover Institution was partisan, there were a series of reports by various committees. One headed by Robert Ward (political science professor and Hoover senior fellow) was critical of the political science department for its unprofessional conduct in the handling of a proposed joint appointment. The Ward committee had been established to provide information to the president and the trustee committee on the Hoover Institution. (The Hoover Institution has frequently cooperated with the University in granting joint appointments; there are now about 21 such appointments.)

In reaction, the Faculty Senate established its own committee headed by sociology professor Dornbusch. That group's report recommended several changes, most of which would make the Hoover Institution more like a university department. Several would alter the basic agreements regarding the Hoover Institution.

Three Dornbusch findings were interesting. While they said they could find no partisanship at the Hoover Institution, they admitted that that was not the main thrust of their inquiry. They also said that we were too boastful regarding our many connections with the Reagan administration. Their report ended with an incredibly intolerant and arrogant statement. In effect they said that if progress was not made in making changes they recommended and if cooperation between Stanford and the Hoover Institution did not improve, then maybe consideration should be made to divorcing the Hoover Institution from Stanford University.

First the Stanford professors created an environment of dissension and mistrust and then THEY tell us that if WE don't improve the relationship (which they control), the Hoover Institution should be spun off from the University.

Regarding being too boastful about the Hoover Institution, I will plead guilty to that charge. A high university official and a Hoover scholar warned me when I was public affairs coordinator not to publicize too much the fact that many Hoover scholars were advising the Reagan administration. My reaction to that was that if they were intolerant that was their problem, not mine.

The Hoover scholars' reply to the Dornbusch report noted that (a) most of the recommendations had been in place for many years, (b) others were not necessary, while (c) still others would violate long-standing agreements and contracts.

Another reason why the Hoover Institution appears to be more conservative than it really is due to the fact that much research concerns Communism. Most scholars conclude that it is not a very good system of governance.

Hoover scholars are free to reach any conclusions they wish. However, the liberal Stanford faculty long ago seized on Herbert Hoover's statement about "the evils of the doctrine of Karl Marx" to label all of Hoover with having "a mission." No amount of facts to the contrary can change the wrongful interpretation which serves the faculty's ideological purposes.

Liberal professors frequently exhibit guilt to anything our country does or stands for. It's amazing how such professors can distort the facts. One alum wrote the following in the *Stanford Magazine:*

> As evidence for his contention that since 1945 the U.S. has been more militarily aggressive and expansionistic than the U.S.S.R., Professor Bernstein cites the presence of U.S. bases in more than 40 countries. He chooses to ignore the obvious distinction between

bases in countries that freely permit them and thereby suffer no loss of autonomy and the continuing Soviet presence in Eastern Europe that relies on actual or threatened military force.

The most disturbing aspect of the article is that its sources are Stanford faculty, probably tenured. Presumably, alumni have the maturity to recognize shallow thinking and political bias, but students are typically younger and more impressionable.

The poisoned relations between Stanford and Hoover produced other negative results for Hoover scholars. Hoover senior research fellow Admiral James Stockdale was to repeat a popular philosophy course that he had taught with emeritus professor Phillip Rhinelander. Instead, the course was dropped. I believe it was due mainly to the fact that Stockdale is a Hoover fellow, but a university investigation concluded it was just a bureaucratic mix-up. There is no question in my mind that this was just another white-wash of an out-and-out case of discrimination against a Hoover fellow.

Professors Manley and Rebholz have even gone so far as to suggest that the dissemination of the research of Hoover fellows be squashed. They were referring specifically to a Hoover program that distributes articles to newspapers written by Hoover fellows. They have urged the university leadership to put a stop to this practice.

I think it is an infringement on my academic freedom for a university professor to even make such an intellectually intolerant proposal. What really bothers me is that they have made this proposal over a period of years and not once has the university administration or other faculty ever publicly rebuked them on the impropriety of that suggestion.

However, I am happy to report that two students have blown the whistle on the Manley/Rebholz intolerance. In recent writings in *The Stanford Daily*, one student noted that, "Hoover scholars are regularly criticized for publishing op-ed pieces, that is, for exercising their constitutional right of free speech. Sadly, this campus has come to accept only one form of public discourse."

Another student (in the business school) wrote: "Perhaps Manley and Rebholz would be more successful at limiting Hoover's influence if, instead of seeking to limit their colleagues' academic freedom, they worked a little harder at promoting their *own* views in the political and public arena."

The loss of the Reagan library at Stanford is quite a serious blow to scholars who were looking forward to using its documentations and facilities, as well as enjoying the electronic access which such a library would have given us to similar presidential libraries around the country and to the National

Archives. Although the Stanford Board of Trustees had welcomed the facility, the faculty frequently signaled that it really did not want it there.

Several events this year brought about the end for the Reagan library. Political Science professor David Abernethy urged in January that the university reconsider the library invitation. A university's reputation, he said, depends in large measure on the public perception that it is a non-partisan institution. He pointed out that the university already had the Hoover Institution image with which to contend.

It seems incredible to me that a political science professor from a department in which 92% of its members are registered Democrats should be concerned that the Hoover Institution is perceived by the public as having a Republican or Reagan connection. The fate of the Reagan library was further sealed when twelve former chairmen of the Faculty Senate urged that the Reagan library be reduced in size and removed to a more remote location. My research shows that eleven of the twelve chairman are registered Democrats.

The Faculty Senate voted a resolution agreeing with the former chairman's proposal. In addition, they further insulted the President by welcoming his library but not him personally!!

There is no need to speculate about what caused the withdrawal of the library. The partisan opposition of much of the faculty, which through the faculty senate insulted Reagan, was the reason for the withdrawal. It is ironic therefore that Stanford president Kennedy is trying to point the finger of blame at Hoover Institution director Glenn Campbell.

It is bad enough for the partisan faculty to deliberately seize upon Campbell's words regarding a "Reagan connection" and to distort their meaning to incite colleagues. But for the Stanford president to make the same interpretation speaks louder about the politics of the university administration than it does about those of the Hoover director. (See Appendix D, "Stanford's Ideological Hostility" by Dr. Thomas Sowell.)

It is ironic that Professors John Manley and Ronald Rebholz (both Democrats) charged that the Hoover Institution is partisan when a survey by the nation's foremost authority on political polling showed Hoover scholars are registered almost equally as Republicans and Democrats.

When the loss of the library was announced, Manley and Rebholz could hardly contain their glee. Manley said that "a lot of people will be full of elation tonight." Rebholz revealed more fully his political coloration by calling the decision "astonishing, surprising and wonderful. It's one of the few political victories I've had in my life."

The President of Stanford is a registered Democrat. A recent study reveals the magnitude of the problem faced by the Hoover Institution and others who are trying to maintain balance within academia. My research assistant and I conducted a research of public records to determine the political party registration of all of the assistant, associate and full professors within the social science faculties at Stanford University. Of those who were registered with a political party, the following are the percentages of those who are registered Democrat: Sociology 100%, English 96%, History 96%, Political Science 92%, Philosophy 83%, and Economics 75%.

Again, I wish to state that there is nothing wrong with anyone being registered a Democrat. I am simply reacting to charges by professors from these departments that we at Hoover are partisan. They are so uniformly to the left of us that to them we appear to be "far right." Actually, we are as balanced as the public in general.

The evidence is overwhelming, let's drop all the pretense about why Stanford lost the Reagan library. It will not be located at Stanford because of the partisan and intolerant nature of Stanford's administration and faculty senate.

What is lacking at Stanford is the leadership to temper the one-sided nature of vocal partisan professors in order to maintain an environment of academic freedom where diversity of views are not only tolerated, but indeed welcomed.

And who says that history does not repeat itself? This is the second time in its 100-year history that Stanford University has lost a presidential library. The first time was in December 1960 when former President Hoover, Stanford University's most renowned alumnus, grew tired of constant carping and criticism from a small group of faculty members. Rather than locate his presidential library at Stanford as he had promised the Stanford trustees, he chose to locate it at his birthplace in West Branch, Iowa.

What should one conclude from this analysis? First, that there will be continued conflict between Stanford and Hoover because of the very liberal faculties in the social sciences. However, there is no need for illiberality if Stanford will just apply the same affirmative action policies toward conservatives that they eagerly grant to leftist minorities.

Second, since the balance of political power in the U.S. will continue to shift westward, the Stanford faculty should get used to having "connections" with presidents — Republican and Democrat.

Third, parents and students should be aware that when they select the social science departments of America's most elite universities, they are probably not going to get an unbiased "balanced" point of view.

Fourth, financial supporters of institutions of higher education should do at least a minimum amount of investigation to ensure that they are not supporting the teaching or research of one-sided values which are contrary to their own beliefs.

George Marotta is a Hoover Institution research fellow, specializing in U.S. foreign policy regarding developing countries, world trade and finance. He joined Hoover in 1975 after 26 years with the federal government including several overseas assignments. Mr. Marotta, who helped launch the Peace Corps during the Kennedy years, also served on the National Security Council staff in the Eisenhower administration, specializing in U.S. programs in the Middle East, Africa and Latin America. Mr. Marotta is a graduate of Syracuse University, where he also received an M.A. in Public Administration.

CHAPTER FIVE

THE MARXIFICATION
OF THE AMERICAN ACADEMY
CAN IT BE STOPPED?
by ARNOLD BEICHMAN

No Socialist country enjoys a smidgen of academic freedom. Marxism-Leninism precludes academic freedom. So where, as far as the Marxist Left is concerned, is academic freedom endangered? In the United States, the only country in the world which allows academic freedom to be used to subvert academic freedom...Marxist predictions have proven 100 percent false — there has been no pauperization of the proletariat...there has been no collapse of capitalism and there has been no world revolution...[yet] its doctrines are taught in major universities not as part of intellectual history, but as the sole and immutable truth.

THE MAIN AUDITORIUM of Moscow University carries the slogan: "A Leninist cannot simply be a socialist in his favorite branch of science...he must be an active participant in the political leadership of his country."

Substitute the word "professor" for the epithet "Leninist" and the quotation would be regarded as almost a cliche to many American academicians. Its assertion, however, as a mandatory political obligation upon a scientist could not — to state the obvious — be made by the government of any democratic country. If by chance such a dogma were ever to be propounded by any government official, no scientist would pay it the slightest heed.

Yet such corollary Leninist themes and variations have become a commonplace in the American university. They are not asserted by the U.S. government, university boards of trustees or university presidents. They are asserted by members of the academy themselves. There are professors at reputable universities who insist that it is not enough merely to teach Marxist radicalism but the teacher must also be "an active participant," an actor to bring about the coming revolution.

Professor Howard Zinn argues that "to be a radical and not an activist is a contradiction." Then he adds that only activists can write the best "history" and that "the binding power of social action itself" will bring about "value-directed history." Professor Zinn writes that "in a world where justice is maldistributed, there is no such thing as a 'neutral' or representative recapitulation of the facts...truth must be shaped by present conditions and future developments."

Another opposite example of the New Campus Politics is an article by Richard Lewontin, a Harvard biologist, in which having asked: "What does Marxism have to offer the bourgeois university?", replies "preferably, nothing." He explains:

> That is, Marxism, can do nothing for the university; the real question is what can Marxists do to and in the university...for the natural and social scientist the answer is very clear. The university is a factory that makes weapons — ideological weapons — for class struggle, for class warfare, and trains people in their use. It has no other leading and important function in the social organization."

Or listen to this:

> The social university is not primarily concerned with the abstract pursuit of scholarship, but with the utilization of knowledge obtained through scholarship to obtain social change. There, it does not recognize the right of its members to do anything they wish under the name of academic freedom; instead it assumes that all its members are committed to social change. To give an example, a course in riot control would simply be declared out of place in such a university, while a course in methods or rioting might be perfectly appropriate.

I cite these statements, among others, in order to raise the most significant question which confronts the American university today: How much longer can non-Leninist, non-Marxist, non-Communist academics continue to ignore this crusade organized within the university against truth, against knowledge and against the fundamental ideas of academic freedom? This is a crusade which wants to establish a system of "adversarial education," as Professors Stephen Balch and Herbert London call it, on a Marxist infrastructure.

Nobody would suggest that the majority of American academics are radicalized Marxists: it simply isn't true. What one could suggest is that the non-Marxified academicians who believe in the ideals of the university are doing little to resist a widespread and relentless Marxifying campaign which seeks the subversion of our academic institutions. This campaign proceeds with little bang or whimper from them.

While "the enforcement of the academic ethic must rest with the faculties themselves," writes Sidney Hook, "...I have been saddened to observe a reluctance upon the part of faculties to correct abuses of the academic ethic." Condemning the "systematic politicization of the university classroom," Hook writes:

> Few can be proud who are willing to take disciplinary measures against individuals who have clearly violated the responsibilities of honest teaching. There seems to be a complete indifference to the behavior of teachers who use their classes as a bully-pulpit for the propagation of political and other ideas that have no relation to the subject matter of their courses, or whose one-sided, extremely partisan commitments to controversial issues are reflected in biased reading lists and unscholarly assignments... Since [the late sixties], far from improving, the situation has worsened in that the violations of the academic ethic have become more widespread if less dramatic.

For example, at a recent convention of the American Political Science Association in Chicago I heard the Marxist-Leninist Michael Parenti discourse on the superiority of Soviet trade unions to U.S. trade unions. There was nothing remarkable in Parenti's pro-Soviet position; he is as open about his Stalinism as Angela Davis is about hers. What was remarkable is that the non-Stalinist members of the panel, all distinguished academics, plus the audience of several hundred political scientists, listened stolidly to Parenti's propaganda without a murmur. Had another speaker suggested, say, that trade unions in South Africa (which actually do exist) were superior to those of the United States let alone to those of the Soviet Union, he would have undoubtedly been booed off the platform as an intolerable racist and the panel members would have led the booing.

When I inquired as to why political scientists allowed this palpable pseudo-Marxist-Leninist schlock to be dispensed at a scholarly meeting without some attempt at rebuttal, I was told that the Marxist academics are losing the battle everywhere and, therefore, why bother to debate them.

However, it is my thesis that while the Marxist academics may debatably be losing in the world beyond the academy, they are most definitely not losing their crusade to establish a

Marxist infrastructure in the social sciences and the humanities.

More than three decades ago Lionel Trilling wrote:

> This is the great vice of academicism, that is concerned with ideas rather than with thinking and nowadays the errors of academicians do not stay in the academy; they make their way into the world and what begins as a failure of perception among intellectual specialists finds its fulfillment in policy and action.

In fact, I would say that the Marxist academics are today's power elite in the universities and, by the magic of the tenure system, that academic power elite has become self-perpetuating. Instead of a proletariat to be liberated from their shackles, we today have a professoriate which has already liberated itself from the academic mandate and successfully perverted the goal of learning, which is to seek objective truth, to the dogma that the goal of learning is to convert the university into an instrument of Marxist social change. The influence of the Marxist professoriate and their New Campus Politics extends to other sectors of the "New Class," opinion leaders and institutions, the radio and television networks and the prestige press.

In the face of such Marxist domination one can say that the life of the anti-Marxist or conservative faculty member without tenure is today, to use Hobbes' memorable description of life in a state of nature, "solitary, poor, nasty, brutish, and short."

One of the earliest social scientists to recognize the intrusion of the "adversary" culture into the university was Dr. Evron M. Kirkpatrick, former director of the American Political Science Association. In a speech, he summarized the position of the "new critics" on the left arrayed against contemporary political science. These "new critics", he said, were arguing that non-left political scientists had accepted the "false gods of reason, objectivity and freedom." The non-left political scientists were condemned by the New Campus Politicians "for making understanding, not action, the goal." As far as Dr. Kirkpatrick was concerned the "new critics" were opposed to "scholarly inquiry." While he didn't name names, it was obvious from the context that he was talking about the Marxist invasion of the university campus.

Professor Bertell Ollman of New York University's Institute of Marxist Studies is quite correct when he said that "[a] Marxist cultural revolution is taking place today in American universities. More and more students and faculty are being introduced to Marx's interpretation of how capitalism works...it is a peaceful and democratic revolution, fought chiefly by books and lectures."

59

The field of American history, says Professor John P. Diggins, "has come to be dominated by Marxists and feminists...What killed liberal historiography, whether political, intellectual or diplomatic was Marxism."

At Harvard we have a strange situation, Professor John Womack, who recently was the chairman of the university's history department, has said publicly, "In politics as I was ten years ago, so I remain — a Communist. This keeps me busy." Harvard President Derek Bok said Womack's political loyalties didn't trouble him so long as Womack didn't "seek to indoctrinate his students." But that grants an immunity to a man who by being an active Communist is doing more than merely participating in a ordinary political act. Being a Communist today is a meta-political decision since there can no longer be a dispute that Communism is the most serious threat to freedom today.

"Can there be a Nazi," asked William F. Buckley, "who is also qualified to teach in a community of scholars?" The answer is no and, adds Buckley, "Nor is there such a thing as a Communist qualified to teach in a community of scholars." Dr. Bok called Professor Womack "a conscientious and principled person." How principled can a man be who associated himself "with the doctrines of a slave empire," as Buckley put it?

It was not so long ago that Harvard professor James Q. Wilson was arguing that what passes for a liberal education today is inconsistent with liberalism and its traditional values, civility, free speech, equality of opportunity and "the maintenance of a realm of privacy and intimacy from the constant assaults of the political and the societal." Writing in 1972, he said:

> In the last two or three years, the list of subjects that cannot be publicly discussed there [at Harvard] in a free and open forum has grown steadily, and now includes the war in Vietnam, public policy toward urban ghettos, the relationship between intelligence and heredity, and the role of American corporations in certain overseas regimes...To be specific: a spokesman for South Vietnam, a critic of liberal policies toward the ghettos, a scientist who claimed that intelligence is largely inherited and a corporate executive who denied that his firm was morally responsible for the regime in South Africa have all been harassed and in some cases forcibly denied an opportunity to speak.

So what else is new? In May 1987, assistant professor Randall Kennedy of Harvard Law School defended a student blockade which prevented a South African diplomat from speaking on the Harvard campus on the grounds he said, that "Toleration has its limits." Professor Kennedy, who is a board member of the Massachusetts Civil Liberties Union and a black, was asked how he would respond if a lecturer he didn't like was beaten or killed during a protest. He replied: "It's a close call, something I'd have to think deeply about."

Half a century ago the American philosopher, Arthur D. Lovejoy, one of the founders of the American Association of University Professors, said:

> A member of the Communist Party...is engaged in a movement which has already extinguished academic freedom in many countries and would — if it were successful here — result in the abolition of such freedom in American universities. No one, therefore, who desires to maintain academic freedom in America can consistently favor that movement or give indirect assistance to it by accepting as fit members of the faculties of universities, persons who have voluntarily adhered to an organization one of whose aims is to abolish academic freedom.

In the 1950s, the New School of Social Research graduate faculty and the general faculty adopted a statement which I doubt they would adopt today:

> The New School knows that no man can teach well nor should he be permitted to teach at all unless he is prepared "to follow the truth of scholarship wherever it may lead." No inquiry is ever to be made whether a lecturer's private views are conservative, liberal or radical, orthodox or agnostic; views of the aristocrat or commoner. Jealously safeguarding this precious principle, the New School strictly affirms that a member of any political party or group which asserts the right to dictate in matters of science or scientific opinion is not free to teach the truth and thereby is disqualified as a teacher.

The politicization of the university just didn't happen yesterday. The attempt to endow it with a dangerous attribute — corporate identity — has succeeded beyond the wildest dreams of its fomenters. The mutation of the American university has been going on for a long time and it has been going on openly with little opposition to those who are transforming the university into Marxist agit-prop revolutionary theater. For example, the left-liberal John Kenneth Galbraith was boasting almost twenty years ago that "it was the universities...which led the opposition to the Vietnam war, which forced the retirement of President Johnson, which are leading the battle against the great corporations on the issue of pollution, and which at the last Congressional elections retired a score or more of the most egregious time-servers, military sycophants and hawks."

How did this coup against the traditions of the University begin and why has Marxism become the driving motor of this coup? At a time when Marxism has over and over again demonstrated its failures on every level, it is more influential than it has ever been before in the U.S. and British social sciences. As to its failure, here are the words of one of the leading scholars of Marxism, Professor Eugene Kamenka:

> Marxism has failed us. It has failed as a science of society, as an ethic (ethics is conspicuously absent from Marxist theory) and as a political movement promising and working toward that "true Communism" in which alienation, exploitation and dehumanization would disappear...Socialist democracy and justice, and socialist conceptions of human rights, have come to mean the opposite of justice, democracy and human rights.

How the Marxist professoriate has reached its pinnacle of power particularly in the social sciences is a long story and an old story; the willingness of modernist intellectuals to serve the interests of power when that power promises drastic societal change. A.J.P. Taylor described the revolutionaries of 1848 as those who believed in "movement: therefore only those elements who desired change were democratic [and] since movement and democracy were synonymous, only those who desired socialism were the people."

But there were later intellectuals, in the 1920s, who found reaction and the early fascism congenial, because like the appeal of socialism, fascist doctrines seemed to them to afford an opportunity to establish their pre-eminence as custodians of morals and culture. The fact that these doctrines were anti-democratic made them particularly appealing to an extraordinary number of leading artists and writers, among them Yeats, D.H. Lawrence, Wyndham Lewis, T.S. Eliot, Ezra Pound, Paul Claudel, Celine, Henri de Montherlant, Georges Bernanos, Martin Heidegger and Oswald Spengler. The latter two both supported Hitler.

In the United States, there was a surprising amount of support for Italian fascism among leading American intellectuals. The liberal *New Republic* in the late 1920s was urging "a sympathetic hearing" for Italian fascism because it promoted "national cohesion and national welfare." As it later waffled on Stalinist terror, the liberal weekly even justified fascist violence as necessary to end internal strife and disunity. Among Mussolini's backers were such leading intellectually known figures as Bruce Bliven, Alvin Johnson, Robert Little, George Soule, Wallace Stevens, Henry Miller, Irvine Babbitt, Charles Beard, Horace Kallen, William Lyon Phelps, George Santayana, Ida Tarbell, and Lincoln Steffens.

What we have seen in this half-century is not only a crisis of authority but a crisis of authority in relation to mind and "the right exercise of its mental powers," as Lionel Trilling put it. It has reached the point where "it has become possible to claim...credence for the idea that madness is a beneficent condition, to be understood as the paradigm of authentic existence and cognition." It is a view, he said, which is advanced "by a notable section of post-Freudian psychiatric opinion with wide influence in the intellectual community."

The power of the university is such that academic spokesmen of what has been called the Freudo-Marxist left have contributed to the alteration of perceptions and ideas of opinion-makers so that one can almost talk about a Marxist fellow-traveler takeover of our powerful media institutions. The print and electronic media are replete with what are called "double standard" judgments on socio-political issues of the day.

In recent years, thanks to former U.S. Ambassador Jeane Kirkpatrick, we have heard a good deal about the concept of "moral equivalence." This concept seeks to prove that both superpowers are equally guilty, immoral and ominous, both scorpions in a bottle. In actual fact, "moral equivalence" is a rhetorical device to demonstrate the moral superiority of the Soviet Union over the United States. What you then see is a double standard: What the U.S. does is unforgivable, what the USSR does is understandable.

George Orwell noted this double standard among British "pacifists" at the end of World War II. In 1945, Orwell wrote:

> Pacifist propaganda usually boils down to saying that one side is as bad as the other, but if one looks closely at the writings of the younger intellectual pacifists, one finds that they do not by any means express impartial disapproval but are directed almost entirely against Britain and the United States. Moreover, they do not as a rule condemn violence as such, but only violence used in defense of the western countries. The Russians, unlike the British, are not blamed for defending themselves by warlike means, and indeed all pacifist propaganda of this type avoids mention of Russia or China.

Here are some contemporary examples of the double standard. Ask yourselves how did our political culture become so transformed that such nonsense becomes received truth. For example:

• When Nicaragua's Daniel Ortega on a visit to New York buys several dozen eyeglasses, the media treats it as a venial oddity, but when it is learned that the Marcos family stored vast quantities of shoes, furs, jewels, perfumes and other baubles it is regarded as a mortal sin. We can assume that the Marcos' looted the Filipino treasury. Has anybody checked to see who pays for Ortega's purchases and for Señora Ortega's?

• The U.S. is always, so goes the cliche, propping up unpopular dictators. The Soviets never prop up unpopular dictators whether in Afghanistan, Angola, Mozambique, or Nicaragua. It is certain that General Jaruzelski could not win a popularity contest in Poland. He is most assuredly being propped up by the Soviet Union, yet to accuse the USSR of such a transgression is to interfere in the internal affairs of the Polish people.

• Oliver Tambo, apostle of violent revolution, ally and stipendiary of the Soviet Union, is a Left culture hero, but Jonas Savimbi is a Western stooge. Why Castro, "si", but Pinochet,"no"?

• Nobody ever emerges from Chile, South Africa or South Korea with hope for the existing government and its "reform" program. People are always emerging from the USSR or Poland touting their reform programs. Soviet leaders are always becoming more enlightened. Afrikaner leaders are always becoming more benighted.

• Soviet military power and continuing rearmament is ignored. On the other hand, U.S. military power is too great, too expensive, reckless, non-essential and imperils world peace. The Soviet Union marshals huge military parades on the anniversary of the October revolution. No complaints. When was the last time you saw a military parade in front of the White House, the Capitol or anywhere else?

• Fidel Castro has the respect of men like Senators Dodd and Weicker even though there are no elections in Cuba. But Napoleon Duarte is a leader who was suspected of rigging El Salvador's elections despite impartial observers who said it was a fair election. There were predictions of a small vote because the people would be intimidated into not voting. But there was an unexpectedly large turnout; ah, yes, the people were intimidated by the military and forced to vote. There hasn't been an open competitive election in any Communist country from the day of takeover but only in El Salvador or South Korea is there an election problem.

• If the United States brings evidence of the use of chemical or biological warfare against the people of Laos, Kampuchea or Afghanistan, it is disbelieved. However, when the Soviet Union accused the U.S. of introducing AIDS as part of biological warfare, Dan Rather, the CBS televangelist on March 30, 1987 played this smear as news but offered no evidence. Soviet disinformation is all the evidence Dan Rather needed.

• Under the Brezhnev Doctrine, all Communist countries are off limits to any attempt to introduce western democratic influences. However, under the doctrine of Marxism-Leninism, the West and non-Marxist Third World countries are a free-fire zone for Soviet penetration and subversion.

• Why are "wars of national liberation" or "liberation" movements only legitimate against non-Marxist countries and illegitimate and counter-revolutionary when they are directed against Soviet colonies? A liberation movement in captive nations like Estonia, Latvia or Lithuania or Poland and the Ukraine or suppressed nationalities like the Kazakhs and Uzbeks is illegitimate, but the Moscow-Cuba-Nicaragua axis can insist with lots of UN support on freedom for Puerto Rico from U.S. colonialism.

• Senator Alan Cranston and other Congressmen insist that no aid be given to El Salvador until the government starts to negotiate with the Communist guerrillas. No such threat is heard about stopping aid to Poland unless General Jaruzelski starts to negotiate with Lech Walesa and Solidarity. The El Salvador Communist guerrillas are legitimate in the eyes of Cranston and his allies because they have the support of the Marxist-Leninists. The contra freedom fighters in Nicaragua are granted no such legitimacy because they are fighting a Marxist-Leninist dictatorship. Imprisonment of Communist guerrillas in El Salvador is a violation of human rights, while jailing or killing Nicaraguan contras or sentencing critics of Castro's Communism to twenty years in solitary is protecting a constitutional regime.

• President Reagan is criticized for his "alarmist anti-Soviet rhetoric," but when did you hear of attacks on the Soviet Union for its "alarmist anti-American rhetoric?" Attacks on the USSR always endanger world peace, attacks on the U.S. safeguard world peace.

• To call capitalism "the focus of evil in the modern world" or some variant of that epithet would be sound Marxist analysis to be heard on any American campus. But to similarly characterize Communism as President Reagan once did demonstrates political irresponsibility and a desire for an imperialist war.

• Why is it almost a national crisis for the left when a Colombian journalist is refused a U.S. visa because she was involved in terrorism, but there were no "Free Lech Welesa" committees ready to spring into action at the shocking announcement by the Polish government that Lech Welesa, then under house arrest, would not be allowed to attend his daughter's christening?

• Why does the phrase "death squads" always signify right-wing terrorists and the word "junta" always mean right-wing militarists? Are there no left-wing "death squads", no left-wing juntas?

• How come Marxist academics who say they aren't Communists are always on the side of Soviet foreign policy and always against U.S. foreign policy? If you cast doubt on Soviet good faith, you're a cold warrior: if you cast doubt on U.S. good faith, that's understandable realism. If a summit is on the horizon, criticism of the Soviet Union for whatever reason means you don't want the summit to come off. Criticism of the U.S., however, means you want a summit.

• To talk about the "fascist" danger in the U.S. means you understand the dark side of American life. To talk about the danger of Communism to freedom means you're (a). a red-baiter (b). a cold warrior or (c). blind to the danger of nuclear war. Why is it alright to be "anti-fascist" but not "anti-Communist."

• It is easy to ignore an open letter by 30 Soviet scientists and physicists now in the west who say the USSR is researching Star Wars; after all, they're disaffected emigrés and, anyway, how would they know what's going on back in Russia? However, the writings of any ex-CIA officer, like Philip Agee are always credible. The mere accusation of alleged CIA wrongdoing is probative evidence of CIA guilt.

• The Soviet Union can, it seems, do anything: from shooting down a passenger airliner to using napalm or biological warfare against the Afghan freedom fighters — whatever the atrocity, an immediate cry for understanding is heard in the West — "you know the Russians are paranoid about their border" or "it was an act of self-defense" or "the CIA was involved, you know." However, the U.S. has no right to be paranoid about its borders especially the Rio Grande, and it certainly has no right of self-defense so that when the U.S. bombs Libya or successfully invades Grenada, we are bullies, terrorists, imperialists, fascists, militarists and war-mongers. The inhabitants of the Kremlin are paranoid: that's why they had to build the Berlin Wall. Too bad, but that's life among the paranoiacs.

• Reports of Soviet atrocities in Afghanistan are, for the left, always false because the American media does not assign permanent correspondents or camera crews to the battleground. So the atrocities don't exist because the reports come from Afghan refugees and they have no film anyway. On the other hand, reports of atrocities by Nicaraguan freedom fighters are always true because correspondents and camera crews are permanently assigned to the Sandinistas.

• No Socialist country enjoys a smidgen of academic free-dom. Marxism-Leninism precludes academic freedom. So where, as far as the Marxist Left is concerned, is academic freedom endangered? The United States is the only country in the world which allows academic freedom to be used to subvert academic freedom. How many faculty protests were organized after it was announced at a PEN Congress that the Soviet Union, together with Vietnam and Turkey, are the three countries with the highest number of writers or journalists in prison or some form of detention?

• Marxist predictions have proved 100 percent false — there has been no pauperization of the proletariat: there has been no proletarianization of the bourgeoisie: there has been no collapse of capitalism and there has been no world revolution. The capitalist countries have not gone Communist and their peoples are more strongly wedded to a market economy than in Marx's time. Despite the disaster of Marxism, its doctrines are taught in major universities not as part of intellectual history but as the sole and immutable truth.

• Isn't it remarkable that all anti-nuclear demonstrations occur at bases in the U.S., Britain and West Germany but never at bases behind the Iron Curtain? Wouldn't it be an idea for nuclear disarmers in the West to write to Mikhail Gorbachev for a parade permit outside the Kremlin against nuclear reactors, Chernobyl style? And if they can't get a permit, they could have a sitdown on the Kremlin cobblestones as an act of civil disobedience.

• When President Reagan was overwhelmingly re-elected in 1984, our televangelists, editorialists and columnists had to tell the American people who had just voted for this landslide that the results did not mean that the president had a mandate for his program: They had voted for his personality not his program. The same concern for a mandate was invisible when it was announced that Mikhail Gorbachev had been chosen by the Politburo to be the Soviet Party General Secretary. For the media President Reagan was a usurper on the throne but Gorbachev was a legitimate successor to somebody named Chernenko who had been the legitimate successor to Andropov to Brezhnev to Khrushchev to Malenkov to Stalin to Lenin. They all had mandates but not President Reagan.

• Why are women's movement leaders, who are as desperately concerned about the allegedly low achievement status of women in a market economy society as they are opposed to U.S. foreign policy, so unconcerned about the visibly low achievement status of women in socialist societies, especially in the Soviet Union? How many women are there in Communist Politburos?

• Why is it that when we argue with Third World intellectuals and their Marxist admirers in the west on behalf of the values of democracy, as enshrined in the Bill of Rights or the Rights of Man or the British constitutional order or the efficiency of the free market, we are told that we should not try to impose on Asian, Latin or African peoples our western political culture because it is so alien to their values? Yet it is perfectly proper to hawk Marxism in the Third World even though Marx is as much in the Western tradition of philosophy and political theory as are Locke, Hume, Adam Smith, or James Madison.

How are we going to stop this Third Marxist invasion of the American University? (The first invasion began in the 1930s and continued through the mid-1950s; the second began in 1968, ebbed and then intensified in the 1980s.) Academics of good will stood on the sidelines in Spring 1968 and said the revolutionary whirlwind couldn't last and would blow itself out in a few days. They were quite wrong. I am reminded of the pithy comment by Professor Werner Dannhauser: "I am a political scientist and the safest generalization about the predictions of political scientists is that they are always wrong." The same, I dare say, could be said for sociologists and other social scientists.

The first thing we can do about the third Marxist Invasion is to encourage associations like the University Center for Rational Alternatives and Accuracy in Academia to broaden their activities and to keep the spotlight on the activities of the enemies of academic freedom. We cannot expect the AAUP, the National Education Association or for that matter even the professional organizations in the social sciences and the humanities to resist the Marxification process. They are trapped because the sense of ethics which pervades the university means that any left extremist must be mantled by the dogmas of academic freedom. In practice, however, this indulgence does not cover conservatives whose socio-political positions are defined by campus Marxist caucuses as racist, war-mongering or counter-revolutionary. Academic freedom should not be regarded as a faculty comforter only; the principles of academic freedom should also benefit students.

Second, alumni associations must be brought into the campaign against the subversion of academic freedom. Obviously, alumni who are a permanent source of revenue for their alma mater have a stake and certainly an interest in the future of their university. But they must be kept informed.

Third, the work of the Institute for Educational Affairs in subventioning and sponsoring pro-democratic and anti-

Marxist campus newspapers is of crucial importance and should be encouraged and broadened. A dissident voice in the age of an intrusive campus Marxist conformity is a *sine qua non* in beating back the Marxist tide.

Fourth, wherever it exists the dissident campus newspaper should be sent to the families of students so that the grave situation in which a given university finds itself would be made known to parents.

Fifth, wherever possible a campus guide to faculty and courses should be published as an aid to incoming students in selecting their programs.

Sixth, studies of grading particularly in graduate school departments should be undertaken with outside help if necessary, to see whether non-Marxist students are being penalized for their opinions as expressed in classroom work.

Seventh, notes taken in class, syllabi and reading lists should be anaylzed and discussed by students to see if the teacher is using the classroom as a "bully pulpit" or whether he is playing by the rules laid down by Max Weber, the great German political theorist:

> To take a practical political stand is one thing, and to analyze political structures and party positions is another. When speaking in a political meeting about democracy, one does not hide one's personal standpoint; indeed, to come out clearly and take a stand is one's damned duty. The words one uses in such a meeting are not means of scientific analysis but means of canvassing votes and winning over others...It would be an outrage, however, to use words in this fashion in a lecture...*[T]he true teacher will beware of imposing from the platform upon the student, whether it is expressed or suggested.*

Eight, if it is a state institution, get in touch with state legislators and keep them informed. The dissident campus newspaper should be mailed to legislators.

Nine, keep in touch with the local newspaper, television and radio stations and the reporters who normally cover campus affairs.

Ten, run for campus offices.

Eleven, organize (with faculty help where possible) serious academic symposia on socio-political issues. *Try to get all sides and positions represented.* Watch for attempts to break up such meetings. Have a telecamera ready in case of trouble.

It is quite probable that many faculty members and the university administrations will be hostile to such campus reform movements. The cry of "invasion" of the classroom will be heard on the campus. University administrators, cowed by a powerful faculty, will rush to the rescue against the students seeking academic freedom. As I said earlier, so what else is new?

Arnold Beichman is a research fellow at the Hoover Institution. He received his B.A., M.A. and Ph.D. in political science from Columbia University. He has taught at the University of Massachusetts, the University of British Columbia, the University of Calgary, and was adjunct professor at Georgetown University. Dr. Beichman is the author of four books, including Nine Lies About America.

THE MARXIFICATION
OF THE AMERICAN ACADEMY:
A MARXIST'S PERSPECTIVE
by SIDNEY GLUCK

Marxism did not have to beg its way into academia. It came in through the front door, supported by legitimate academic concern by outstanding academicians and public figures long before the Palmer raids and official anti-Communism (1924). Although a minor factor in our history, it was, nonetheless, significant and always an influence on the side of progress for working people.

I WANT TO SAY FROM the outset that I am not a Stalinist. That should give you a little comfort. I am somewhat of a maverick in the Marxist movement. I tell you this so anything I say will not be held against any other Marxist. I appreciate the opportunity to debate the topic of your choice: "The Marxification of the American Academy." But first let us talk about Marx and Marxism.

I have been teaching Marxism for many years. I have poured through my volumes of *Capital* — there are four — and other classical works of Marx, Engels and Lenin, many times. I have made notes in the margins, always with different colored pencils, and often wondered how I found new meanings as I read the same section at different times as the dominant world conditions changed. It is that aspect of Marxism that has always impressed me. The philosophy of Marx reflects change openly and frankly, from a partisan point of view; that is, the interests of the working class.

Yet Marx and Marxists after him absorbed the teachings of philosophers, social scientists, political economists and socialists who came before them, evolving a consistent

71

philosophical materialist approach to conflict in human relations and between mankind and all else in nature, not a crass materialism but one that is totally humanist, objective, self-critical, and cognizant of individual subjectivity in the process of social change. All other ideas in the past century have been, in a sense, in a debate with Marxism.

Furthermore, Marx and Engels adopted Hegelian dialectics as their method of social analysis; the concept of individual elements in nature existing independently and inter-dependently at the same time; the recognition of conflict and contradiction as natural consequences of diversity and unity; the inevitability of change following shifts in the relative strengths of combinations of opposing elements. There are changes within the existing structure and changes that fundamentally alter the balance of forces, negating the existing balance and establishing new sets of elements and structures. Nature and society evolve in a series of negations of the negation — with no guarantee that every negation is a forward motion to a higher state.

Marxist philosophy, Dialectical Materialism, combines methodology with conceptualization. Applied to historical analysis, it views property rights and class conflict as levers of social change. Marxism itself is inherently growth oriented.

C. Wright Mills, the eminent sociologist, expressed "the ideological message of Marxism" in an early work *The Marxists* (1962):

> You do not have to be poor any longer...you are poor not because of anything you have done or anything you have failed to do, not because of original sin or the Will of God or because of bad luck...you are poor and you are exploited and you are going to be exploited as long as capitalism prevails...you do not have to be poor. The conditions that make you poor can be changed. They are going to be changed. Inside capitalism itself are the seeds of its own destruction...you can enter into a socialist society in which mankind conquers nature. And no man any longer will know poverty and exploitation.

> Little wonder that clergyman regularly complain that that Communists "have stolen our stuff." Indeed, Marxism as ideology is less a message than a "gospel," which in the literal sense means "glad tidings."

> The work of Marx taken as a whole is a savage, sustained indictment of one alleged injustice: that the profit, the comfort, the luxury of one man is paid for by the loss, the misery, the denial of another.

I may shudder at the futility of addressing this message to an organization like AIA, whose centerpiece is anti-Marxism: but it is a tribute to the appeal and strength of Marxism. For me, it is a compelling scholarly responsibility to rise in its defense.

We are all aware of differences among Marxists, between the Soviets and the Chinese, and residual frictions in Eastern Europe. We are also aware of conflicts generated by the introduction of elements of market economics and enterprise initiative concomitant with the dismantling and reordering of bureaucratic centralized decision-making. Socialist societies are more and more recognizing serious and destructive deviations from theory democracy and basic humanism by none less than Stalin and Mao, which had effects beyond their own borders. Nevertheless socialism as an economic system is here to stay. Just as there are variants in the capitalist system, which pre-conditions socialist formations, there are and will be variants in socialism.

Now what can I tell you in twenty-five minutes when you have spent a life time being conditioned as conservative purists? There are different kinds of conservatives. A Barry Goldwater is a defender of the Constitution, a pragmatist with give and take propensities. You are radical conservatives, fundamentalists, bent on changing the Constitution into a restrictive document. In the name of "original intent" you ignore the amendment process which showed concern for changing times and expanding democracy. You say you fight for truth. Whose truth? One of your speakers finds your truth in Nietzsche whose social criticism ended in nihilism and inspired fascism.

Is your "truth" to be found in the report prepared for the annual meeting of the Tri-lateral Commission report in Tokyo in 1974 and summarized by its authors in a publication at New York University? I quote from a British newspaper review:

> The democratic surge against the Vietnam War withered away confidence in existing authority regimes, caused a "democratic distemper," the withering of confidence in government, a decline in faith and a threat to the governability of democracy.

> The theme that runs through the report is that the threat to governability is an "excess of democracy" and if the system is to correct itself, this "excess of democracy" must be reduced. There must be limits to economic growth and political democracy. What has to be done to restore "balance" to democracy? Among other things, there must be restrictions on democracy, such as restrictions on the press. "There is no need to assure to the government the right and ability

73

to withhold information at the source." Education should be cut back because democratization should be related "to economic and political goals," and if it is offered to the masses, a "program is then necessary to lower job expectations of those who receive a college education."

These are the themes which run through the conservative Reagan administration, and are these not a springboard for Accuracy in Media and Accuracy in Academia, spawned by the far right.

Philosophically speaking, I cannot possibly change your point of view. I can attempt to reason with you through the accumulated wisdom expressed in homilies at the core of American pragmatism. It is said that the more investment you have in your beliefs, the harder it is to change them. It is also said that most of the time we don't communicate, we just take turns talking. I have listened carefully, and believe you are now. We are not compelled to support opposing views; we are compelled to know them. But we do reflect contradictory group interests. How else would we distinguish our antagonists?

There is a legitimacy to the pluralism of ideas. But the agenda for social debate is not set by one group alone. It is dictated by human needs and problems. Your big gripe as conservatives and neo-conservatives is that you could not and never will set the agenda in academia, as you did for several years in the Reagan administration.

Not that you have not tried. You have had more than equal time and more than equal opportunity, with unlimited funds and organizational effort. We can point to thirteen conservative organizations aimed at the campus: Morton Blackwell's Leadership Institute (LI), the Council for National Policy (CNP) and the International Policy Forum (IPF), which are dedicated to training technically proficient conseratives; the Institute for Educational Affairs (IEA) bestowed $200,000 on young journalists in a two year period and made contributions to over fifty college newspapers; The United States Business Industrial Council (USBIC) sends technical assistance and releases to the newspapers; The United States Industrial Council Educational Foundation (USICEF) supplies campuses with anti-union leaflets among a host of other anti-labor hand-outs; the Committee for Responsible Youth Politics (CYRP), another support from off campus; the U.S.A. Foundation and Students for America, with no acronyms; three more campus efforts, the Young Americans for Freedom (YAF), The Intercollegiate Studies Institute (ISI), and Students for a Better America (SBA); and lastly, hardly least, the Heritage Foundation, which brought over 100 conservative foreign speakers to campuses in a period of three to four years. And then you launched the AIA which has been universally resisted on every campus.

All of these are financed individually or collectively by the Hunts, Coors, Simon, Olin, Krieble, etc.

Arnold Beichman believes, on your behalf, that there are 10,000 Marxists who are setting the agenda on American campuses. I believe there are 15,000. With 650,000 full-time and 250,000 adjunct professors in the nation's institution of higher education, Marxists *of all kinds* represent only 1% of the total 900,000. Are you suggesting that this 1% tail, if they are all agreed, and you know that they are not, is wagging the body politic in academia? You make a mockery of efforts in academia to teach challenging philosophies and balance an *already* conservative atmosphere. If not, pluralism loses it meaning, education becomes warped, and ethics fade into personal greed.

Lester C. Thurow, Dean of Sloan School of Management at M.I.T., recently wrote:

> Ethical questions arise because we live in communities that function according to rules and laws that promote the long-run interests of the community...The doctrine that one should sacrifice self-interest for the collective good, however, is a message that is seldom preached in America.

In *The Left Academy* edited by Bertell Ollman and Edward Vernoff, it is noted that:

> Marxism viewed as a serious alternate approach is finding its way into the courses of an increasing number of *non-Marxists* in practically every discipline...
>
> For, in order to effectively transmit the knowledge, skills, and values required by our advanced capitalistic society, in order for students to learn willingly and believe that what they learn is true, in order for ideas which emerge from scholarly research and debate to be respected by the public at large, universities must allow for the presentation of opposing points of view, including those which contradict the prevailing values of society...Marxism could not be purged from the academy without seriously undermining the ideological support for capitalist ideas...What would "academic freedom" mean if Marxist scholarship were explicitly forbidden, and what is a "free society" without academic freedom? In this way, the continued presence of some Marxist professors has become an absolute requirement to legitimize the university in the eyes of students, faculty, and the general public alike as a "real" university.

Marxism did not have to beg its way into academia. It came in through the front door, supported as a legitimate academic concern by outstanding academicians and public figures long before the Palmer raids and official anti-Communism (1924). Although a minor factor in our history, it was, nonetheless, significant and always an influence on the side of progress for working people.

Many of Marx's early works were first published in English in our country before and after the Civil War. He was a contributor to the *New York Tribune* from 1852 to 1861 (with the tacit assistance of Engels), and a probable influence on President Lincoln, in whose State of the Union message of 1861, one finds:

> Labor is prior to, and independent of, capital. Capital is only the fruit of labor, and could never have existed if labor had not first existed. Labor is the superior of capital, and deserves much the higher consideration.

Marx's activities on behalf of workers' organization inspired Socialist movements and early labor leaders such as William H. Sylvis, head of the first national federation of trade unions in the United States, the National Labor Union (founded 1866). He supported a shorter work-day and particularly the demands of American labor for an eight-hour day. Although the Haymarket Massacre at the International Harvester strike for an 8-hour day in Chicago occurred on May 3, 1886, three years after his death, the organization he had led, The International Workingmen's Association, moved to commemorate the day as May Day, celebrated still by workers around the world.

Nor should it come as a surprise that in American universities, culture and science, also influenced by European antecedents, should have produced social thought accompanying or corroborating Marxism.

Lewis Henry Morgan (1818-1881), pioneering anthropologist and President of the American Association for the Advancement of Science, author of *Ancient Society*, was admired by Marx and, in effect, became a co-worker through Frederick Engels use of Morgan's interpretations in *The Origin of the Family, Private Property and the State.*

Henry Demerest Lloyd (1847-1903), economist, authored *Wealth Against Commonwealth* (1894), decried the crimes of great wealth, independent of but in the same direction as did Marx.

Gustavus Meyers (1872-1964) wrote the definitive work, *History of the Great American Fortunes*, which was brought up to date by Matthew Josephson's *The Rober Barons* (1934) and then by Ferdinand Lundberg in *America's Sixty Families* (1946).

In academic sociology, Lester F. Ward (1841-1913) and, a generation later, Charles Hunt Page recognized the "significance of class divisions in society" in their respective works, *Applied Sociology: a Treatise on the Conscious Improvement of Society by Society* (1908) and *Class and American Sociology: From Ward to Ross* (1940).

Dr. W.E.B. Dubois (1868-1963) complained after his studies at Harvard where there were no references to Marx, "I was astounded and wondered what other areas of learning had been roped from my mind in the days of my 'broad' education."

Herbert Aptheker, the renowned Marxist historian, in his *Marx and American Scholarship* (1954), covers six outstanding figures in the social sciences: Charles A. Beard (1874-1948), John R. Commons (1862-1945), James Harvey Robinson (1863-1936), E.R.A. Seligman (1861-1939), Albion W. Small (1854-1926) and Thornstein Veblen (1857-1929). Beard was a foremost historian, Veblen a foremost economist. Small was founder of the *American Journal of Sociology* and for a long time its editor. Robinson, a professor of history at Columbia University, was a president of the American Historical Association. Commons was a professor of economics at the University of Wisconsin for nearly thirty years. Seligman, a professor of economics at Columbia University for forty-five years, was editor of the *Political Science Quarterly* and a president of the American Economic Association.

Thorstein Veblen, in a series of articles, told academicians that Marx was "neither ignorant, imbecile or disingenuous," and that "[T]here is no system of economic theory more logical than that of Marx." He often said, "Read Marx. Uncover the roots of the problem."

Beard wrote: "I freely pay tribute to the amazing range of Marx's scholarship and the penetrating character of his thought...He not only interpreted history, but he helped to make history."

Commons called Marx "One of the three or four greatest minds who have contributed to the progress of economic science." And Small is quoted: "Marx will have a place in social science analogous with that of Galileo in physical science..."

"They were not themselves Marxists," says Aptheker, "but always they dealt with Marx respectfully and with a sense of responsibility. They did not use Marxism as an epithet; rather they treated it as one of the great seminal systems of world thought."

James Robinson, the last of the six, addressed future generations when he wrote:

> It was not a professional student of history who suggested a new and wonderful series of questions which a historian might properly

77

ask about the past, and moreover furnished him with scientific explanations. I mean Karl Marx.

That was written in 1908. A generation later, despite official anti-Communism and the Rapp-Coudert campus witch-hunts of the 30s, students and professors found the scientific explanations of Marxism more apt than the fascist doctrines (operating in the guise of socialism) which led to World War II. Marxism had a mass appeal. Hundreds of thousands joined political, student and labor movements. Marxists, socialists and Communists were accepted as dedicated Americans in the fight to protect and extend our democratic institutions. There were five major schools of Marxism, coast to coast; the largest, the Jefferson School of Social Science, in New York City, where I was chairman of the Economics and Politics department for a number of years, had seven thousand registrations in the 1946/47 Fall term, as large as the New School for Social Research at that time. But in 1947 the Cold War started before the ashes of war had cooled.

The Smith Act of 1941 and the McCarran Act of 1950 (passed over President Truman's veto for its unconstitutionality) were brought down on Communists only and many who had associated with them in good causes: against Jim Crow and racism, in building industrial unions, and in exposing and fighting fascism "prematurely" — before 1939. These laws, as with the earlier Alien and Sedition Acts, now lie dormant because of constitutional inconsistencies with the Bill of Rights, but they had done their damage.

Under McCarthyism, the Taft-Hartly Labor Law was amended to require declarations which automatically barred Communists and sympathizers from the collective bargaining process, supplanting them with class-collaborative leaders. The Walter-McCarran Immigration Act of 1950 has successfully kept active anti-fascists from visiting our country through all successive administrations. By applying a double standard, they have been admitted through one or another subterfuge. Seventy-five percent of "subversive" FBI infiltration into left-liberal organizations centered in the Communist Party which was subjected to harassment, prosecutions and imprisonments. It was decimated by the end of the 50s.

Yet, students in the 1960s, without Communist leadership, began to construct their own Marxism in the search for answers to a democratic society. The legacy of objective historiography and social science, and a bounding literature with high moral principles, concerns for the poor and our quality of life helped shape a liberal cultural pattern as American as apple pie — with ice cream.

Need I remind you of Jack London's *Iron Hell*, or Upton Sinclair's *The Jungle*, Steinbeck's *Grapes of Wrath*, or *An American Tragedy* by Theodore Dreiser who, incidentally, joined the Communist Party? Remember Edward Bellamy's *Looking Backward*, a Utopian socialist projection and best-seller of its day, and Hemingway's anti-fascist *For Whom the Bell Tolls*, and the many others including theatre and films. One could go on to emulate serious theatrical productions, musical comedies, and motion pictures which mirrored the same ideas.

In preparation for this program I recently learned to my astonishment that an overwhelming number of major publishers, especially the university presses, have issued works on Marxism. There are today at least 15 specializing in this subject alone and scores of periodicals that have networked for decades.

There are, in fact, two cultures in our society, one that is liberal to revolutionary and the other conservative to neo-conservative. They exist side by side, independently and in conflict.

Liberal and revolutionary reflections today are imprints on the American psyche which have been reinforced by the events and views of recent decades: Keynesian economics and New Deal ideology; the victory over German fascism and its allies; the observable demise of colonial empire; the successes of the civil rights and other minority movements; competition from existing socialist nations; the assassinations of President John F. Kennedy, his brother Robert, Martin Luther King and Malcolm X; the sense of a peoples' victory in bringing the unpopular Vietnam War to an end; and the Watergate fiasco which revealed the shoddiness and selfishness of undemocratic elements in government. These are as indelible as the illegal usurpation of government power will prove to be in the case in the Iran-Contra deals of the NSA and the CIA.

Conservatives, especially the radicals, choose to forget certain facts which bred racism and chauvinism as features of our national character:

1. "Insider deals" of Alexander Hamilton and his associates on the redemption of the Continental debt and the support of piracy in the post revolutionary era.

2. Failure to eliminate slavery in the Declaration of Independence and in the Constitution; legalization of the slave trade until 1819 and slave breeding thereafter; and permitting a plantation system following emancipation which gobbled up

79

the allotted 40 acres and the mules enforcing share-cropping and peonage.

3. Tens of millions of acres of land grants to canal and railroad barons, two miles wide and tens of thousands of miles long.

4. Genocide against American Indians, gun-running, land-grabbing and unfair trade.

5. Indenture and deceitful immigration as the source of cheap labor by railroads, industry and mining.

6. Unjustifiable wars against Mexico and Spain where "virtue" lay in victory over weak neighbors, the annexing of much of Texas and New Mexico, the conquest of Cuba and the Philippines, and the silent absorptions of Puerto Rico and Hawaii.

7. Gunboat diplomacy in the Caribbean.

8. Official government support of anti-unionization.

The United States has had the bloodiest and most violent labor history of any industrial nation in the world." There have been few sections and scarcely any industries in which violence has not erupted at some time...(from "Violence in America" researched by a grant from the Ford Foundation).

Is it any wonder that C. Wright Mills in his work, *Power Elite*, observed about conservatives: "Those who grope for ideologies with which to explain their conservative mood — as well as themselves — in some solid tradition feel that they have somehow been trickled by liberalism, progressivism, radicalism, and they are a little frightened. What many of them want, it would seem, is a society of classic conservatism."

There are deep moral and ideological differences between the two cultures. You attack the liberal intellectual community for its claims to humanism and make a pejorative of "secular humanism" to blanket them all in what you regard as pretense and sham. Do you consider humanism to be a strictly religious phenomenon?

For Marxists, humanism is a process — the recognition and emancipation of the individual within a hostile social structure. It is a social development — just as is democracy. It first found its expression in religion, in the "cry of the oppressed," in the faith of a "chosen people" in a single deity with *social* commandments, and evolved into a concern for the poor and unfortunate in a divided society. Did not Jesus preach against the "money changers" in the temple? Were it not his enemies who argued, "If we let this one alone, all men will believe in him," and did not his enemies conspire to put him to death? I believe in Jesus the man — not in the religious

80

figure — for he epitomizes the ongoing struggle to eliminate the exploitation of the majority by a relatively small group in society.

As the Western world evolved from early Christianity and extended feudal states into national consolidations of widening economic interdependence, Protestantism and the Enlightenment brought new meaning and new concerns for the rights and responsibilities of individuals. The wealth of nations was hence to be measured in wage-labor and capital.

The arena of beliefs changed. Agnosticism and skepticism were accepted as industry and science emerged. Non-religious beliefs in human dignity competed with religious philosophy. Humanism was shared in the social-political sphere. Notwithstanding the history of the church institutions controlled by economically dominant groups, the Judeo-Christian precepts fostered sects and church movements, from a purely humanitarian basis.

Marxism is one of the philosophies which embraced these humanitarian concerns with faith in people, not in a deity. It is not the only humanist philosophy outside the official religious communities. It joins others in the stream of social conscience. The Ethical Culture Society believes in no specific deity, yet rejects none. It has an overriding humanist content in its social philosophy. The American Humanist Society is non-religious yet finds its heroes from Jesus to Paine and all who took the cause against "man's inhumanity to man" to heart and to the streets. You cannot strip "humanism of its progressive liberating essence."

Marxism, too, is an advance in humanism. The arena of beliefs has changed again. Socialism seeks to eliminate the economic exploitation of individuals by other individuals, restricting the use of accumulated wealth as private capital, to live off unearned income. Everyone must work in order to consume. It is an advance in human freedom — a trade off, if you will — limiting the freedom of a small group, yet, freeing them to share in their own humanity.

"Secular humanism," which you intended as a shibboleth, has real substance as a concept. Liberals and Marxists stake legitimate claims to humanism.

Democracy, too, is a historically developing social order with its own contradictions. It has always been flawed by class or bureaucratic state power.

While the practice originated with freemen in slave-based antiquity, in modern times mercantilism and capitalism promoted democracy out of necessity to hasten free market relations and uproot feudal political and economic restriction.

The juxtaposition of democratic and anti-democratic tendencies has been the hallmark of the capitalist era. Vigilance, it has been said, is the price of liberty, and every generation must safeguard the gains of its predecessors or suffer regression.

From the Boston Tea Party to the framing of the Constitution, our founding fathers structured a white, propertied, male-only government, an edifice reaped in republicanism, out of fear of a majority rule; and ever since, all minorities (who constitute the majority) have been in a struggle to gain personhood and equality before the law.

The Constitution was first rejected by some states, notably Virginia, where independent producers of whisky rebelled against ratification of the Constitution, demanded guarantees of freedom of trade and personal liberties as protection against what they perceived as "wealthy merchants" from the north. The Bill of Rights had to be added as the first ten amendments. We must still defend them against encroachments.

The amendment process from the beginning conceded that changed circumstance would demand expansion of constitutional rights when a minority or group of minorities can no longer tolerate injustices.

The pursuit of happiness presupposed the right to constructive labor, personal freedom, possessions in home and habit and cultural satisfaction. As the complexities of advanced technology required greater skill and knowledge, the right to basic education was won. Today this right is marred by failures in lower grade levels among minorities, notably in inner city schools. As a consequence, they are locked out of the higher education required by the scientific and technological revolution that burst on the world after the war. The right to a job with fair compensation — not welfare — is on today's agenda to fulfill the promises of the early declaration.

Our countrymen are proud of our democratic and revolutionary tradition. Witness President Reagan's calling of the anti-Nicaraguan mercenaries as "freedom fighters," while polls show that well over 70% of our people are against involvement in Central American hostilities. Many despair at the impediments and legal traps in capitalist democracy.

On the other hand, the "right to a job" is guaranteed in all socialist countries. This represents a form of economic democracy that does not exist under capitalism (even the Japanese "life-time" labor contract for a segment of its force is being broken under current international competitive pressures.) Notwithstanding problems at growth, socialism has erected societywide safety nets. Yet those in the USSR who fear "perestroika's" initiatives while clinging to these safety nets will find themselves — like those bureaucrats who persist in maintaining excessive centralized controls — institutionally frozen. Both impede the mid-course correction in the theory and practise of socialism, in economic restructuring, and in the democratic revolutionary changes now under way. But Mikhail Gorbachev has made it clear that changes will proceed within the Socialist social contract, which protects the right to a job to which will be added variations in renumeration and protection of the individual.

Democracy is not Socialism, but a socialist might say that democracy — if understood as the people's rule — is the preparatory stage for socialism. The historic transition to socialism expands democracy and creates a balanced economic development influencing all social-economic systems — which continue to exist side by side, despite their differences.

* * *

Having warned you about "Marxification," Dr. Beichman now compounds your fears by conceiving a "Leninization" of the campus — a further threat to democracy. Is this intended as an eye opener to liberals or as a fund-raiser for neo-conservatism?

Last spring I delivered a keynote address at a Marxist Scholars Conference funded by Duke University. This institution offers a two-year certificate in Marxist Studies comprising a basic series and a number of electives. Each department contributes at least one course in its particular discipline. Duke is proud of its initiative, yet it did not stop the administration from denying tenure to a participating anthropology professor whose brother is a Communist editor and Marxist-Leninist.

If that campus, with its "Marxist Studies," had been "Leninized," the students and faculty would have risen in protest, for Lenin had taught that "the struggle for Socialism is a many sided struggle for democracy."

I should hardly be worth my salt were I to fail to counter your fear of "Marxification" and/or "Leninization" with a sober warning against the consequences of "Militarization" of the campus. Basic research is being diverted from probing the outer limits of human knowledge intended to improve the quality of life into narrow objectives whose end product is human destruction. Both government and private corporate funds are ensnaring academic brain power. Student aid is subjected to "militarization of tuition" by government withdrawal of loan and grant programs and offers of paid tuition for participating in ROTC. Job searchers are now confronted by CIA recruiters as another negative brain-drain. The National Education Association devoted the entire first issue of its quarterly journal *Thoughts and Ideas* (Fall, 1985) to the effect of military projects in the reduction of free choice in studies, research, creativity, equity and justice, and ultimately academic freedom itself.

Marxism proclaims that the massiveness of means of destruction — the threat of nuclear war by design or by human or computer error — has made human survival the imperative of our times. Humanity is at the crossroads. It has lost its immortality in the nuclear age. There cannot be another Noah's Ark. The ashes of a capitalist or a Communist — a conservative or liberal — are all the same color, gray. A nuclear war would negate all upward movements of humankind — the ultimate backward negation of the negation.

Listen to the words of Lenin, who is echoed by Gorbachev in more dangerous times: "We only know too well the incredible misfortune that war brings...We are ready to make the greatest concessions and sacrifices in order to preserve the peace for which we have paid such a high price...We are ready to make huge concessions and sacrifice, but not any kind and not forever."

World economic integration is a powerful positive force. It can serve both capitalism and socialism. The untraveled road to economic expansion in trade and investment between the two economic systems — to bring the USSR into Western institutions such as the World Bank and GATT (USSR will have to establish a transferable ruble.) and to invite cooperation with COMECOM, the international organization of socialist economic integration.

Listen once more to Lenin: "There is a force more powerful than the wishes, the will or the decisions of any government of classes of any governments or classes that are hostile... That force is world general economic relations, which compel them to make contact with us."

The younger generation today, before it reaches the campus, is already participating in people to people exchange, expressing aspirations that envisage new world relations.. The campus of tomorrow will not be less liberal, it may be more revolutionary. Marxism in our country had a history before the Russian Revolution. It cannot be wiped out of academia or out of the conscious or reflexive actions of the working populations in all its stratifications.

"Whereas making things, and the activities related to products, were the main preoccupations of prior generation," wrote Felix Rohatyn, "making money and the activities related to money, are the driving forces of our society today...when such a culture grows cheek by jowl with extreme poverty, it is potentially dangerous."

Neo-conservatives blame the victims and not the system. Poverty is systemically generated by class exploitation and callousness. Look at the diversity and complexity of our traditions. Recall another homily, "When you blame others, you give up your power to change." Stop looking for a Marxist evil and look instead to your own humane survival. "The fault, dear Brutus, lies not in our stars but in ourselves that we are underlings." History has not betrayed you. You have not caught up with the overriding balance in our times. Recognize co-existence of two distinctly different social systems and two morally different social contracts. Both are in transition. Only an open democratic attitude on all sides will ensure survival. We need a worldwide *glasnost*.

Recognize that liberalism on campus is a natural condition and Marxism occupies its legitimate grounds. As an intellectual, I am proud to espouse a philosophy that best serves the working class — the majority in our country, and I thank you for this opportunity to express it.

Sidney Gluck is a member of the political science staff of the New School for Social Research in New York City. He is also a lecturer on fabric design and technology at the Parsons School of Design. Mr. Gluck, a board member of the National Emergency Civil Liberties Committee, is also the coordinator of Scholars Against the Escalating Danger of the Far Right. He is a frequent keynote lecturer at Marxist scholars' conferences.

CHAPTER SIX

PEACE: CAN IT BE TAUGHT?
A DISCUSSION OF THE ROLE OF PEACE STUDIES
by HERBERT LONDON
and COLMAN MCCARTHY

A peace studies course is not propaganda, it's not trying to convert anybody...It's about studying those who have a philosophy of non-violent force which does not involve fists, guns, armies or nukes. And it's risky either way. There's no fool proof system. We live in a violent world, but the lesser risk and more effective approach is non-violent force.

- Colman McCarthy

Since I am a defender of academic freedom, I don't oppose anyone who teaches peace studies, but what I don't understand is why peace studies at a university I am familiar with includes the work of Carl Sagan, Helen Caldicott...and virtually excludes Robert Jastrow and Herman Kahn. And I was told that not only am I challenging academic freedom by even raising this objection, but that I should be drummed out of the academy for taking this stance for the argument of balance. This is what academic freedom has come to.

- Herbert London

MCCARTHY: I WANT to tell you about my work with the teaching of peace through non-violence. I began five years ago when I went to a District of Columbia public high school in the fall of 1984 and then took my course to American University where I was invited by the government department.

I started out with 12 students. Then we had 50 students in the spring. Finally after the second year I was up to about 250 in two classes, on Wednesday evenings. And I was always heartened by the students' openness to new ideas, particularly among the conservative students. I had the president of the American University chapter of Young Americans for Freedom in the class. He would come a little bit braced, naturally, and you could see that he was a bit rigid in the first few classes, but gradually he loosened up. The next semester, he took another course from me, and then a third course. He came to me after the final class and said, "You're really the first liberal that's ever listened to my view points about things." We developed a friendship and he often came to my home for dinner. I met his mother and she thanked me for teaching her son about non-violence.

The conservative students, I found, often were the most receptive to studying Mustie, Merton, Day, Schweitzer, Rankin, Addams, Amos, Isaiah, Gandhi, King and all the others in the long list of pacifists and teachers of non-violence that we studied. It was new material. They came from schools and families where they hadn't heard much of the other side. Many would come to me and ask, "Why haven't we heard of these people — Jane Addams or Day or Merton or Mustie or Isaiah or St. Francis and people like that?" I would answer, "It's simple, you went to American schools, where they are good at giving you all the history of wars and the lives of Robert E. Lee and U.S. Grant and Caesar and the generals."

Children are taught the history of warfare with great efficiency — they know about the battles we've had — our seven declared wars and a lot of our 140 undeclared wars, the Grenadas, Libyas and Nicaraguas. The kids are well-informed about these, but they don't know very much about the alternatives to violence. Many would say, halfway through the course, "Well, we're glad you're here professor, we're glad you former 60s flower children are still active, but in the real world..." and then give you the usual line, "but we have to defend ourselves and be strong." The usual slogans and cliches. I answered, "No I believe in strength, I believe in defending myself, and defending you and defending our values and defending freedom. I believe in non-violent force as the better way to do it. Violence has been the worse failure."

The purpose of a course in peace studies is to develop a philosophy of force. We have two choices in any conflict, whether it's at home with our family or our friends or among governments. A course in non-violence is not merely how to coexist with alleged enemies, the Soviet Union, or threats like that, real or imagined. It's also how to deal with conflicts domestically. We have a high rate of family violence, teenage suicide, 10,000 handgun homicides a year, and economic violence that corporations inflict on the weak. We have environmental violence. We have homelessness. So the course is about that also.

The goal is to develop a philosophy of force. You're either going to solve conflicts violently or nonviolently. Those are the only two ways. And so we talk about that. In class, we talk about the nonviolent options. A perceptive student will usually say, "Yeah but what about Gandhi — he was killed and King was murdered. And Jesus Christ was killed by the government." That's true, which leads to the conclusion that we're dealing with two failures; the failure of violence and the failure of non-violence. Which do you want to commit your heart to?

I'm not trying to convert. I'm not trying to preach. In class we read some King, some Merton and Day and Mustie and Schweitzer and Jane Addams and Jeannette Rankin. I give them a quiz the first class, where I list 5 people — U. S. Grant, Robert E. Lee, Caesar, Eisenhower, Westmoreland. Identify those. The kids know them all. Then I put down Mustie, Merton, Day, Rankin and Addams. Rarely do they know who they are. Its obvious the kids have been cheated in school. Their education has been one-sided, violent-sided.

It's not for me just to criticize Reagan and his war machine or Gorbachev and his war machine, or Castro and his war machine, or Chile, or any of the other governments that are spending cumulatively $900 billion a year on armies and armaments and war-readiness. The U.S. government alone spends nearly $300 billion a year, or $2 trillion in the Reagan years. Numbers too high. Military spending comes out to about $13,000 a second in this country.

It's not enough to criticize. I try to go beyond that. I've tried to learn a new word over the years — the word "I." What am I doing about this, instead of what you should be doing. That's why I'm in the schools, to teach this and offer students an option, to keep and broaden their choices so they can choose. You can't choose if you don't know about the options. You can't develop a philosophy of force if you don't study the available forms of force. Ideas are a force. Love is a force. Truth is a force. Organized resistance is a force. I think those are the more effective forces. They aren't fail-proof forces — they are only better than the violent forces.

In this century alone nearly 80 million people have been killed in wars. More than 40,000 people are slaughtered every month in the some 40 wars and conflicts in the world today. Most of this is the poor fighting the poor. Under this current administration weapon sales have increased I think about 100%, including the black budget. We had a president who came into office vowing to re-arm America. It was already over-armed, but he re-armed it anyway with the approval of Congress. If you believe in that, fine. Gandhi always admired soldiers because they were disciplined true believers. He'd rather have a disciplined soldier than an undisciplined pacifist.

It takes a long time to develop a philosophy of force that doesn't rely on violent force. To teach that is to give the young an option. Most of my students are grateful to have had that chance, including the conservatives.

I was never concerned with their biases. I never viewed them as "those right-wing kids with closed minds." Not at all. I found that they were often the ones most receptive. My wife and I included them when we had students to dinner every Friday night. You can imagine it was a lively time we had. The head of the College Republicans, along with the Young Democrats was there. Jewish kids and the children of Arab shieks. One fellow came in his ROTC uniform. He took the course and had his head opened up a bit. He's not in ROTC any more. I'm not saying he wised up because of what he learned in my class, but the boy did say of non-violence, "I've never heard this before." I said, "Of course you didn't. You go to American University, you went to Exeter. You came down to Washington full of the history of violence."

A Peace Studies course is no more than that. It's not propaganda, it's not trying to convert anybody. It's just trying to offer some fundamental truths: There's something else out there, young friends, and if you want to study it, let's get started. I would always tell my students the first time we met: "Is anyone here just to get a grade? If you are, say so. You can take your A now and leave. I promise I'll give you one at the end of the course. But if you want to study non-violence, stick around and I will help educate you." Out of 1200 students, everyone's always stayed. That's what the Peace Studies course is about. It's about studying those who have a philosophy of force which does not involve the violent force of fists, guns, or armies or nukes. It's a risk either way. There's no foolproof system. We live in a violent world made that way from street criminals to corporate criminals to governmental criminals. We know there's violence. How do we deal with it? That's what I've been asking as a journalist, and non-violence is what I've been answering as a teacher.

London: In listening to Colman McCarthy, I'm reminded of a story that my students first told me. A student walked up to me one day and said, "Dr. London, I wonder if you could describe the difference between an optimist and a pessimist?" And the student said, "An optimist is one who believes that this is the best of all possible worlds, and the pessimist says, 'You're right.'"

The reason why this story is particularly instructive is because what I think we've heard from Professor McCarthy is an unalloyed, unvarnished statement about peace studies. Is this what peace studies is all about? It is the study of non-violence. It is the study of Gandhi, Thoreau, Francis, Merton, Day, Mustie, and some of the other people that were mentioned. What it is not, however, is scholarship, and I'll attempt to explain why.

If one were to look at the essence of scholarship as seen from the point of view of Einstein, for scholarship to truly be scholarly, there has to be a hypothesis and a null hypothesis. There has to be a way of proving that it's not true, that is, you are not engaged in propaganda. You are not preaching, you're teaching. You are presumably there to provide various points of view. Karl Popper made the same point, as you may recall, about Freud, by suggesting that it is impossible to prove there is a super ego. In that sense it is not scholarship.

If one were to read the works that Mr. McCarthy has for his students, they all represent exactly the same point of view. Now I should add, rather hastily, I am not opposed to students reading Martin Luther King's Birmingham statement. I am not opposed to students reading Thoreau. In fact, I assign these works in my own classes. It is just as important, however, for students to read the works of Clauswitz and Freud and those people who want to defend the interests of the West, not only those who are engaged in acts of non-violence.

Colman McCarthy's response about students is also very instructive to me. He said he conducted a poll about generals and those who would represent positions we might describe as conscientious objection. Mustie, Day, Merton are on one side, Eisenhower, Lee, Grant are on the other side, and students presumably know about Lee, Grant and Eisenhower, and don't know about the others. Well, that is clearly an indication of two things. One, the general ignorance of students, and two, how the deck was stacked.

Let's assume for the sake of argument, I asked students to identify, on one side, Shai Meyer, General Burnside and

Sherman, and on the other side St. Francis, Gandhi and Thoreau. And then asked, how many of you are familiar with the first group as opposed to the second group? If I were to ask that to any random group of students, I suspect I'd get a much higher response in the case of the second group than the first. So it's just a question of who you decide to list as your generals and who are those that represent non-violence. Again, this poll is rather indicative of the rather propagandistic techniques that very often surround peace studies. Peace studies is to peace what military music is to music.

What you are doing in peace studies is trying to create the illusion, usually done rather effectively, I might add, that you are engaged in a dispassionate analysis of what is happening in the western world. How dispassionate is it when, in fact, the readings are all about the same point of view?

How do you teach peace? Well, teaching peace in American universities is a little bit like teaching salvation. Indeed you can teach about salvation, you just don't know whether it occurs. In the case of peace, you've got the very same condition. You can teach about peace, but you don't know whether it's going to occur in this lifetime. It's a rather utopian idea. I'm all for the idea of peace. Again, I certainly don't want to be misinterpreted. It's important to understand that what has happened in American universities is not that students are unfamiliar with peace studies, but that they are only given peace studies. Mr. McCarthy talks about his experiences at Georgetown, American University and the University of Maryland. Let me relate some of the experiences that I've had very recently.

I wrote an article a couple of years ago about some of my colleagues who started a peace studies program. I said, since I am a defender of academic freedom, I don't oppose anyone who teaches peace studies, but what I don't understand is why peace studies here include the work of Carl Sagan, Helen Caldicott, and of course I don't even have to tell you about the others who are on the list, and virtually exclude Robert Jastrow and Herman Kahn and some people who obviously represent a point of view that I happen to favor. And I was told that not only am I challenging academic freedom by even raising this objection, but that I should be drummed out of the academy for taking this stance for the argument for balance. This is what academic freedom has come to.

Several weeks ago I gave a lecture at Wesleyan University. I was asked by the Republican Club at Wesleyan University to speak about SDI. I presented a defense of SDI. Several of the students came up to me afterwards and said, "You know, this is astonishing. We've been at Wesleyan for four years, we're all seniors, we've never heard a point of view like yours expressed here."

I then went to Vassar University about a month ago and met a young man who described himself to me as a triple minority. He said, "I'm black, I'm conservative and I'm a male at Vassar." This young man proceeded to tell me that he is in the political science department at Vassar and there was recently a debate on aid to the Contras. He was the only person among the faculty and in the student population who defended the proposition that aid should be given to the Contras. Now Mr. McCarthy says that the point of view he expresses isn't to be found on American campuses? It's my experience that it is ubiquitous on American campuses. The real problem is that another point of view representing the defense of the West does not exist.

> I'm not opposed to Mr. McCarthy teaching his course. I'm opposed to the idea of its one-sidedness. I'm opposed to the idea that the readings are all very similar. I'm opposed to the idea that only one point of view is expressed in the class. Earlier today we heard a discussion about Marxist scholarship. It was suggested, and I agree, that it's oxymoronic. It's oxymoronic for the following reason: The Marxists themselves say, and I quote from Bertell Ollman's book *The Left Academy,* "If non-Marxists see my concern with such questions as an admission that the purpose of my course is to convert students to socialism, I can only answer that in my view...a correct understanding of Marxism (or anybody of scientific truth) leads automatically to its acceptance." Now, if that is true, then what Bert is doing is simply assigning books that will lead to his end. But is this teaching? Max Weber said that the point of teaching is to provide a variety of viewpoints without necessarily imposing your own view on the student so that he arrives at a conclusion that you would regard as desirable. And yet we are told by Mr. McCarthy that it's precisely his aim.

Let me refer to one of those people Mr.McCarthy regards as a hero — a hero not only in the course, but a hero to a great many students as well — Gandhi, whose notions of passive resistance undoubtedly have received an extraordinary amount of attention among the student population in the United States. That passive resistance was successful in India in the 1940s suggests as much about Gandhi as much as it does about British rule. Notwithstanding the moments of brutality, and clearly they must be recognized, the British were put in the reluctant position of having to escalate the violence of that period, of that rule, in order to maintain control. That price openly became too high for any British government and for the sensibilities of the British people, just as the price of maintaining order in the South with Martin Luther King's passive resistance became much too high a price for this nation to pay. The venality of both the British and many Southerners is perfectly clear to us, even to those on the right. But the point is, that had Gandhi lived under the colonial rulers like the Soviet Union, had Gandhi attempted his passive resistance during the period when Stalin was in power, or even when Gorbachev is in power, he would have ended up in the gulag, he would have ended up in the bowels of the Soviet system.

To suggest that that form of passive resistance can work everywhere in the world is patently naive. Moreover, it's worse than naive, because it destroys the resolve of American students at the very time when they should understand the realities of the present world condition. Gandhi is quoted as having said, "Ultimately, tyrants are defeated by love and truth." When he is confronted by an interlocutor who asks if he would apply his tactics to Hitler, he responds by saying yes, even a Hitler would succumb to this approach. What is not asked is what happens to those generations who are overrun by Hitler's army? What happens to those generations who are waiting for love to emerge as the way in which people engage in human intercourse? The difference between passive resistance against an essentially democratic foe and against a totalitarian enemy was not considered by Gandhi, and is not considered by Mr. McCarthy. The British response to Gandhi's violation of law was imprisonment. Not once, but several times. What would have happened if Gandhi had resisted Hitler? It wouldn't have been imprisonment — he'd be dead!

To suggest that Gandhi's methods are universal is to confuse wishful thinking with thoughtful approaches to change. There is nothing wrong with love. The love of Jesus, the love of McCarthy, the love of Thoreau, the love of Merton, is indeed admirable. What is not admirable is to suggest that you can throw flowers at Soviet tanks. What is not admirable is to not recognize what is the real problem in the world. It is not the distinction that Mr. McCarthy points out — the distinction between violence and non-violence. The real distinction in the world is between those who want freedom and those who don't. The real distinction is between those who want freedom and will fight for it and those who don't and won't. *That is* what we have to confront as students. That is what we have to confront as citizens in western civilization. The way to peace is to prepare for war. We do not want to fight as a nation, that has been clear for decades. But there are times when this nation is obliged to fight in order to protects its interests. If we lose that

93

resolve, if we become a nation very much like the British empire in the 1920s where the prevailing point of view was pacifism, then we not only will not fight, we cannot defend ourselves, we cannot sacrifice for freedom, we cannot defend the very values on which this nation is based. I thank you for being so attentive.

McCarthy: Those were forceful views, Herb. I want to talk a little about what we study in my classes, and we do study Gandhi. I've never told my students that what happened with Gandhi in India could be applied every where in all situations. The closest I've come to any absolutes is when we discuss an earlier movement in solving problems without violence and using the force of other strengths. We discuss early Christianity which was founded by an absolutist on not using arms or swords or violence.

Early Christianity was, for the first three or four centuries, a small sect in the outer reaches of the empire where a group of people believed that they wouldn't resort to arms. You couldn't join the Roman army, and the Roman army didn't want you. Of course the Christians were killed — Jesus was killed, Stephen was killed, along with other martyrs of the early church. Many were jailed. You can conclude, see, it really didn't work, did it? You can say that as you can say it about Gandhi in India, and Denmark in 1940, and some of the French villages in the 1940s that resisted without violence. You can say that they all failed. I said before, we're dealing with a choice of two failures. When I study early Christianity with my students, we try to think about what happened then. How did this one small sect which was committed to what Jesus instructed them to believe in — love our enemy, share our wealth, do good to those who hurt you, pray for those who offend you — evolve into a new way of thinking? We study that, and go into it more deeply than what is given in the usual courses about religion. The idea is offered that early Christianity was a successful spiritual and social movement. It worked then, and many who believe it can still work are around today — the Plowshares movement, the Berrigan brothers and others who are actively putting their souls and their futures at risk.

The idea that somehow the campuses are being overridden by people like me is absurd and unfactual. ROTC, a Pentagon program funded for $535 million a year, is on about 1,200 of our campuses now. Only about 50 or 60 campuses offer degrees in peace. That you have 1,200 schools teaching the science of war but only have about 50 or 60 offering a peace degree doesn't quite seem like equality. Perhaps it does to others, but not to me. I've interviewed a fair number of ROTC students.

They say, "Look, I'm just in it for the dollars. I can't get through school otherwise." Of course they can't. The Reagan administration has been taking money away from higher education loan programs on one hand; and on the other hand they're funding this ROTC soldier-boy program lavishly. College students say, I've got to get through school some way, so I'll put on a uniform, and sign away four years of my life when I graduate. The Peace Corps is trying to get a program similar to that so that rather than going into the military after you graduate, you go in the Peace Corps. It will pay your tuition for your junior and senior years. Why don't we have a similar enthusiasm for that program? It receives about $10 million. It deserves the $535 million the ROTC gets.

So we talk about that in class. The kids think it's a fine idea. That's part of what goes on in the peace studies courses that I'm teaching — I can't defend what the other professors are doing. I can only answer for my own courses, for my own students.

London: There are indeed about 60 programs in the United States that offer degrees in peace studies. However, I defy you to find one campus in the United States that does not have a peace studies program. They're everywhere. Not all of them lead to degrees. Some of them are minors, some are majors, some are just courses. Some are given in schools of continuing education. But peace studies in a very short period of time have become a very powerful tool to be used by those who share one point of view about the nature of our society.

Let me also refer to ROTC programs. I think Mr. McCarthy rightly pointed out that many of the young people who go into ROTC programs go for a variety of reasons, very often to simply have the tuition paid. To describe these people as engaged in the science of war is patently absurd. Most of them don't know what war is about. If you examine the curriculum in ROTC programs, you would find that many don't deal with the science of war at all. Many deal with management questions. One of the great controversies that I've had with people at West Point is that they are no longer engaged in the science of war. I wish they were, but in fact they are discussing what are primarily management issues: how do you place ordinance in one place as opposed to another. Let me deal, however, with an issue that I think bears comparison, and that is how Soviet students are trained.

While Mr. McCarthy is talking about the need for more non-violence in our society, I don't know where the Colman McCarthy's are in the Soviet Union. I think that it's interesting to point out that starting in what is equivalent to our kindergarden, students in the Soviet Union learn about the use of weapons. Every student is obliged to learn about the use of weapons. By the time they come to high school every student must be conversant with the use of an AK-9. Now that is part of their training. Compare that kind of martial arts training with what goes on in this country. Not only do students generally not know about weapons, students who take ROTC are very often unaccustomed to the use of weapons.

Let's talk about these two failures that Mr. McCarthy refers to. Obviously the two failures being the failure of violence and the failure of non-violence. Passive resistance has worked. It has worked in the United States. Martin Luther King can point to that. It works largely because democratic governments are unwilling to pay a high price in violence in order to restrain those who engage in this form of conscientious objection. And so it does work. Where it doesn't work is in totalitarian regimes, the very places that Mr. McCarthy refuses to acknowledge. There, passive resistance cannot work. Jesus could not be successful in a regime that would simply destroy Him and destroy His followers. There it could not work. And so, passive resistance works in societies that allow for a variety of flowers to bloom.

Let me refer to the third point, and that is, in looking at the idea of non-violence, people like Mr. McCarthy always say, some time in the future we will live in a non-violent world. And indeed, he may be right, since his crystal ball is obviously as good as mine. But what is not said, and what is not addressed, is what do you say to the Jew who is on that freight train to Buchenwald? What do you say to him? "Some time in the future your children, or the children of your children will live in a non-violent world"? Is that the answer? We simply write off a generation? Do we simply say to those people who end up in the bowels of the gulag, well, we're not going to defend ourselves, we're just going to turn the other cheek. You can shoot us once on one side, and then on the other side. Is that the answer? I wonder. I wonder if this is what we should be telling students in our classrooms.

Csorba: I just want to read a short letter from a former student of Professor McCarthy's before we begin questions. This letter reads, "As a moderate-to-conservative Republican, I do not agree with most of Colman McCarthy's beliefs, but he is teaching me about peace and non-violence. These are subjects that we never really touch upon in our normal course of study. That is important. But most importantly he is challenging my ideals. He encourages students to respond to his ideas. He presents his case so strongly and convincingly that it forces

96

the students to think deep down, 'Are my ideals really what I believe? If they are, how do I support them in the best way I can?' The aim of this university (American) is to teach, to stimulate intellectual growth. In the classes that I have had with Colman McCarthy I have gained the most valuable part of my education — I have learned to think."

Question: Do either of you teach in your courses the great peace movement at the beginning of World War II when Hitler and Stalin were allies, and the peace lovers in this country did everything to disrupt our help to the British and to our army. The peace movements dissolved when Hitler invaded Russia...Do you all teach that, and do you consider this was a peace movement, or was it a Soviet plot?

McCarthy: The book I use to teach about World War II is by Phillip Hallie of Wesleyan University. The book is called *Lest Innocent Blood Be Shed.* It describes de Chambon, one of the French villages which armed itself against the invasion of the Hitler army in southern France. They armed themselves without violence. It's a beautiful book and it describes how there are options to facing an army without guns. This village was a leading center of hiding Jews who were fleeing Hitler. It's a wonderful book, and the students love it...

London: Part of the problem is the Hallie book. Again, it represents the one-sidedness that I was referring to before. This period is a very important period. It suggests that the totalitarians of the Communist variety and the Nazi variety had more in common than they had differences between them. This is a point that's very often overlooked in our schools. Even the Hitler-Stalin pact of 1939 is overlooked in our schools. I was amused when Tony Podesta suggested that he has come across textbooks that make the point that many blacks look to South Africa as the Promised Land. That's patently absurd. I've gone through every American textbook that's used in the United States and a statement of that kind won't be found. I assure you that you can also look through most American textbooks and find that there is scant attention given to the 1939 pact between the Soviet Union and Hitler's Germany. And that I think is part of the problem — this rather naive view that many students have that is based ostensibly on historical amnesia of not knowing about the past. For most American students in 1987 the past began with the Gulf of Tonkin resolution in 1965. That was year #1 of our history.

Question: I am very interested in what I'm hearing from Professor McCarthy about his reading list which includes, apparently, a great number of Christian writers on questions of war and peace. As I recall from my own education, the

Catholic tradition on these matters is called the just war tradition, and part of the just war tradition includes a recognition and a respect for pacifism. I was wondering if Professor McCarthy, in his course, addresses the traditional Catholic position of the just war tradition, or if this is only an excursus into the teachings of some pacifists who are within that tradition.

McCarthy: Sure, we talk about the just war theory. St. Augustine, I think, was one of the ones who began that, but we try to emphasize early Christianity...

Question: (by the same questioner) By what books, sir?

McCarthy: We read the Scriptures. I refer the students to the Christian Scriptures, which I think is a fine flammatory document. And then we read about Francis of Assisi, we read some Benedict. I talk about some of the saints who refused to bear arms...St. Francis, as you know, deserted the army. We talk about the Catholic pacifist movement of this century.

Question: (same questioner) If I may, sir, there's a bit of a jump between the thirteenth and twentieth century. If I could simply recall to you that in the Scriptures we would hope that we would be able to "beat our swords into plowshares," but the fact is that later in the Scriptures there is recognition that quite the opposite is possible and probable, and that there is every necessity to defend one's intellectual freedom and one's religious beliefs when that becomes appropriate, and I would submit to you that the more balanced teaching might simply be an excursus into the 1983 pastoral letter of the American Catholic bishops, "God's Promise and Our Response," because that includes some of the major writers as well as some of the minor writers you have mentioned here. In addition, you might wish to recommend to your students the journalism of Dorothy Day and the writing of Thomas Merton, especially where he recognizes (and he never accepts in fact absolute pacifism) that at some point we need to defend ourselves.

McCarthy: Thank you.

Question: Is it not academically wrong and morally wrong to offer any student an A even though his work would not include any exercise of the mind greater than that of deciding at the outset not to attend the lectures of the class?

McCarthy: I guess that's directed at me. I could talk to you for quite a while about grading...When the students evaluated my courses at American University I think I got three times a higher rating on the question of how much was learned in this course, so I don't think about grades too much...and I don't think it's immoral to do that. I merely tell the students that if you're not taking the course with enthusiasm, if you're not

98

here with an interest in being open-minded, be honest about that and say so. Don't clutter up the classroom if you don't want to be here. If you're here to scam and hustle around to get grades, be honest about that.

Csorba: Do you think that the popularity of your course on peace studies is due to the fact that you may be perceived as an easy grader?

McCarthy: You have to ask my students. All I know is that they like the course. They rated the course very highly after they took it, regardless of what grades they received. I've been invited to teach at other schools. I don't want to waste my time on the issue of grading.

Question: Dr. London, you have no problem with peace studies classes, it's the pacifist bias in those classes that gives you trouble, is that correct?

London: Yes, it's the pacifist bias that generally exists in those courses, but I have some difficulty with the discipline of peace studies, primarily because it's trying to achieve a goal without any understanding of how it's achieved. Peace is very often achieved by preparing for war. That's how it's achieved. Since that point of view very often does not appear in peace studies courses, I find that attitude reprehensible. But I was, and you're going to be shocked to hear this, a peace studies student when I was at Columbia years ago, long before you were around. And what we studied was Herodotus, Thucydides, Gibbon and Shakespeare. There's nothing wrong with reading those works, and those works include the ideas of peace, because you learn about why wars are fought, what brings people to the brink of war. I think that has to be a dimension in these courses and very often is not.

Question: If the peace classes are biased in a pacifist sense and you want to add in another influence, peace through strength, and have intellectual underpinnings of that whole philosophy, does it need to be incorporated in a peace — meaning non-conflict — kind of class? Can't that happen in a conflict class, a separate class?

London: Absolutely not. There used to be something called National Security Studies. Unfortunately, that's now an anachronism, no one uses that word. But that was a true Peace Studies program. National Security dealt with the same issues that Mr. McCarthy is dealing with in his classes, but grafted onto it a lot of other matters as well. As I suggested to you before, I don't understand why Edward Teller isn't acceptable in a peace studies class. His work certainly should be. I don't understand why Herman Kahn's *On Thermonuclear War* isn't read in the peace studies class. It certainly should be. The central problem is that these courses are often taught by leftists and the word peace has been preempted by the left. That is what concerns me. It concerns me because it represents a one-dimensional approach to the study of peace. We have to regain that word for our side now that we've lost it.

Question: I am the director of the Association to Unite the Democracies; it aims at a federal government for the democracies; it takes after Alexander Hamilton rather than after Jefferson or Thoreau; for example, it believes in the organization of power rather than in the contempt of power. It is a very important problem in our society that what is called non-violence has become so pervasive. It's very distinct from the classical Socratic conception of nonobedience to an illegal or immoral command. It consists of setting out to violate the law in such a way as to bring it into disrepute. That, by the way, is not what Martin Luther King did. He stood by federal law, a very important distinction. Do you draw this distinction to your students, or do you just go from Socrates to Jesus to Gandhi and make them believe that it's all the same thing?

McCarthy: I don't make the kids believe anything. We just read some of the best writing I can find on the subject of non-violence. It's a 14-week course, and I come out of the course, and the kids do also, very frustrated because we haven't gotten to very much. I tell the students that you can lead a horse to water but you can't make him drink, however, you can go upstream and put a little sugar in the water, and then the horse will usually drink. Now a course like this is just designed to put a little sugar in the water. If you want to drink, fine. But I tell the students, "Listen, come to this class, it's going to be very short, 14 weeks is not a lot..."

Question: I take it your answer is no. My follow-up question to that is do you feel responsibility for people who go out and break the law to draw attention to themselves and call it non-violence? Don't you feel sometimes that it goes a bit far?

McCarthy: (laughter) No, we read Berrigan and the Plowshares movement, and we read Thoreau. We read a lot of lawbreakers, and there are a lot of laws that deserve to be broken, and we read about people who have broken them and have been jailed, we read about the 10,000 conscientious objectors who have been jailed in this country because they refuse to solve problems through violence...

Question: Dr. London, earlier in your speech you mentioned that part of the problem on today's college campuses is that students are suffering from general ignorance and historical amnesia. Well, as a student, I'm going to try to overcome that by asking this question. Keeping in mind that passive

100

resistance and non-violence would be unsuccessful under tyrannical regimes, and that the history of the British government and the British people is one of rabid imperialism, and they are perhaps the most tyrannical and imperialistic country that has ever existed, they've had to be physically removed from almost every country of the world at the cost, in most cases, if not all, of a great many lives, including this country...the fact that Gandhi was able to overcome that oppressive government through non-violent resistance would seem to lead us to believe that in fact that can be successful even against the most tyrannical and militarily strong countries in the world. Wouldn't you agree even further that the release of Soviet dissidents within the Soviet Union was due to something other than the pulling of a trigger? I think the Soviet people and even the most tyrannical governments can be persuaded by this type of thinking. With that in mind, don't you think that we should at least entertain the alternatives on college campuses, that we should at least say, all right, we'll let ROTC go on campus, we'll study military science, but on the other hand, we've seen so much effectiveness in the past, don't you think we should at least entertain the study of non-violence if it's been so effective against these countries?

London: Let me start with your assumptions. I think it's a good question, but I think your assumption is absolutely wrong when you talk about the British as being the most tyrannical government in the world. That is patently absurd. The reason why it's absurd is this: If there is sufficient political pressure placed on the British regime, as was the case in the 1940s, the British government relented. It relented in India. Tell me about the political pressure that will be applied on Gorbachev so that Soviet troops will be released from Afghanistan. You see the comparison that you are making is false. It's a comparison that is often made by students who do not recognize the true tyrants of the world today. The difficulty that I have with your question is that political pressure in a constitutional system, even a limited constitutional system, is possible. But if you're talking about totalitarian regimes, there is no political pressure that would have that government relent. Once those troops are abroad, once the adventurism has occurred, once the gulags are created, they are there permanently.

The Brezhnev doctrine is, "Once a Communist government, always a Communist government." When is the change going to occur?

You tell me about the release of Soviet dissidents in the Soviet Union, and clearly you can point to a couple of illustrations, like Sakharov and Scharansky. But what you have to also understand are the political motives behind the release of these prisoners. If you can gain the kind of press, the media attention that you do in the West, with the belief that *glasnost* exists, a *glasnost* that represents openness in the Soviet Union, then in fact you've won a great victory. You've won a victory over minds like yours that now believe the Soviet Union is not a great menace. And so there are propaganda purposes behind it.

Keep in mind that the real definition of *glasnost* is publicity. That is the exact definition of *glasnost*, not openness. And so the Soviet methods are exactly the same that Lenin used before. Propaganda is very important in extending the reach of the Soviet Empire.

Herbert London is Dean of the Gallatin Division of New York University and a Senior Fellow at the Hudson Institute. He is a graduate of Columbia University and received his Ph.D. from New York University where he is also a Professor of Social Studies. Dr. London is the author of ten books, including Myths That Rule America, *which inspired an NBC-TV series of the same title. Dr. London writes a syndicated newspaper column, is a frequent guest on radio and TV talk shows and has made several appearances as co-host of CNN's "Crossfire."*

Colman McCarthy has been a syndicated columnist for The Washington Post *since 1969. He has taught "Alternatives to Violence" at American University, Georgetown and George Mason Universities, and in 1987-1988 taught at the University of Maryland, as well as Wilson High School and Georgetown Day School. Professor McCarthy, whose articles have appeared in* The New Yorker, Reader's Digest, *and* The Progressive, *is also the author of three books. He and his family founded and direct the Center for Teaching Peace in Washington, D.C.*

CHAPTER SEVEN

THE ACTIVISM OF THE SIXTIES AND THE EIGHTIES: A LOOK BACK AND A LOOK FORWARD

STUDENT ACTIVISTS: THEN AND NOW
by DAVID HOROWITZ

What does Marxism have to offer the bourgeois university? Preferably nothing. That is, Marxism, can do nothing for the university; the real question is what can Marxism do to and in the university?
- Harvard professor Richard Lewontin

ON APRIL 15, 1980, as invading Soviet armies poured across the Afghanistan border, a thousand students assembled for a "'Stop the War' Teach-in" on the University of California campus at Berkeley. Their protests were not addressed to the Soviet invader, however, but to the Carter White House which had condemned the attack and had requested defense increases and a military draft as deterrents to Soviet aggression. Speaker after speaker rose to denounce these measures as manifestations of a resurgent American militarism and anti-Communist paranoia, and to condemn them as preludes to "another Vietnam" and threats to the peace.

The echoes of a radical past were far from incidental at the teach-in which served to kick off the activism of a new political decade. Those in the crowd who were too young to make the allusions for themselves were guided by the parade of middle-aged political veterans who mounted the rostrum at the invitation of the protest organizers. Communist Party leader Angela Davis and Berkeley radical Congressman Ron Dellums may have played minor roles in the sixties political drama, but they were center-stage at its eighties revival.

Recalling how similar "teach-ins" and anti-draft protests had changed history in Vietnam, they applauded the symbolism the organizers had contrived: The time had come, they said, to revive the political enthusiasms of the past together with its radical discontents.

If the episode revealed the self-conscious effort of eighties activism to identify itself as a child of the sixties, it simultaneously exposed the contradiction inherent in such a claim. For the radicalism of the sixties had identified itself as a child without political parents. Its most apparent slogan — You Can't Trust Anyone Over Thirty — meant exactly what it said.

Sixties activism was born as a self-conscious attempt to reject one tainted politics (Stalinism) and to atone for the sins of another (liberalism). Therein lay its redeeming originality and its aura of idealism and political innocence. Eighties activism was born in an opposite attempt to revive the tainted politics that had been previously rejected and to appropriate the aura of idealism and innocence that had thereby been gained. Therein lies the seriousness and cynicism of its political commitments and the sinister complexity of its political styles.

The cynicism of today's radicals is immediately visible in their self-preservation as "progressives" and "liberals." Eighties radicals are not only comfortable with these political labels, they insist on them, denouncing as "McCarthyite" efforts to penetrate their deceptive surfaces. But, as an ancient wisdom shrewdly observes, all political justice begins with clarity about names.

The radicals who laid siege to the "System" in the 1960s and today's activists are in fact successive generations of the American left — a left which is itself a branch of an international Marxism whose roots lie in the solidarities of the Soviet Revolution of 1917; it is a left which, having been shattered by the traumas that followed Stalin's death, embarked, as the sixties began, on a long and painful process of rebirth.

Sixties radicals situated themselves squarely within this tradition by identifying themselves as a "new left" — a term which had been adopted by Communists all over the world who had decided to repudiate Stalin's crimes, but not the cause that he had left to them. By calling themselves a "new left," they declared their intention to distance themselves from the old pro-Soviet Left of their parents generation, but also to pick up its ideological pieces — to begin politically where they had left off. On the one hand this meant a renewal of faith in their old left ideals. On the other, it meant the adoption of a political style that was radically new.

Since they had rejected the old left's loyalties to the Soviet Union, the new leftists had no need to disguise their agendas or to pose as progressives as their predecessors had done. They could be radical and proud. They had no desire to infiltrate liberal institutions in order to shape and influence the democratic process. They would make, instead, "a revolution in the streets."

As the sixties began, these new leftists were joined by another group of political orphans, the offspring of their parents' liberal antagonists, whose anti-Communist crusade had incurred a debilitating taint in the McCarthy excess. The two groups joined forces at the outset of the sixties in a conflict that defined their relation to the political future.

The scene of the conflict was SDS, (Students for a Democratic Society) which was to become the pre-eminent organization of sixties radicalism, having begun the decade as the student arm of the Socialist Party, a liberal anti-Communist faction of the left. The conflict was over the radicals' determination to include Communists in their political ranks and their rejection of "anti-Communism" as a political principle. This caused a break between the SDS young Turks and the over-thirty veterans of SDS' parent organization. In short, the rejection of anti-Communism was the self-evident truth with which the new left declared its independence at the outset of its radical career.

The new left's earlier rejection of the scourges that had been associated with Stalin and McCarthy at first fostered an ethos — non-violent, democratic, idealistic, "American" — that allowed radicals to join the civil rights movement in its early triumphs. But deep in their political hearts the radicals at the same time regarded these truimphs as ominous subversions of their real agenda. The democratic passions and non-violent tactics they had embraced were obstacles to political desires that could never be satisfied by mere reforms.

But by mid-decade, America had become engaged in a war against Communist aggression in South Vietnam whose tribulations would provide the radicals with the rationale they needed for discarding the liberal ideals which made them uncomfortable and returning to their political roots. By the end of the decade the radicals had relinquished any commitment they might have had to the purposes and values of American democracy. Proclaiming themselves Marxists and Leninists and at war with "Amerikkka," the radicals embraced America's totalitarian enemies and revived the Communist loyalties of the past. With these twin betrayals of country and self, the new left's ten year effort to make a "revolution in the streets" ended in political defeat.

As in a previous era, a radical politics had discredited itself and died. But, as before, the radical faith had survived. During the seventies, radicals began a "long march through the institutions" of the American mainstream. While liberals wrestled with their guilts over America's anti-Communist effort in Vietnam, leftists struggled to come to terms with the Communist heritage they had previously rejected. While liberal sentiment congealed in the recriminations of a political divorce, the community of the left was enveloped in the nostalgia of a political reunion. In a cultural and literary outpouring, which included films like "The Front" and books like *The Romance of American Communism*, leftists attempted to rehabilitate the forbears whose politics they had once rejected and to celebrate the old "reds" whose corrupt and divided loyalites they once had scorned.

It is this reunion that has given birth to the left we see now before us.

The sixties' left had no political teachers. It did have a political guide: its memory of the crimes and treasons its predecessors had committed and justified in the Revolution's name. The eighties left has no such guide, but it has plenty of teachers in the hardcore survivors of the sixties who betrayed their own political ideals and embraced a discredited past. The teachers of today's left are the political diehards whose radicalism is defined in solidarities with Communist totalitarianism and an anti-Americanism immune to the lessons of its own experience. The most dramatic civil rights revolution in the history of any 20th-century nation, the most spectacular display of democratic process in a self-inflicted defeat in Vietnam, the most expansive demonstration of political tolerance in a postwar amnesty for its "enemies within," — all served merely to harden the hatred for America that these radicals felt.

In sum, the eighties left did not originate, like its predecessor, in a rejection of Communist politics and the Soviet empire, or in renewed appreciation for American democracy. Under the malign tutelage of its political elders, the eighties left began in apologies for Soviet aggression in Afghanistan, refusals to condemn Communist oppression in Vietnam, and denunciations of America's democracy as racist and militaristic, and a threat to world peace.

Where the new left has begun with traumatic lessons in the nightmare realities of Marxist liberations and had rejected the old left's subversive loyalties to Marxist regimes, the eighties left was the beneficiary of no such guides. In the political school of its radical teachers, the lessons of Vietnam contained no instruction in the brutal consequences of Communist victories, or the imperialist expansions of Communist empires, or the costly human toll of American defeats.

It has been more than a decade since American armies have been at war in Vietnam or anywhere else. But while America has remained militarily passive, the Communist victors have been on the march. In Indo-China, Hanoi's armies have blazed a trail of military conquest and colonial occupation; in Africa, Cuban expeditionary forces have spread famine and bloodshed and Communist oppression; and in Afghanistan, Soviet marauders have torched a nation and made refugees of half a population in one of the most savage invasions of modern times. But, from its inception, the eighties left has been deaf and blind to these events. Through all these years of Communist conquests and human suffering, the United States has remained the only real enemy of American radicals.

In the radicals' school, the lesson of Vietnam is just that: America is the enemy; America can be defeated. Vietnam Has Won, El Salvador Will Win. Vietnam Has Won, South Africa Will Win. All that is necessary is a Communist guerrilla army backed by the Soviets on the field of battle, and a political force in solidarity with the Communists inside the United States.

The solidarity left of the eighties begins where the sixties ended: *in a politics of secession from America's democracy and service to the totalitarian cause.* Because its politics is Marxist, it is a continuation of a war begun in 1917 by other means. Because its politics is war by other means, there is no room for candor in its rhetoric or integrity in its agendas. These pay lip service to humane goals and liberal values in order to manipulate democracy's publics. But liberality and humanity are not the real commitments of the American left. Its real commitment is to America's future defeat and to Communist victories like Vietnam.

The strategy of today's radicals is a strategy invented by the old Communist left in its heyday as a fifth column for Josef Stalin. It is strategy that forms "progressive" coalitions for "Peace and Justice in Central America" in order to further its real goals which are to provide support for a Marxist police state in Nicaragua and a Communist war in neighboring Salvador.

107

The eighties left invokes democratic principles and America's interests only to promote its covert agendas which are anti-democratic and anti-American. That is why it is eager to deny democratic rights to its political opponents whenever the opportunity appears. The radical left is a fascist force with a human face, the carrier of an ideological virus as deadly as AIDS. Uncontained, it will first subvert and then surely destroy the immune system of the body politic.

What can be done to strengthen democracy's defenses against this attack? The sixties provide the relevant lesson. The sixties left was numerically small and politically weak. Not a single one of its political successes would have been possible through its own efforts alone. Its successes were in fact made possible by a single factor: the collapse of the liberal center of American politics, the surrender of the establishment to which it had laid siege.

Crippled by guilt over Vietnam the liberal center lost the will to defend itself and its traditional values, and thus conferred legitimacy on the radicals and their political agendas. Instead of maintaining the radicals' isolation, the liberal establishment gave the radicals access to the very institutions — the media, the universities and the Democratic Party — that they had so diligently attempted to destroy.

Today the legacy of this political masochism is everywhere evident — above all in academic institutions. Radicals who violated the canons of intellectual discipline and the principles of academic freedom are not promptly expelled from the community they despise. Instead their political savagery and contempt for academic values are treated as expressions of idealistic concern that the academy ought to heed and respect. Administrators at Columbia University have devised a specially lenient disciplinary code for students whose offenses occur in the course of political protests. In this way, an institution which had been brought to its knees by radicals in the sixties now encourages the destructive agendas of their political heirs as an integral part of the educational process. The short term result is that every spring Columbia radicals find a pretext to lay seige to the university and bring its functions to a halt. A year ago the occasion was the radicals' desire to inflame a racial conflict in Southern Africa, this year to ignite a race war at home. The longer term result is that the radicals' agenda is accepted as legitimate by the very community they seek to destroy. By failing to enforce its principles and standards, the academic community not only strenghtens its radical enemies, but weakens its own foundations and accelerates its decline.

In the last two decades there has indeed been a precipitous decline in academic standards and institutions. In classrooms across the country ideological indoctrination has supplanted intellectual inquiry as academic discipline. Marxism, long consigned along with flat earthism and other fallacies to the intellectual mausoleum, has been raised from the dead to a place of respect in the university curriculum. Racial and gender discrimination (against Asians and white males) has been institutionalized as enlightened academic policy. Professional associations once devoted to the promotion of scholarship have been turned into political lobbies for totalitarian causes and terrorist elites.

The problem that faces the university community is the problem that faces democracy itself. A community which refuses to recognize its enemies is a community which has lost its will to survive. The continuing failure of the liberal center to withdraw the cloak of legitimacy from the illiberal shoulders of the hate-America left, is a reflection of the continuing failure of liberal nerve that began with Vietnam. Its root cause is a loss of faith in the liberal values of American society and in the role that American power must play in the fate of liberal hopes in the world at large. It is only when liberal America is once again able to believe in itself that it will be able to recognize its radical enemies and to join with American conservatives who have begun to wage the battles that are necessary if America's democracy is going to survive.

Anthony Podesta came to Accuracy in Academia's conference on academic freedom in June of 1987 as the head of an organization calling itself "People for the American Way." I remain unconvinced. Or perhaps I missed the news item describing how Mr. Podesta led his troops up the hill at Northwestern University to do battle with the campus fascists who had prevented Adolfo Calero from exercising his rights of free speech; or at Harvard, Columbia, Berkeley, Minnesota, and other campuses where the same type of repression has taken place in recent days; and perhaps I didn't see the account of Mr. Podesta's suit against Columbia University for its dereliction in failing to expel the racist Black Students Organization and the racist Coalition for a Free South Africa after they attempted to incite a citywide lynch mob against a group of white students their members had already attacked; or perhaps I wasn't informed about Mr. Podesta's campaign against the use of university funds and resources by radical groups attempting to provide propaganda and intelligence support and even material aid to terrorist agents and regimes in the Communist bloc. Finally, I may have missed the announcement by Mr. Podesta and his patron Mr. Lear of their forthcoming effort to promote the adoption of a mandatory curriculum in American schools on the evils of Communism, the hostile empire which has posed the principal threat to the American Way since the cold war began.

If I missed all this I apologize. But until Mr. Podesta assures me that I have, I will continue to regard his organization as People (some well meaning and some not) For Undermining the American Way.

David Horowitz, formerly the co-editor of Ramparts *magazine, was a radical campus activist during the 1960s. He is the author of nine books, including* Empire and Revolution: A Radical Interpretation of Contemporary History, Student, *and the best-selling* The Kennedys: An American Drama *and* The Rockefellers: An American Dynasty. *He is a graduate of Columbia College and received an M.A. from the University of California, Berkeley. Mr. Horowitz is presently co-director of the Second Thoughts Project at the National Forum Foundation in Washington D.C.*

MISUNDERSTANDING THE SIXTIES
by ANTHONY PODESTA

There are no heroes on the campuses in the 1980s. Reed Irvine has tried to become a hero. I've tried to become a hero. But none of us has succeeded in becoming a campus hero. But all of us are frustrated with the fact that the investment bankers are thought about more on campus than the leaders of political movements.

IT'S A PLEASURE to be here this morning. I didn't know rightwingers got up this early. But I wanted to see for myself. I enjoyed hearing about Berkeley in the sixties from David Horowitz. I personally was never there during that time and instead spent my campus days at the somewhat less glamorous University of Illinois in Chicago. The campus was at the Navy Pier, which was an old World War II facility that was used to train GIs during the war. Unlike the many movements that occured during the sixties at Berkeley, we were proud of the fact that we were the only university in America that could have been torpedoed.

Those times, I think, are important in understanding American political history and thinking about where we are today, both on campuses and off campuses in the country. I think it is misleading to suggest that all of the most radical, extreme people in the sixties, somehow or other, led every single person who became politically active in the sixties. I didn't follow Tom Hayden into the streets. I followed Martin Luther King into the streets of Chicago as we demonstrated for civil rights laws in Chicago and all across the south. So I think that it's important to recognize that the campus activism was not activism that strictly led all of us to be followers of Tom Hayden or Rennie Davis.

I think that the Eugene McCarthy campaign is another important moment in the history of that decade in which literally tens of thousands of young people left their campuses and went out and knocked on doors — not out of a desire to destroy democracy, but out of a desire to practice it. And I think that the McCarthy campaign stands as a model for responsible political activism in service to democratic values.

If you look at other movements in the sixties, like the Vietnam War Moratorium, which crept into the seventies, you see a number of people who were from the McCarthy campaign and a number of others who were deeply troubled by what was happening in Vietnam — and not out of a desire to serve international Communism, but out of a desire to serve this country who found the war to be morally reprehensible.

I was thinking as we were talking about the evils of the sixties and the duplicity of those people who have all of these double standards. One of those people was David Hawk who was one of the four national leaders of the Vietnam War Moratorium and was probably more than anyone else single-handedly responsible, in this decade, for bringing the Cambodian genocide to the attention of the American people. I think he was the person who very articulately argued against the war in Vietnam and brought photographs back from Cambodia that became the first public awareness of the awful Communist rule in Cambodia. So I think that it is convenient and clever and easy to get a couple of applause lines attacking all of these people, but as with the seventies, the sixties were somewhat more complicated than we might make them seem.

But I think that there were a couple of figures who tended to the media of the sixties. I don't know if Tom Hayden or Stokely Carmichael capture them the best. But there are no heroes on the college campuses in the 1980s. Reed Irvine has tried to become a hero. I've tried to become a hero. But none of us has succeeded in becoming a campus hero. But all of us are frustrated with the fact that it is the investment bankers who are thought about more on campus than the leaders of political movements.

I think the campuses today are dead. I think there are a few little glimmers of activity. Dartmouth is one you heard about. And there have been speakers from the right, or positions from the right, shouted down on college campuses. That happened to the left as well when the right wing students tore down the shanty towns put up by demonstrators. And I know that you don't see that quite the same way, but I want you to know that I do. And it seems to me that if you try to say, well, this is one kind of speech and this is another kind of speech; if you shout down Pat Robertson, that's a bad thing, but if you take down the shanty demonstrations of the anti-South African individuals, that somehow is on a different moral plane. I think you end up on a very slippery slope and end up really being very similar to some of the people from the sixties whose excesses are justly condemned.

So I confess that I am a liberal. But I think that I am a true one. I like coming to Accuracy in Academia's meetings. I try to speak the truth and criticize the left when it needs to be criticized. We have criticized textbooks for sugar coating the repressive regimes of the left in this country which I think you would applaud. I would hope that you too would join with us, however, in criticizing textbooks for portraying South Africa as the promised land for black people.

Finally, on behalf of intellectual consistency, I think that these kinds of meetings and an exchange of views are helpful and healthy, and I appreciate being here this morning.

Anthony Podesta is founding President of People for the American Way, a national citizen's organization that seeks to protect constitutional liberties, especially in the areas of religion and education. Mr. Podesta is a former political science teacher and director of admissions at Barat College, Lake Forest, IL. He is an honors graduate of the University of Illinois, Chicago, and received his law degree from Georgetown University.

ACTIVISTS OF THE SIXTIES AND THE EIGHTIES
by PETER COLLIER

When I hear students at Berkeley and other campuses mouthing a saying of the official Sandinista Youth Organization, "To follow the Soviet Union is to know how to conquer, to follow the United States is to know defeat," I get a nasty case of the deja vues. I listen to the rallies and hear the same ignorance, the same intolerance, the same infatuation with anti-American styles and language that I heard two decades ago. It is like stepping into a time warp.

FIRST, THE SIXTIES. Those of us for whom it was — for better or worse — the time of our lives should have been more vigilant about who got custody of the memories. Instead we surrendered the history of the era — to nostalgia merchants and socialist realists, to pop historians and radical ideologues.

These people keep assuring us that the sixties was a time when, to turn the famous Yeats line around, the worst lacked all conviction and the best were full of passionate intensity. It was a time when those in control of America led it cynically down the path of war and racism; a time when the nation had to be rescued by its heroic youth — those huddled idealists whose only dream was to give peace a chance. A whole generation was forced to spend itself in political activism, we are told, because of the moral iniquity of its elders.

Were there young idealists finally driven to extreme remedies in their quest for peace and justice? It was because the world they were pledged to change was one of cruelly entrenched power. Did they finally turn to violence? It was in violation of their better natures and in support of a higher law.

I don't know about the rest of you, but I'm bored by these cliches about the sixties. There were indeed well-meaning young men and women who became involved in what we

114

called the Movement. But they were bit players, the stage dressing and cannon fodder. The sixties as I remember it was a time of heavy hitters, freelance nihilists who became addicted to the sense of moral superiority their opposition to the war gave them and who used the war as justification for whatever destructive acts they chose to engage in.

Vietnam justified annointing the Black Panther Party, a ghetto gang that never overcame its gangsterism, as an *avant garde* and acceeding to its reign of terror against moderate blacks — those "Uncle Toms" who had been trying to do something about the condition of their people long before the Panthers were discovered by radical whites, and who would continue their patient work long after the Panthers had burned themselves out in violent histrionics and self-dramatization.

Vietnam justified Tom Hayden announcing to a small meeting of us radicals in Berkeley that fascism had arrived and it was time to think about beginning the civil war against "Amerika."

Vietnam justified the fifth columnism of Weathermen, whose cadres returned from Havana in 1969 having promised the Cubans and the North Vietnamese they had met there that they would begin the guerrilla struggle and would "bring the war home."

Vietnam justified everything, every excess, every insanity, every self-indulgent thought and deed.

When I think back to those times, I remember the mobs that frequently formed on the University of California campus — I was usually a part of them — and worked themselves into a frenzy before marching into Berkeley to trash the windows of the local merchants — a blow, by out tortured logic, against the petty bourgeois capitalism that supported the war against the Vietnamese. I remember so called "activists" (we had pressured the press into using this value-free term) shouting down speakers they didn't agree with, threatening people whose views were unfashionable, and laying plans to blow up research institutes whose work they regarded, in one of those odious little phrases borrowed from the thirties, as "objectively fascist."

Think of these images the next time someone shows you melodramatic photos of the candlelit faces of peaceniks in tremulous vigil and says that they summarize the sixties. If that era was the best of times, it was the worst of times too.

Indeed, one of the problems confronting us in the eighties is that student radicals of the sixties got such good press — both by contemporary journals and, as time passed, by historians and social critics who ought to have known better. In fact, as a group, the activists I ran with were allergic to ideas or creative discussion. They pursued a politics of narcissism which was based on an infantile adversary posturing against the democratic values of the culture which protected them even as they sought to destroy it. Harranguing each other about "freedom" in rooms whose walls were covered by posters of Che, Mao, Lenin and other tyrants, they made cognitive dissonance into the dominant political style of the era.

One might forgive them of some of this if they had later on, as the thought and deed of the sixties came unravelled, created a balance sheet for their acts, let alone a profit and loss statement. But this was beyond them. It would have required a maturity, not to mention a courage, which they lacked. They admitted only those "lessons" of Vietnam into the curriculum of American life that made them look good. These were not the lessons involving the Cambodian genocide and Hanoi's imperialism, as you can well imagine. They were only the lessons of American guilt and the inevitable triumph of Third World "nationalism" that we try to forestall.

The case of Fidel Castro shows the sixties left's inability to come to terms with its commitments. Many of us who ultimately became active in the Movement cut our political eyeteeth supporting the Cuban Revolution. Just as we said at the beginning of the sixties that we wanted to build a movement that would not follow Ike's tired and trite Americanism on the one hand, nor the Stalinism of the old left on the other, so Castro said that his revolution would follow neither the red, nor the red, white and blue. His would be distinct and independent — olive green. (The color of Daniel Ortega's as well.) He was a new leftist like we were! No wonder we supported the New Society and the New Man we were sure were evolving in Cuba.

As we know now, of course, Castro was a Leninist from at least 1956, long before his tiny band of diehards came out of the Sierra Maestre. And what is he today, that fearless and independent hero we worshipped in the sixties? An aging pimp who sells his young men to the Soviets to use in Africa in return for a huge subsidy to keep his corrupt island afloat. He has turned Cuba into a gulag, a place so horrible that 10% of its population has left since he took over, with that many more ready to depart if he would let them. You would think that my old comrades would regard the fate of the Cuban Revolution as a cautionary tale, a tragic development requiring a reassessment not only of Castro but of themselves. But not only do they fail to look back in anger at the way they missed the truth about Castro, but wish the same totalitarian fate on the

Nicaraguans that has sunk the Cubans in a misery incomparably worse than anything they experienced under Batista and other "American puppets."

It is this sixties tradition, unfortunately, that I see the emerging activism of the eighties emulating. Young people ought to want to step away from the preceeding generation and look at it critically as part of a process of self-definition. Instead, current "activists" have accepted the left-over radicals of the sixties as culture heros and gurus. Thus Abbie Hoffman, the Mortimer Snerd of the new left, has become pied piper to Amy Carter and other ingenues, an indenture that shows as well as anything else their political incompetence. Thus Tom Hayden, whom we said among ourselves twenty years ago gave opportunism a bad name, now has cachet among young campus leftists. People like Hoffman and Hayden pour old, fermented, possibly poisonous wine into new vessels.

Campus leftists today have bought the whole myth about the sixties. They seem to think of it as the last good time, a time they weren't able to experience first hand and thus must experience by resurrecting its worldview.

When I hear students at Berkeley and other campuses mouthing a saying of the official Sandinista Youth Organization, "To follow the Soviet Union is to know how to conquer, to follow the United States is to know defeat," I get a nasty case of the deja vues. I listen to the rallies and hear the same ignorance, the same intolerance, the same infatuation with anti-American styles and language that I heard two decades ago. It is like stepping into a time warp.

When Berkeley students chant, "No Vietnam in Central America," it is more than an admonition. It is, at a deeper level, a wish-fulfilling fantasy, the unconscious revelation of their desire for another tragic engagement between the U.S. and a plucky band of Third World nationalists that will, like fairy dust, turn the complex and ambigious world of the eighties into what their activists believe was the morally monochromatic world of the sixties when there were only good guys (like Ho Chi Minh and Danny Ortega and Winnie Mandela) and bad guys (like Ollie North and the rest of us).

They want to see a return to what they regard as the good old days. They want the self-indulgence people of my generation enjoyed in their own lives — the excitement and also the power. They want also another humiliating defeat for this country that will justify their hand-me-down anti-Americanism. Their "No Vietnam in Central America" has the same spirit as Abbie Hoffman's recent lament to the *New*

York Times: "It is awfully hard to have an anti-war movement without a war."

There are some differences between the activism of the sixties and the eighties, of course. The mass of today's students, for instance, are not hostile to America — not yet anyway. They realize (as indeed their radical peers do at a more cynical level) that this country's position in the world is more precarious than it was twenty-five years ago, and because it is more precarious it must be defended with more determination.

The mass of students want to be integrated into America's future, rather than alienated from it. But they face a tremendous juggernaut. On the one hand there are figures outside the campuses — people like Hoffman and Hayden — telling them that they are boring and complacent and ought to get with it. More malevolently, there are also voices from within the academy urging the same message. My generation had to force its radical ideas into the university, breaking down the defenses of the faculty and the administration. Today that current of propaganda has reversed directions. The professoriate — many of them former new leftists who in the seventies got into tenure tracks at the very universities they had failed to burn down in the sixties — lay their political ideas on their students, ridiculing anything they regard as conservative or patriotic, and inducting the young into the mysteries of radical scholarship, an oxymoron if I ever heard one.

In the eighties, moreover, the university is no longer a center of authority, making a stand, however ineffectual, against ideas that are silly, dishonest or downright destructive. The university is pathologically unsure of itself, the wounds we inflicted twenty years ago never having healed. Witness all the Marxist, Peace, Gay and Women's Studies departments that have bloomed like toxic flowers in the academy of today. The university does not tell students — as it tried to do in the sixties, before caving in — about standards and values. It is a fearful, emasculated institution filled with double talk and double standards.

Now my generation had its faults, but lack of candor was not one of them. We said that we were radicals, insurrectionists, revolutionaries. We were frank about what we had in mind, as our slogans showed — Up Against the Wall, Bring the War Home, Tear the Mother Down.

Eighties radicals, by contrast, like the role of the wolf in sheep's clothing. They have adopted the popular frontism of the thirties. Instead of admitting who and what they are — a force out to destroy American power — they posture as sincere liberals who are only in favor of peace and justice. They do this even as they work for totalitarian solutions, in the manner of their newly canonized martyr Benjamin Linder.

This is, to say the least, an alarming tendency. Alarming too are the popular fronts today's "activists" work through. I have in mind an organization like CISPES, The Committee in Solidarity with the People of El Salvador. This organization has chapters on campuses across the country. Student radicals either don't know that CISPES was formed in 1979 by an El Salvadoran Marxist guerrilla agent working with Cuban intelligence, or they don't care. Perhaps they don't know and wouldn't care if they did. But this is the kind of left that they seem to like — one that works through apparently "objective" fronts which actually are intelligence organizations set up by America's enemies.

So, it looks as though we are on the threshold of a leftism that is like that of the sixties in its romanticized affection for totalitarian movements like the Sandinistas, the FMLN in El Salvador, and the African National Congress in South Africa. And like the left of the thirties is its intention to work through deceitfully layered organizational arrangements.

The worst of the sixties and the worst of the thirties — that's a combination to be wary of.

Peter Collier, a former radical and campus activist during the 1960s, was co-editor of Ramparts *magazine with David Horowitz. He has collaborated with Horowitz on numerous articles and books, including the best-sellers,* The Kennedys: An American Drama *and* The Rockefellers: An American Dynasty. *A former lecturer of sociology at the University of California, Santa Cruz, Mr. Collier has been a visiting professor of English at the University of California, Berkeley. He graduated* cum laude *from Berkeley where he also received an M.A. Mr. Collier is co-director of the Second Thoughts Project at the National Forum Foundation in Washington D.C.*

THE MOVEMENTS OF THE SIXTIES AND THE MOVEMENT IN THE EIGHTIES
by CURTIS GANS

"I am tempted to ask the question of the sixties, which movement, and about the eighties, what movement?"

I COME HERE (AS A LIBERAL), a true one; one that is concerned when both a professor from the ideological right and a Marxist professor are denied tenure because of their beliefs. As Reed Irvine knows, I can in my writings be equally critical of misrepresentations of facts by liberals like Bill Moyers as I can be of misrepresentations of facts by Evans and Novak. I care that anybody has the right to speak at any university and I think that goes with the entire spectrum and that is the nature of academic freedom.

I hope that I will lend a little light, rather than heat, to this debate. Given the topic, which is the movements of the sixties versus the movements of the eighties, I am tempted to ask the question of the sixties, which movement, and the question about the eighties, what movement? Which is to say, in the sixties, you could trace essentially four different movements. There was a movement of liberal activism that owes its genesis in 1960 to the sit-in movement. It owes its intellectual and institutional underpinnings to the articulated consensus of liberal thinking presented by Adlai Stevenson in 1952 and 1956 and to the development of that thinking in institutions ranging from the National Council of Churches and the Newman clubs and the California Democratic Council and the Americans for Democratic Action. And that movement carried through to 1968. Its characteristics were in a sense, self-discipline. If you remember the sit-in movement, a lot of students wore shirts and ties. They talked politely. If you remember much of the activity surrounding something called the teach-ins, it was civil dialogue in universities, it was orderly expressions in peace marchers, it was trying to find ways through the political system, ultimately in the Johnson movement and the Eugene McCarthy campaign, for trying to persuade people that points of view ought to be different on certain issues.

There was a second movement which was in reaction to that movement which was similarly disciplined, which had its national manifestation in the Barry Goldwater campaign and its campus manifestation in an organization called Young Americans for Freedom.

And there was a third movement which was an outgrowth and an offshoot, but something fundamentally different, from the first movement, which emerged somewhat out of Students for a Democratic Society and Student Non-violent Coordinating Committee and which emerged out of the pessimism of their experiences in fighting injustice in Mississippi and which led to an attack on the American system. Those were the people who demonstrated at the Pentagon. Those people were not in the convention, but out of the convention, in Chicago. Those were the people who believed in confrontation. But they were of a different strain.

And there was finally another movement, that was totally in chaos, which was the counter-culture movement. Those were the people who were the beats; the people who were into drugs, longhair, into calling cops "pigs."

Both the first two movements were healthy developments in American society. When I started looking at the 1980s I say what movement? — because I spent a lot of time looking at voting statistics — and I found that 16.6% of those age 18 to 24 voted in the last election. When we are talking about movements, we are talking about a very small segment of American society.

I have to compare the early sixties' movement somewhat favorably to the eighties' movements because of the concern for institutional integrity and their discipline. But I think they had some advantages. One advantage was that we weren't fully into the television age and people weren't competing to get on the evening news with extreme action. The second advantage was that there existed both nationally and locally mediating institutions; organizations like Student Government, the National Student Association, the U.S Youth Council, the Newman Clubs. Groups that served as training grounds for leaders gave them a means of honing their dialogue for persuasion of majorities and gave them respect for institutions. I think that some of that has been lost.

I also think that in many ways you were dealing in the sixties with much more definable issues. You were dealing with segregation which was something that could be seen by a large number of people as wrong. I know that people here believe that the Vietnam War was the best thing since sliced bread. But there are a lot of people who could believe as I believed that the Vietnam war was wrong, not because we like the Communists, but because it was a bad place to extend American self-interest.

I think the third thing is that we have a different sense of values operating today. My parents and all the parents of people my age come from a generation who were either immigrants or who had to struggle through the depression. And those people by and large dedicated their lives to making their children's lives better than their own. Those of us who were grateful for that translated that to a commitment to our society. Today, on all sides of the fence, you have more people concerned about their own lives without a commitment to society, partially because of the lack of a value structure that is larger than the self and partially because of the lack of mediating institutions; partially because of television, and partially because the issues are somewhat more intractible now. The movements of the 1980s, such as they are — and that is reflected in the voting statistics — are much less than the movements were in the 1960s. And I don't think that it's my nostalgia speaking.

What may be done to re-instill a sense of institutional integrity, a sense of rational dialogue, a sense of commitment to the marketplace of ideas for free competition? I think those are the critical questions we face in terms of developing an activism in this generation.

Curtis Gans, the former staff director of Senator Eugene McCarthy's presidential campaign, was a campus activist during the 1960s. A former member of the Democratic National Policy Council, Mr. Gans has served as a consultant to the Woodrow Center for International Scholars. He has written for several major publications and has appeared on nationwide TV talk shows. Mr. Gans is presently the Director of the Committee for the Study of the American Electorate. He graduated from the University of North Carolina with degrees in English and Philosophy.

CHAPTER EIGHT

FREEDOM OF SPEECH AND ADVOCACY IN ACADEMIA
THE DEBATE ON "STAR WARS"
by EDWARD TELLER

An institution devoted to the search for truth must insist on doubt and the development of opposing points of view. Those who are firmly convinced that they are the sole possessors of truth have no chance of finding truth. Ways and means to inject skepticism into our academic institutions are sorely needed. It is a most difficult and most important challenge. Only if academia succeeds in replacing advocacy within its community with real debate will academia have a chance to make a contribution to the search for and defense of truth.

ACADEMIC INSTITUTIONS, AS they grew up in the Middle Ages, were closely related to the Church. The Church in turn was the guardian of truth as it was perceived in those times. Academic institutions started and remained not only guardians of the truth but seekers of new truth and shapers of the means that lead to truth. In that respect, the claims of academia have remained consistent. Being closely connected with the search, recognition and defense of truth imposes a particularly heavy responsibility.

One crucial question concerning truth in academia concerns the ways in which the great influence of our universities is used in the debates on important public issues. The response of academia to the war in Vietnam and to the discussion of the Strategic Defense Initiative occured decades apart. Considering them individually raises a question about the quality of the debate. Considering them side by side suggests an obvious and simple improvement.

In the late 1960s, our universities were in turmoil; by May of 1970, some had even abandoned the attempt to function as institutions of learning for the rest of the academic year. During that spring, thirty-three presidents of great universities publicly protested the policy of the nation. That deed was defended as a right of free speech. Whether the national policy was right or wrong is beside the point. The issue at question is the role of academia.

Academic freedom is the highest distillate of freedom of speech. The fight for academic freedom — that is, the right to present any point of view for examination — has been rightly and remarkably extended in the past few decades, and its specific defender should be the academic community as a whole. Freedom of speech also guarantees the right to advocate a particular course of action. At first glance, there seems to be no contradiction between the two aspects of freedom of speech — academic freedom and freedom of advocacy, but there is actually a considerable difference between them, and the difference leads to a paradox. Both aspects of freedom of speech are necessary for the proper functioning of a democracy, but it is impossible to use and maintain both at the same time and place.

Academic freedom makes it possible to get to the bottom of things, to reach a true understanding. As a scientist, as a teacher, and as an intellectual, I am obligated to be a skeptic. I should doubt all my convictions. I should be ready, willing and eager to listen to objections — never being free of passion and of emotion, but as aware and as critical of passion and emotion as humanly possible. The purpose of that exercise is to arrive, through doubt, at as great a certainty as can be attained. Academic freedom carries an inherent obligation — the obligation to listen in as careful and openminded a manner as possible.

Freedom of advocacy is very different from academic freedom. It is the freedom that provides a means to mobilize our society for action. Preparing for action means that at a specific time — the end of the year, next month, tomorrow — an action will occur. There is a deadline. We cannot listen to endless speeches. Freedom of advocacy needs to be clearly distinguished and separated from academic freedom.

For the proper functioning of congress, freedom of advocacy is essential. Freedom of speech in its complete sense cannot and does not exist on Capitol Hill. Members of Congress have cloture; they don't have time to listen to each other; they must decide and do. Often many of us disagree with them. That is in the nature of a democracy.

In 1964 a free speech movement was organized on a great university campus, the University of California, Berkeley. It claimed freedom of advocacy and destroyed academic freedom. The group was willing to listen but only to itself. It refused to tolerate even the simplest, briefest expression of the views of its opponents.

The group forced the resignation of several good teachers from the university. The professors were not reactionaries; one was an old Social Democrat. He was forced to leave because he was for true freedom of speech. The activities of the Free Speech Movement, a tiny minority, were discomfortably similar to the activities of the Nazis in the late 1920s and early 1930s, and to the behavior of Communist movements prior to takeovers. In this case, freedom of advocacy led in a short time to violence, to burning and bombing, and even to bloodshed. When freedom of advocacy is given into the hands of inexperienced young people, such excesses are probably unavoidable. The proper place for freedom of advocacy is in responsible political bodies and in the press and media.

The heads of our universities are responsible for defending academic freedom. The university must be allowed to discuss anything, explore anything, in order to clarify ideas. As is true of every other freedom, academic freedom can be defended only if it is limited. In my opinion, academic freedom in a democracy does not mean that the intellectual speaks and everyone, including the President of the United States, obeys. That is not academic freedom, and that is not democracy.

As individual citizens, those thirty-three presidents had the right to criticize our administration. They all were men of great reputation; their views would have been heard had they chosen to speak up without using the names of their universities. Nevertheless, they found it necessary to band together and speak as presidents of their great schools. Thirty-three presidents failed in their responsibilities as leaders of their great institutions. The university must abstain from advocating action in the day-to-day development of politics. Without that appropriate limitation, academic freedom is not going to survive. Without it, respect for the intellectual will evaporate. Great decisions deserve debate. As citizens, we have the right and responsibility to speak up. But if we are part of academia, we must do so as private citizens. As a professor, one should confine his remarks to his field. As a university president, one should respect his responsibility to the institution of learning. If the ivory tower becomes a soapbox, it cannot be a citadel of reason.

What happened two decades ago in connection with the debate on Vietnam is being repeated in connection with the Strategic Defense Initiative. Inside the academic community, differences of opinion seem to have disappeared. Instead of careful discussion and debate, there is a call for action. One case in point is the report by a panel of the American Physical Society (APS) on directed energy weapons — special products of high technology on which physicists, due to their professional abilities, can deliver truly valuable judgments.

The start of the investigation was auspicious. Several scientists of international repute participated. In a field in which there is too much secrecy and too little judgment, these scientists were given access to all the relevant classified information. They worked hard for more than a year. At the same time, the bias of the group was unmistakable. Many members of the APS had publicly opposed all attempts at strategic defense as not feasible, and useless.

The conclusion of the study was not to endorse such an extreme position. Instead of condemning directed energy weapons — lasers, x-rays, beams of particles, electrons or microwaves — as impossible, these projects were described as difficult, and it was estimated that success might require many years of work.

Some of the scientists involved in directed energy device work raised objections to pessimism expressed in the conclusions of the report. They pointed out errors and ambiguities that had emphasized the difficulties. In response to the criticism, the eminent authors of the original APS report, though sometimes admitting the correctness of arguments on the other side, remained completely adamant about their conclusions. Such rigid opinion about difficult technical questions concerning future developments is not compatible with good science.

The real objection, however, is the complete absence of a single positive suggestion in the entire report. The members of the panel had produced many excellent ideas in the immediate past in the basic sciences; they did not come up with a single idea for accelerating the development of directed energy devices. During World War II, such suggestions abounded in connection with radar and nuclear explosives.

When the report was handed over to the council of the APS, political considerations got into the driver's seat. Instead of confining attention to the object of the study — advanced devices of high technology — conclusions were given to the press about short-term engineering projects, which in fact were not studied by the panel. The Council seems to have taken its cue from the thirty-three presidents.

The same spirit guided an attempt in 1986 by Cornell University to take a poll of the members of the National Academy of Sciences (NAS) for their opinions about SDI. Each NAS member received three solicitations by mail, and those still not responding were called personally by telephone. In all, about two-thirds of the members responded.

Although only a handful of respondents claimed familiarity with the scientific work in question, less than one-tenth of the participants declined to respond because of inadequate information. In publishing the poll, not only were the opinions of a number of very difficult scientific questions voted on, but the comments of the respondents were appended.

The most frequent comment expressed was distress over the damage that SDI would do to progress in science. The claim is that SDI diverts scientists from work on important, pure and peaceful research. An indication concerning the validity of that point can be found by looking at *The Physical Review,* a journal that reports summaries of the research each year in physics. In 1986, the two volumes of *The Physical Review* contained a total of about 13,500 pages. In 1982, the year before SDI began, the two volumes included 11,000 pages.

During World War II, it may properly be said that national defense drew talent and other resources away from basic research. In 1939, *The Physical Review* contained 1,400 pages; in 1944, the publication had shrunk to about 300 pages. However, the corollary that is usually attached to the concern about drawing talent away from basic research — that such a drain will have an adverse effect on future scientific and technological advances — was patently false on that occasion. In the mid-twentieth century, the United States was far ahead of the rest of the world in practically every branch of science and technology.

Today, the degree to which academic scientists are helping with SDI work is very slight. Such participation, or lack of it, has an effect on the rate at which progress can occur. During World War II, the immensely difficult jobs of separating isotopes, of building the first nuclear reactor, and of building the first nuclear explosive, were accomplished in less than seven years, including three initial years of indecision. But at that time, the scientific community of the United States was united. Today the community is divided.

The second most common comment had to do with the regret that SDI might take attention away from disarmament talks.

One remarkable and characteristic view of a member of the National Academy of Sciences was:

> The whole SDI project appears to me as a fairy tale. That grown ups, let alone the President of the U.S., could take it seriously, is flabbergasting to me. I see this SDI thing as a boondoggling enterprise, whose net effect is to increase funding for the military, waste vast sums of money, and to prevent people from discussing some basic issues in other terms...STOP THE BOONDOGGLE.

Clearly, the basic issues the respondent had in mind did not include questions about the effect of deployed Soviet defenses and ongoing Soviet research on national security, or the effect of international protective defense — even so limited an ability as stopping an accidentally fired missile — on international tensions.

The strong view expressed by the poll is certainly not a convincing argument. What is really disturbing, however, is that, within the poll, it was hardly challenged. It is remarkable that in the debate between Gorbachev and Reagan, the academic community is taking Gorbachev's side. It remains to be seen if Gorbachev's recent statement that the Soviet Union has worked on strategic defense and continues to do so will modify the attitude of contemporary American academia.

In the examples mentioned above, political advocacy either replaced the search for truth or at least has prevented such a search from playing the central role that it must have if the purpose of our institutions is to be fulfilled. No individual should be faulted for having strong and polarized opinions. But an institution devoted to the search for truth must insist on doubt and the development of opposing points of view. Those who are firmly convinced that they are the sole possessors of truth have no chance of finding truth. Ways and means to inject skepticism into our academic institutions are sorely needed. It is a most difficult and most important challenge. Only if and when academia succeeds in replacing advocacy within its community with real debate will academia have a chance to make a contribution to the search for and defense of truth.

The greatest adventure of my life was understanding the uncertainty inherent in explaining atoms. That our universe is not built on machine-like, predictable components is the great new scientific insight of our century. The concept still is hardly assimilated by most intellectuals. Similarly, our search for truth must be based on doubt and the exploration of all possibilities. There is plenty of evidence that the tolerant society of the United States draws strength from admitting doubts in most of its decisions.

Academia has deviated from this difficult but important approach to truth. It has repeatedly embraced the fixed point of conviction and advocacy rather than the flexible approach, which admits imperfection. Using our rational powers fully requires patience, even sympathy for the opposing view. Members of the scientific community should be aware of how difficult that process is, because they are applying it consistently to their work in science.

The academic community rightly insists on its freedom to differ from the rest of the society. The practice of differing is even more difficult if exercised not by a community but within a community. That practice is also more important.

Edward Teller is the co-founder and associate director emeritus of the Lawrence Livermore Laboratory. His recent book, Better a Shield than a Sword, *is published by the Free Press. He serves as a National Advisory Board Member of Accuracy in Academia.*

PART TWO

The Liberal Ethos

CHAPTER NINE

THE CAMPUS ETHOS:
STUDENT TESTIMONIALS

ABBIE, AMY AND THE CIA CAPER
by GREGORY ROTHMAN

Not only did the protesters shut down the university, destroy school property, attempt to prevent an arrest, steal money from university employees, break a wooden banister from the stairway in the building, kick a hole in the wall of the building, leave cigarette burns in the carpet and break trespassing laws, they broke a constitutional principle. This violent minority...denied students their First Amendment rights of association and freedom to hear.

FOR YEARS, THE University of Massachusetts at Amherst was known, as Jesse Jackson coined it, "a bastion of liberalism." I have never viewed the situation so moderately. If the sixties still live in America, they live in Amherst; the most liberal town, in the most liberal district, in the most liberal state in the union. In the two years I have been attending U. Mass, Amherst, I have witnessed the rallies for "gay rights" and the terrorist African National Congress, an anti-SDI rally where the speaker claimed that the Soviets were more self-righteous than the United States, and even a rally which defended Muammar Khaddafi where a professor called the US attack against Libya, "racist-inspired." I have witnessed the Residential Administration promote homosexuality and fight the Student Government Association over student rights and fiscal responsibility, but I have never seen anything like the anti-CIA protests that took place on our campus during the 1986-1987 academic year.

It was a cold November night when I showed up outside the career center at the University of Massachusetts. I had always been enthralled with the CIA and secret agents, but I was outside that evening for a different reason. As a conservative activist and a student government leader I knew there would be people at the career center that had no intention of ever working for the Central Intelligence Agency — destroying the agency, but never working for it. There were no more than thirty radicals leftists in attendance that evening, but they were successful in temporarily defeating the CIA. I had no idea what I was getting involved in; my grades were about to take a drastic dive, my name was about to become known in every corner of the university, and I was about to learn about how powerful a violent minority, glamorized by the media and driven by hate for America could take away the fundamental rights of students on my campus.

During the next month there would be many rallies, protests, stories in the daily paper, and discussions in classrooms and dorm rooms regarding the CIA and their presence on our campus. As a point of listening in and taking part in as many of these as possible, I was also able to be present at all of the rallies and protests and made sure that the left was not the only side seen in the UMASS CIA debate.

Eleven members of the Radical Student Union were arrested on one occasion and on November 20th, the infamous Abbie Hoffman, a convicted drug pusher and sixties leftover, appeared on campus to put on a workshop on effective protesting and civil disobedience. I attended the workshop and watched the Peter Pan of the sixties protests spill his wisdom to a group of about one-hundred leftwingers and assorted malcontents. Immediately following the workshop Abbie addressed a group of over two hundreds students. Many of the students in attendance were opposed to the radicals' recent tactics against the CIA.

From the rally, the protesters along with Abbie Hoffman, marched to the Whitmore administration building. November 20th, 1986, had happened to be the last day for students to turn in their pre-registration forms for the next semester's classes. On the last day, nearly 90% of the 18,500 undergraduates students turn in their forms. The campus radicals, many of whom were from Boston University, Boston College, Brandeis University, Smith College, Hampshire College and Brown University, had succeeded in shutting down our administration building. When the marchers reached Whitmore they found the same thing that many students wanting to turn forms in had discovered; the building was locked shut.

The angry protesters turned and took over a smaller building. The building housed the University Public Relations office. Radicals, once inside, perched themselves on employees' desks, destroyed papers and created the chaos which led to the closing of the office. The angry students, unable to turn in their forms, turned and looked to a group of twenty conservatives holding signs and chanting "USA, USA, USA." Slowly the group of counter-protesters grew and at one point even outnumbered the two-hundred protesters inside. But the media nearly ignored this basic fact when covering the story. *The Boston Globe* said a "handful of couter-protesters stood outside..." The local television stations ran pictures of both protesters and counter-protesters without sound — the commentators indentified the students as simply anti-CIA protesters.

On that day, 60 radicals were arrested inside the building. I stayed until the last bus was filled with arrested protesters and the police were about to lead the buses away. It was at this point when I had my first encounter with the daughter of Jimmy Carter. I must refer to this experience, because if it wasn't for the fact that her father was once President, she would be just another malcontent feminist — in her own words, another "socialist-feminist." As a friend pointed her out to me in the crowd — they all looked the same to me — she sat down infront of one of the buses and was quickly arrested.

Since that courageous act, Amy Carter has become a celebrity in America. Over and over she has stated in interviews that she does not like to be the center of attention that she does not enjoy the spotlight. I strongly question that. I would submit, based on my experiences with her activities, that Miss Carter needs the attention or she would not only be ineffectual, but also ignored. How many reporters would listen to a rabid feminist with multi-colored hair and rhetorical talents which resembles Elmer Fudd's? Amy Carter is a media-hound who has precious few intelligent things to say about international matters, besides the mere rhetoric and propaganda which comes out of the KGB handbook. (See Appendix B, "Amy: a Left-wing Microcosm.")

Not only did the protesters shut down the university, destroy school property, attempt to prevent an arrest, steal money from University employees, break a wooden banister from the stairway in the building, kick a hole in the wall of the building, leave cigarette burns in the carpet and break trespassing laws, they violated a constitutional principle. This violent and noisy minority, made up of many people who were not even students at the University of Massachusetts, denied students their First Amendment rights of association and freedom to hear. Indeed, it was a sad day for freedom of speech. But we've had a number of those days on campus here at the University of Massachusetts.

The greatest crime of the CIA/Amy Carter episode was not commited until the trial. A jury, after hearing testimony from leftwingers and self-proclaimed experts on the CIA, found the protesters not guilty. Amy Carter was included in the gang acquited by this Northampton jury. Northampton, once the proud home of President Calvin Coolidge, is filled today with hippies, lesbians, and bleeding heart Smith College "women." Though no representative from the CIA testified, the protesters were found innocent based on the "necessity defense." The prosecuting attorney even said after the trial that he didn't bring up the objection to all of the "expert witnesses" testifying, because he was a big fan of Ramsey Clark and wanted to hear him speak. The "necessity defense" said that the crimes that the CIA has committed are greater than the crimes of the defendants. The jury completely ignored the facts of this trial. The CIA was not on trial. Amy Carter, Abbie Hoffman and some frustrated malcontents who have no regrets for our constitution, judicial system or democracy were. Not only did the real students in America (those who attend their classes faithfully everyday and study hard to improve their career chances) lose. Free speech was a victim.

Gregory Rothman is a student at the University of Massachusetts, Amherst. Mr. Rothman is chairman of the U. Mass Conservative Alliance and a columnist for the Minuteman.

THE ROOTS OF THE LIBERAL CAMPUS ETHOS:

A PERSPECTIVE FROM THE UNIVERSITY OF TEXAS

by JOHN COLYANDRO

Our universities clamp down on dissent from traditional quarters and engage in intellectual totalitarianism to escape the truth and certitude of intellectual absolutism. While claiming to be tolerant and humble believers in academic freedom, our schools refuse to hear traditional philosophy.

IN THE COUNTRYSIDE OF New Hampshire, there's a small liberal arts college named Magdalen. The school is devoutly Catholic with a miniscule enrollment (100 students, perhaps.). Its purpose is to instill the Roman Catholic faith and prepare young men and women for a faithful life in a secularized world. On the list of required reading are works by Karl Marx — the one political theorist whose atheistic mendacity is (irreconcilable) with orthodox Catholicism. At Magdalen, however, there is no fear of Marx. Marxism to them is a corrupt ideology that can no longer lay practical claim to men's lives; and which could never lay claim to their minds. And yet, Marx is taught.

At our nation's supposedly progressive institutions, where academic freedom holds court, does St. Aquinas, doctor of the perennial philosophy, the defender of common sense, get a fair hearing? Or course not. At the University of Texas and other American universities, 1,600 years of critical Western intellectual and moral development are ignored. The sagas of the Christian era are denied due process, their works discarded and devised, and any mention of the great Scholastics evokes condescending huffs and puffs.

This is the great paradox of our age. The small, absolutist colleges that defend a faith some 2,000 years old are ridiculed as backward and uninformed. The gargantuan state institutions which defend the new faith of the new age are lauded as open and free-thinking. Marx shares the stage with the absolutists; St. Thomas is locked in the closet by the relativists.

Why does this happen? Absolutism reflects reality; relativism creates a disastrous unreality. Our universities clamp down on dissent from traditional quarters and engage in intellectual totalitarianism to escape the truth and certitude of intellectual absolutism. While claming to be tolerant and humble believers in academic freedom, our schools refuse to hear traditional philosophy.

William F. Buckely Jr. wrote in *Up From Liberalism*, "bear in mind the dictum of Etienne Gilson; Tolerance is a meaningless concept except as practised by a fervent believer." If Aquinas and Marx were given equal time at our "modern" schools as they are at Magdalen College, the current liberal or illiberal ethos would collapse, because liberalism has no creed. "How can the modern relativist exercise tolerance if he doesn't believe in anything to begin with?", asked Mr. Buckley. So universities merely retain the facade of academic freedom while issuing the *academic license*.

This attack upon the traditional philosophy (the philosophy propounded by the Greeks which came to fruition in the Middle Ages) commenced in earnest late in the 16th Century with Descartes. Desperate to be original, the rationalists of the 17th Century concluded that man's senses (the foundation of knowledge) are unreliable. The empiricists of the day on the other hand, dismissed reason. The realistic synthesis was destroyed and the floodgates opened. What remained was a wasteland that produced the materialist sensibilities ("We ain't got no soul"), skeptical proclivities ("Who's really to say?") and utilitarian notions (What's it worth to me?") that has subdued man, and made him something less than a man. Today, infecting our universities, are nothing less than the practical by-products of those epistemologies: relativism as intolerance and intellectual disorder.

Professor Bloom, in his wrenching volume *The Closing of the American Mind*, dissects the cadaver of disorder. "The university now offers no distinctive visage to the young person. He finds a democracy of the disciplines — which are there either because they are autochthonous or because they wandered in recently to perform some job that was demanded of the university. This democracy is really an anarchy, because there are no recognized rules for citizenship and no legitimate titles to rule. In short, there is no vision, nor is there a set of competing visiions, of what an educated human being is."

The hairy-knuckled relativism is also much in evidence. At the University of Texas, copies of *The Texas Review*, a conservative alternative to the campus media, were snatched from a campus display in the designated "free speech" zone because conservatives are "intolerant." One writer was spat upon because *The Review* dared assert that AIDS was not likely to affect people besides homosexuals, IV drug users and those who have contact with them. Pro-African National Congress students vandalized property and occupied the President's office demanding divestment of holdings in companies that do business in South Africa. Former Secretary of State Henry Kissinger was verbally throttled because he supported President Reagan's policy in Central America. The administration, to demonstrate compassion, established classes for credit allowing students to teach their peers the "Methods of Contraception." *Ad infinitum, ad nauseum.*

These demonstrations, though, are merely manifestations of liberalism run amok in the classroom. How else can it be explained? Students don't occupy offices in a vacuum. Administrations are not condom-vending in a vacuum. No, they are expressions of what goes on in our lecture halls. Thus, one must return to the intellectual origins of the *Liberal Campus Ethos*. Engaging the philosophy that leads to protests against South Africa, that undermines traditional morality, that screams for tolerance at the expense of values, is to train the guns on the real enemy.

This also heightens the point that the reign of king pseudo-intellectuality has been long in coming. No university is highly regarded today unless students take to the streets. Once our schools rejected realism, student unrest would become a hallmark or university of life. The outspokeness and virulence by which the Left manhandles the campus ethos is nothing new, and Accuracy in Academia and conservative students who found alternative campus publications, cannot think of themselves as fighting something unique. Back in the 1950's, the Intercollegiate Studies Institute, asked the question: "What for instance have your professors been pushing at you?" The next day's headlines: "Professors blast group searching classroom politics." Sounds familiar.

To disregard the historical rise of the Left on campus and its one-sidedness in constructing the ethos, is to place blinders on our efforts. We must understand that the current campus ethos is the consequence of a continuum of thought that gained credence back in the 16th century. From that time, we've had a rotting effect until today universities promote fornication though condom vending.

Our duty then is to create this new ethos; to undo, to the best of our ability, what has been wrought by the materialism, scepticism and utilitarianism of the modern world (that was born of the rationalists and empiricists). Academic freedom only makes sense when there is an end in mind. At Magdalen, the goal is wisdom. What can be said of most of our schools? That social consciouness is the goal? Self-awareness? Modulation at the expense of truth? Sensitivity at the expense of principle?

The war will eventually be won by our best and brightest becoming teachers and not rushing madly into the political arena. We must establish more Magdalens where academic freedom is real because the goal is truth; not more Universities of Texas' where academic freedom is anarchy because there is no goal, other than to lay waster to the best of Western Civilization.

John Colyandro is a political consultant in Austin, Texas. He recently graduated from the University of Texas, where he was the founder and chairman of The Texas Review.

THOUGHTS ON THE UNIVERSITY OF COLORADO, BOULDER
BY JOHN CARSON

The main problem on campuses today is not the degree of leftist ideas and influence, it is the absence of opposing views and the continual attempts on campus to squelch such views when they arise.

IN HIS INAUGURAL address, Joseph Sewell, the first president of the University of Colorado, delivered the following remarks:

> When the University of Colorado shall have an honorable place and name among the institutions of learning of the land, and I shall be sleeping in the shadow of these mountains, or elsewhere, I would ask no prouder eulogy than that some good and true friend shall say of me, 'he was in at the birth, he directed its infant steps, and now behold the full-grown man.

The year 1988 marked the one hundred and twelfth year of the University, and though it is today ranked among the most prestigious universities in the nation, it is far from achieving the status of "full-grown man." The university takes pride in being what it terms a "liberal" institution. Indeed a genuinely liberal university might be termed a "full-grown man." Yet, it quickly becomes necessary to clarify terms.

To many the word "liberal" entails openmindedness, an affection for pluralism, and a general distaste for tyranny. But as proponents of the free market and individual freedom have known for decades, at some point the term was taken from those who genuinely hold these values, and today is used to describe a philosophy and practice of central planning and collective state control.

Today's "liberal" is most powerfully entrenched in the American system of higher education. The University of Colorado at Boulder is but one of hundreds of universities

141

which take pride in their "liberalism." It is here that I spent seven years from 1979-1983, receiving a bachelor's degree in political science, and from 1984-1987 receiving a law degree. It is also here that I became an advocate for the free market, democratic capitalism, and an opponent of Marxist tyranny.

As a freshman I came to the University of Colorado convinced I was in for an intellectual feast. What I got was a sobering lesson in what happens when one political philosophy holds a near monopoly on thought. It very quickly became obvious that the University was dominated by professors, administrators, and student leaders who saw the solution to every problem in the creation and growth of one government program or another. Their "progressive" and incredibly elite views of society were best mandated through the establishment of an ever-present and powerful central government with the primary function of redistributing the wealth. In foreign affairs, the guidepost was "moral equivalence." The United States was no better than the Soviet Union, or any other powerful nation. Though America was freely and regularly criticized for its foreign policy, one had to strain to hear even a whisper of criticism against any Marxist policies. Campus "progressives" had all the answers, at least they thought so. Most of their agenda consisted of what was wrong with traditional American society, and what was particularly wrong with capitalism.

There was often a rejection of structured learning on campus, students were at the University to "find themselves" or to find "the truth." The old view of a university being a place to build character, strengthen values, and train knowledgeable leaders would have been viewed as absurd. Traditional values of family, hard work, and patriotism were often looked down upon by those in positions of influence throughout the campus. Perhaps most humoring was the moral arrogance of those who had convinced themselves that one can only care for fellow human beings through the uncompromising support of a paternalistic government. To entertain the thought that this might not be the case was to be "racist,""sexist,"or even "fascist."

The chancellor of the Boulder campus stated on June 10, 1982 that: "it is important that each student find a particular niche, a special suited social milieu in which to work, to study, to learn, and to play. An institution such as ours must pay attention to the whole individual, to how students live, to encourage campus associations, and to assure that none is left out." Many times just the opposite seemed to be the case. Conservative organizations and associations were

Dartmouth music professor William Cole, who said in class that sexism keeps women out of jazz and who also referred to certain students in his class as "honkies" was once disciplined for banging on the door of a dorm room belonging to a *Dartmouth Review* writer. He has also attacked a photographer of the *Dartmouth Review,* smashing the flash of his camera.

Minneapolis police are forced to spray mace at violent anti-CIA protesters through the shattered door of Fraser Hall at the University of Minnesota, February, 1987.

Anti-CIA protesters at the University of Minnesota.

Former Northwestern University professor Barbara Foley. A self-proclaimed Marxist, Foley interrupted a speech by Nicaraguan freedom fighter leader Adolfo Calero in November, 1985. Foley took over the microphone and yelled, "He has no right to speak. He should feel lucky to get out of here alive."

Sidney Gluck, Marxist professor and founder of Scholars Against the Escalating Danger of the Far Right, with Accuracy in Media and Accuracy in Academia founder Reed Irvine at AIA's conference on academic freedom, June 27, 1987.

Pro-Life students, who were forced to take down their posters of aborted babies by the University of Oregon, put posters back up after a court rules against the University's free speech policy.

Dartmouth students boycotting a local advertiser of the conservative
Dartmouth Review, February, 1988.

University of California, Davis student-activist Jim Burns who
was caught issuing a bomb threat to disrupt a speech by UC
President David Gardner. "I have long advocated non-violence...
I'm sorry the anti-apartheid movement has come to this
point," says Burns.

Nicaraguan contra leader Adolfo Calero is attacked by Tufts University student Joshua Laub during a speech at Harvard. The speech was cancelled by the University even though Calero was willing and able to continue. Laub was released on $15 bail.

Demonstrators raise their arms in protest and shout down Chief
Justice William Rehnquist at Indiana University, September, 1986.

Anti-CIA protesters at the University of Colorado, Boulder tear down the fence in front of the CIA campus headquarters.

automatically "reactionary." Their mere existence was viewed as a threat to the "liberal" and radical atmosphere which dominated campus political life.

When I arrived at the university I did not view it as "left" wing or "right" wing. It seemed logical to assume that such a prominent institution would be required, if only by its own conscience, to provide a balanced and reasonable look at the dominant issues of our time. Yet as William Buckley once commented; "Liberals are forever telling us that they are eager to hear all points of view, they are often shocked to discover that there really is another point of view."

Take for example, the campus Cultural Events Board which was overwhelmingly dominated by leftist political speakers, many brought to campus for upwards of $5000 in mandatory student fees. In a study conducted by our campus organization, Students for a Better America, we discovered that during the period of 1980 through 1985, 82 percent of the political speakers invited to speak at the University of Colorado, by the Cultural Events Board, ranged from liberal to far left. Leftists invited to speak on campus who received hefty honorariums collected from student registration fees included Alger Hiss, who was convicted of perjury for denying that he was a Soviet spy. He was paid $6,000. Noam Chomsky, a far-left professor from M.I.T. did even better. He was paid $6,150.

Michael Parenti, a Marxist professor who taught at Brooklyn College in New York, collected lecture fees of $2,000 in 1984 and $2,445 in 1986. The students were also required to shell out $2,000 to bring Angela Davis to address the students. Davis, an official of the Communist Party, USA, was that party's candidate for vice president of the U.S. in 1984.

The Cultural Events Board also put up $4,885 to put on the CISPES — Central American Culture Week. CISPES is the acronym for the Committee in Solidarity with the People of El Salvador, an organization that promotes the cause of the Communist-led guerrillas in El Salvador. CEB also put up $1,404 for a CISPES film festival.

On the milder side, the Board paid $4,316 to Alexander Cockburn, a writer for the radical *Nation* magazine, whose views generally seem to have been inherited from his father, Claud Cockburn, a prominent member of the British Communist Party. Leonard Boudin, father of convicted terrorist Kathy Boudin and a legal defender of Communists and other far leftists, netted $3,293. Senator George McGovern was paid a mere $2,000 for his appearance, as was Seymour Hersh, the author and leftist reporter who achieved fame from his exposure of the My Lai massacre.

Our report noted that only 17 percent of the speakers, a total of six, could be said to represent a conservative point of view. These included Gen. Alexander Haig, who was paid $10,000 and pro-life activist Joseph Scheidler, who was paid $891. Both of these speakers were met with disruptions caused by leftists in the audience.

In a letter to alumni and members of the Board of Regents, I wrote, "It is time that the students, faculty, administrators and taxpayers who finance the university begin demanding a more balanced presentation in campus 'cultural' programs when they are funded with mandatory student fees."

The Board of Regents responded to our study by passing a motion to set up an oversight committee that would withhold funds from the Cultural Events Board until a better balance of speakers was presented. If there was no significant change in the type of speakers being invited, the Regents pledged to withhold a portion of the fees that are used to finance the Cultural Events Board. But after conservatives had over the course of the year or two raised enough legitimate and potent complaints, the board decided it was time to stop bringing political speakers altogether and concentrate on cultural events. A speakers bureau which involved a healthy debate of ideas would apparently have been too great a threat.

Campus student groups were a significant power base for the leftists, bringing in over $50,000 in student fees through a deceitful mechanism called "negative check-off." This meant that if you did not wish to pay the student group fee you had to check the box at registration. This was also the favorite fund-raising tool of the local arm of Ralph Nader's PIRG. The Colorado Public Interest Research Group as it was called, raised close to $100,000 each year through the "negative check-off." They thrived on student apathy and ignorance in order to rake in their money. Now that's consumer advocacy liberal style. Of course to challenge any of these mechanisms was to be "anti-consumer" or "anti-student groups." Despite this fact, both fees were by 1984 successfully challenged, and forced by student vote in the first case, and by a vote of the Regents in the second, to survive on optional student fees (the PIRG chose to leave campus rather than subject itself to such optional student funding.).

There is not really much to be said of the faculty. It is much the same as the faculties of most major universities in America today. There are a lot of fancy degrees and academic credentials, but no political diversity. In fact, out of hundreds of professors, the number of conservatives willing to make their presence known can literally be counted on one hand.

However, the main problem on campuses today is not the degree of leftist ideas and influence, it is the absense of opposing views and the continual attempts on campus to squelch such views when they arise. The case was probably best exemplified in 1983 when a group of liberals decided it was time to eliminate Students for a Better America, the organization which had emerged as the only strong conservative organization on campus. Though SBA was incorporated in the District of Columbia, the liberals decided to try and steal the name, and thus force SBA out of business. They incorporated the name Students for a Better America in the state of Colorado, took the original SBA to court, and sued for ten thousand dollars in damages. For a while the court bought it, but the game was stopped short of success when the Mountain States Legal Foundation volunteered its services in defense of free speech and the preservation of a genuine political debate on campus.

Though this ploy was a failure, it did not stop the continual terrorist style attacks on everything from SBA posters to its office door, which was continually defaced and posted with rude materials. The labels of "fascist" and "nazi" once again ruled the day as leftists returned to their old tactics.

All the leftist talk one hears about the need to protect the holders of diverse and differing opinions, is rarely applicable in practice. Collectivists cherish, thrive upon, and arrogantly demand a political monopoly. If at any time this monopoly is threatened by proponents of the free market or traditional values, then it is once again time for labels and distortions of reality. Let some unpopular opinion come over the horizon which threatens their dominance of student government, student groups, faculty, or campus publications and they will be glad to lead the lynch mob.

Possibly the most appropriate reply to the political monopoly which has existed on campuses for so long can be found in the words of Reinhold Neibuhr who said: "A healthy democracy never gives all the power to the proponents of any one dogma; it holds all claims to the truth under critical review; it balances all social forces, not in an automatic, but in a continued harmony of power. In this way it distills a modicum of truth from a conflict of error."

It was Aldous Huxley who said: "the truth does not cease to exist simply because it is ignored." It appears that America is waking up to that fact; one can only hope this renaissance of capitalism and genuine liberalism will continue as the years move forward. America may well be the last hope for the survival of democratic capitalism. It is therefore essential that much more effort be directed at our colleges and universities. It is here that our future is being determined. Unfortunately, it is also here that there remains an incredible degree of misunderstanding, disinformation, and ignorance of this political, economic, and cultural system which has produced more for a people than any system ever has, and likely ever will.

It would be impossible for any person to state how Joseph Sewell, the University's first president, would today view it. It is my assertion that he would feel as I do that it is one of the finest universities in the nation; yet he too might find it falling short of the status of a "full-Grown man." For until it first recognizes and then corrects the gross imbalances and hypocrisy it fosters, and begins to explore society's problems in an enlightened and balanced manner, it will never acheive such status.

It was a much later president of the University, George Norlin, who in 1935 made the following observation before the new gradutes:

> What the University purposes to be, what it must always strive to be, is represented on its seal, which is stamped on your diplomas — a lamp in the hands of youth. If its light shine not in you and from you, how great is its darkness. But if it shine in you today, and in the thousands before you, who can measure its power?

The task which remains for all alumni and students who love this, and indeed all universities, is to help ensure that that light remains one of fairness, virtue, and above all an uncompromising dedication to the survival of a diverse and free society.

John Carson is a 1987 law gradute of the University of Colorado, Boulder. As an undergraduate at Boulder, Carson founded Students for a Better America in 1981 and was President of the College of Arts and Sciences in 1982-1983. Carson is now an attorney with the Federal Trade Commission in Washington, D.C.

THE BATTLE FOR WILLIAM AND MARY
by DOUGLAS PHILLIPS

The president of the college, the twenty-fifth President of the College of William and Mary spent the greater part of his inaugural address denouncing Accuracy in Academia. It was only too appropriate that the leader of this institution characterized by academic intolerance would use the historic occasion of an inauguration to denounce an organization consisting of two men and a xerox machine.

ONCE THE VANGUARDS of free speech and academic inquiry, the college campuses of the 1980's have become a breeding ground for ideologically motivated faculty members and administrators intent on politicizing the academic agenda and manipulating the terms of debate.

The problem is three-fold. Not only are conservative voices absent from most of America's colleges and universities, but those voices, which seek an audience, are being actively squelched by liberals, the very same liberals who have proclaimed themselves to be the greatest champions of free speech. This selective approach to education is manifest in the classroom, in the administration-subsidized student groups, and in many of the officially sponsored programs of the university.

In addition to suppressing conservative viewpoints these same people trivialize the nature of higher education by promoting and instituting trendy and politicized advocacy programs like "Peace Studies," and "Women's Studies;" programs which in the words of nationally renowned constitutional scholar Forrest McDonald are "faddish responses to highly vocal minority political pressure." Of the new Women's Studies program at William and Mary educators, Professor Elaine Themo, has been frank about their objectives of advancing radical lesbian-feminist political thought:

I am a feminist. I know all the women teaching these (courses) are feminists, in the sense of feeling very strongly that the existing cultural conceptions of appropriate behavior for masculine and feminine should be changed.

Students interested in pursuing a degree in Women's Studies currently use books like *Radical Feminism and Love, Female Sexual Slavery, Compulsory Heterosexuality* and *Lesbian Experience, Lenin's Women and Society*, and *Imperialism and Sexuality*, as their texts. Consider this statement made by one such Women's Studies text titled *Feminist Frameworks*, published by McGraw-Hill Books.

The development of lesbian feminist politics as the basis for the liberation of women is our top priority, in our society which defies all people and institutions for the benefit of the rich, white, male, the lesbian is in revolt... When politically conscious and organized, it (lesbianism) is central to destroying our sexist, racist, capitalist, imperialist system.

The intolerance by the established campus Left has created a remarkable void on many of America's campuses. Until recently, there were few organized attempts to fill this void. Christian evangelicals and conservatives with their ideological roots grounded in Biblical tradition, are beginning to react to the moral and philisophical bankruptcy of the American campus.

During my tenure at William and Mary, both as the leader of a student organization and as editor of a campus journal, I was privileged to work with a group of students in offering our campus a positive, Biblically-based alternative to the agenda of our professors and administrators.

It was our objective not only to offer an alternative perspective, but to restore responsible debate to the college; to hold the faculty accountable to standards of academic integrity and to effect administrative policy-making decisions.

Our efforts were met with outrage by the campus establishment. In addition to administrators resistance and classroom harassment by enraged professors, our people were subjected to personal threats and vandalism by campus radicals. All this at a college which is generally considered to being quiet, moderate and politically apathetic.

I was first thrust into the battle for academic freedom at William and Mary when as a sophomore I was censured for challenging the accuracy of the claims of the Marxist leadership in Nicaragua. The William and Mary history department was officially sponsoring Ricardo Espinoza to "educate" students on current developments in Nicaragua. Espinoza, a member of the Communist Sandinista

148

government and a representative to the United Nations, made a number of outrageous claims including the denial that Nicaragua received military aid from the Soviet Union.

While I questioned the accuracy of Espinoza's claims, and offered newspaper documentation to the contrary, one professor siezed the podium and in one breath denounced me, President Reagan and slavishly apologized to the Nicaraguan leader for American foreign policy. He dissallowed any further hostile questions.

During this same lecture, $700 scholarships were offered for students interested in traveling to Managua to rebuild homes "destroyed by the Contras," and tickets were sold to join a host of radical homosexual organizations in a march on Washington against the Reagan Administration.

That year the College of William and Mary sponsored a state-subsidized speaker series that included Abbie Hoffman and Communist Party vice-presidential candidate Angela Davis. In fact, the college invited three self-avowed members of the Communist Party to appear on campus that year at the expense of thousands of dollars to the taxpayers of the state of Virginia and the students of the college.

With alarming consistency, William and Mary sponsored radicals posing as "authorities" in a speakers program aimed at "educating" the student body. Randall Robinson, leader of the pro-Marxist TransAfrica organization, was compensated $5000 to speak to students on the issue of South Africa. While condemning South Africa as a "nazi regime," Robinson argued that the concentration camps of Marxist-Leninist Mozambique were necessary to "re-educate" certain elements within that tiny African nation. Robinson received a standing ovation.

All of these events led many students to feel there was a need for a basic shift in the policy of the College. That year, a group of us met to formulate a strategy for change. A three-tier plan of attack was established: (1) Offer alternatives to the college sponsored left-wing propaganda through an independent speakers series, (2) encourage conservative students to take an active role in student government at every level, and (3) create alternative media outlets, (i.e. starting an independent newspaper).

With the establishment of the William and Mary Young Americans for Freedom, an activist group dedicated to providing the College with alternative speakers, came a steady flow of well-known conservative and Christian leaders. Although our organization received no funds from the state or college, in one year we were able to provide guest speakers whose normal fees to the College would have been in excess of $10,000. Our 1985-1986 speakers series included Reed Irvine of Accuracy in Academia, General Albian Knight supporting the Strategic Defense Initiative, an Afghan Mujahadeen freedom fighter, and a leading Ethiopian freedom fighter.

Our speakers were often met with verbal harassment and sometimes violence. During a lecture on the Republic of South Africa by my father Howard Phillips, Marxist and pro-Marxist members of the faculty shouted accusations and profanities, and then disrupted the talk by staging a walk-out. When Jerry Falwell spoke for our group, over three thousand people attended. The William and Mary administration further heightened the pre-existing tension surrounding the Falwell visit by ordering one of the largest turnouts of armed policeman ever to attend a regular speaking event at the College. In addition, Satanists, radicals, and a host of campus and community left-wing activists, staged a protest outside the hall where Dr. Falwell spoke. Although Dr. Falwell's friendly speaking style diffused much of the tension directed against him, it was not enough to stop the radicals from slicing the tires of the car used for his transportation.

The liberal student groups and professors were outraged at what seemed to be a well organized challenge to their preeminence on campus. Class discussions, radio shows and countless newspaper articles were dedicated to attacking YAF. Interestingly, few of these attacks were related to our philosophical stands; rather, they challenged our right to remain on campus. We were even the subject of psychoanalysis by some individuals hoping to discredit YAF members as maladjusted mental misfits. For some professors, anti-YAF sentiment was a welcome means to return to their hippie days of the 1960s. Yes, once again they could unite to denounce the three great evils which were destroying America: God, family and love of country. Only this time they were defending the establishment; their right to impose their morality on others and the legitimacy of the status quo.

The official college paper, whose 1986-1987 editor described himself as "sympathetic with Marxism," declared war on YAF, dedicating its weekly editorial page to challenging any statement by individuals who were, after all, "racists" and "warmongers."

Many of these articles were lengthy pieces submitted by faculty members. In fact, it was the intolerant faculty who most strenuously tried to discredit and censor our speakers program through unruly conduct at the events, insinuation and verbal abuse. The very same faculty that had been so vocal in its denunciations of Reed Irvine and Accuracy in Academia demonstrated their idea of tolerance, by protesting and refusing to turn out for his lecture at the college. Though the auditorium was full the night of his talk, there were no faculty members in the house. The 25th president of the College of William and Mary, Paul Verkuil, spent the greater part of his inaugural address denouncing Accuracy in Academia. It was only too appropriate that the leader of this institution characterized by academic intolerance would use the historic occasion of an inauguration to denounce an organization consisting of two men and a xerox machine.

In 1986, we founded the *William and Mary Observer*, a self-sufficient independent, monthly journal of student opinion and investigative reporting. *The Observer* proved to be the most effective means of reaching the student population and effecting college policy. With a circulation of over 4000, and a fair-sized staff we were able to reach most of the student body with hard-hitting investigative reports and Biblically-based perspectives on current events and student activities. It was the expressed purpose of the *Observer* to bring honor to God by proclaiming truth and exposing evil.

Despite a college radio station-sponsored boycott and harassment of our advertisers, the paper grew. One of our investigative reporters broke a story that would later be picked up by *The New York Times*. When asked about his willingness to comply with Secretary of Education William Bennett's new policy calling for administrative officials to crack down on drug abusers, President Verkuil told our reporter Jarell Wright, "I'm not interested in the big-brotherism that is implied by a drug crackdown." Not long after *The New York Times* article quoting the *Observer* had run, Verkuil appointed the first committee of students to examine drug problems at the college.

In response to an Observer article criticizing the College for inadvertantly using state tax dollars to subsidize the showing of pornography in one of the dormitories, the Office of Residence Life issued a paper to all campus Resident Advisors to be on the look-out for Observer "spies" on the dormitory halls. Shortly after the publication of our article, however, the ORL agreed to ban the showing of smut in the dormitory hall.

The official sanctioning of homosexuality advocacy programs and the use of state tax dollars to advance a radical pro-homosexual agenda is a problem now common to many of America's campuses. In an unpublicized, but flagrant example of the seriousness of this abuse at William and Mary, one freshman was actually rebuked by college officials for suggesting that his roommate, a self-avowed homosexual being tested for AIDS, should vacate the cramped dormitory room they shared. Soon after the victimized student had registered his complaint, the Office of Residence Life sent professor George Greenia, a self-avowed homosexual and advisor to the campus homosexuality advocacy organizations, to address the students and his hallmates. In his talk, Greenia attacked those who would discriminate against homosexuals and AIDS carriers. Reports circulated that the pressured and belittled student eventually apologized for "discriminating" against his homosexual, and potentially AIDS carrying roommate.

Later, in a lecture entitled "Homosexuality and the Judeo-Christian Ethic," professor Greenia, the official college spokesman on homosexual issues, presented students with a "Biblical" study which "proved" that sodomy was sanctioned by the Holy Scriptures. Tragically, I have spoken to many students who leave a Greenia lecture only to say, "if the Bible says it is O.K., it must be O.K." In fact, students have been known to "find themselves" as a result of a Greenia lecture and change their natural sexual orientation in favor of lesbianism or homosexuality. Prof. Greenia is also reported to have said: "You can take a bucket of blood containing the AIDS virus and pour it over your head and you'll never get AIDS."

In the Spring of 1987, the *Observer* published an investigative report about a fraternity stag night, turned into a sexual orgy between one hired stripper and the members of a prominent campus fraternity. The story, based upon the testimonies of members of the fraternity who were ashamed of the event, became a hot issue on campus. With such stories comes a good deal of bad press for the college, and the Administration quickly dropped their investigation, pressing no charges against the fraternity.

Things did not go as easily for the staff of the *Observer*. The reporter who covered the story received no less than fifteen death threats and sexually abusive threats, probably from outraged members of the fraternity. Despite appealing to the college, no steps were made to investigate the threats or protect the terrified reporter.

If William and Mary is in any way representative of the American academy — and all evidence I've seen indicates that it is — then today's college students are facing an educational environment where immorality is institutionalized and academic abuses rampant.

For the student who maintains a world view based on traditional Judeo-Christian values, a secular education has become inherently combative. To exist in such a system means either to become part of it (a product of liberal, anti-God indoctrination) or to actively combat untruth in the classroom and unrighteousness on the campus.

Thanks to the help of many dedicated students and caring parents, the great giant of secular humanism and academic intolerance was wounded for a brief while at the College of William and Mary.

Douglas Phillips, a 1988 graduate of the College of William and Mary, founded the William and Mary Observer *and is the former chairman of the Young Americans for Freedom.*

CHAPTER TEN

THE DARTMOUTH ETHOS

by BENJAMIN HART

Those running the universities are less interested in education than in political indoctrination. The left-wing academy, which has lost intellectually and politically on every important issue, now clings desperately to its icons and to its symbols. Its entire political agenda has been reduced to posturing and name-calling because it is so void of ideas. Its frustrations are being taken out on its students, as its world is essentially imploding around it. The students, of course, being now predominately conservative, young, energetic and full of enthusiasm, represent everything it hates.

IN 1980, A GROUP of students, including myself, founded a conservative student publication called *The Dartmouth Review*; it's been publishing weekly for seven years now. When we first started this enterprise, it seemed innocent enough. In fact, we were naive enough to believe that the Dartmouth faculty and administration would welcome the new publication. Even if they did not agree with us, we thought they would be open-minded enough to see the advantage of having another point of view expressed on campus. It would add stimulus to academic life. Our professors would welcome the new opportunities for students to write, publish and become trained in journalism. We were mistaken. We did not yet understand the *ethos*.

"*Ethos*" is a term I used in my book *Poisoned Ivy* (a campus memoir of my undergraduate years) to describe the intellectual climate that permeates academic life in America.

In essence, the *ethos* is a distillation of sentiments left over from the 1960s. In fact, the kinds of people who were rioting at the 1968 Democratic Convention in Chicago have taken up positions as tenured faculty in our most elite academic institutions. The flag burners and rioters of two decades ago today comprise the academic leadership of America. As the country at large moved right, the academic establishment careened left. There has been a reversal of the generation gap on our campuses. Twenty years ago students wanted to destroy both America and the academy in its traditional design. It was the administration and faculty who were saying "Stop. Don't do this." But today, it's the academic establishment which wants the country and the academy to be destroyed. It's the students who voted overwhelmingly for Ronald Reagan in both elections, and the students who want a solid traditional education. This has caused a serious conflict. How serious this conflict is was not apparent to me until we began publishing our conservative newspaper.

You see, as the left lost politically in the nation, it found refuge on the college campus, which has become a kind of syncure for burned out radicals who want job security. As their defeat became more and more apparent — no one is seriously advancing a socialist agenda or talking about the romance of Communism anymore — the campus left has become increasingly bitter, and has adopted a kind of bunker mentality. Their main concern is not academic freedom, but to preserve the college campus as the last bastion of sixties-style leftism, which I have dubbed the *ethos*.

This *ethos* is a set of unwritten rules that determine and judge the ideologically correct attitudes on every subject. Anyone whose opinion falls outside the boundaries of this so-called *ethos* will not only be excluded intellectually from the college community, but will in all likelihood be excluded physically. The offender will be brought up on charges before the college disciplinary committee, and in all likelihood, will be expelled from school. The most important issues to the *ethos* are not really those issues that carry substance. The *ethos* is far more concerned with issues of a symbolic nature. For example, favoring tax cuts, an ordinary policy issue, would be considered outside the boundaries of this *ethos*, but would not usually be treated as a truly serious offense. Far more important to the campus *ethos*, the guardians of this ideological virtue are affirmative action, gay rights, South Africa, no prayer in school, and condoms, all of which are symbols of the leftist agenda, or what remains of it.

155

Because so much of what the American left stands for today is so self-contradictory, it is actually quite difficult to define precisely what this *ethos* is. I'll try to draw a picture of this *ethos* by citing some examples from own personal experience. To borrow a phrase from one Supreme Court Justice, you'll know the *ethos* when you see it. The Supreme Court Justice was refering to pornography, but I think the same holds true for the *ethos*.

This point was first driven home to me during an episode which I recount in *Posioned Ivy*, and which I call the "Indian Skater Incident." The traditional college symbol at Dartmouth was the Indian, which was adopted because the Dartmouth College had been founded in the Eighteenth Century for the purpose of educating Indians. Hence, the symbol seemed to make sense. But in 1972, the Dartmouth Board of Trustees, under heavy pressure from the organized Left, decided to abolish the Indian symbol on the grounds that it was allegedly demeaning to Indians, whom they called Native Americans. Not only was the symbol apparently demeaning, but it was "racist." And not only was the symbol itself racist, but we were told that the symbol was indicative of a wider pervasive racism that dominated all of American society.

The students, however, were not convinced by this argument that the symbol was an inherently racist icon. Many students ignored the college proclamations on the matter and bought T-shirts with the Indian symbol emblazoned on it, Indian neck-ties, and feathers. They would yell the Indian cheers at football games. The alumni also contributed funds to an organization that was founded to bring back the Indian symbol. Imagine if liberals in Washington organized an effort to abolish the "Redskins" as a symbol for the Washington professional football team. Such a campaign wouldn't fly in ordinary American society because people wouldn't buy those arguments. It would be impossible to eliminate the Washington Redskins as a symbol.

What could the college do to prevent this enormous, popular support for this thing called the Indian symbol? Mobs of fresh-man would run out on the football field dressed in war paint. To the college authorities, this was an incredible scandal. So the administration decided to single out two students whom they viewed as especially egregious offenders. One of the students was a friend of mine, Shaun Teevens. He decided to dress up as an Indian and skate out on the ice at a Dartmouth College hockey game. He believed that this would delight the crowd and bring back school spirit, which he thought important in this instance, because Dartmouth was playing Brown University for the Ivy League championship.

And he was correct. The crowd cheered wildly, which in turn re-invigorated the spirit among the Dartmouth hockey players, who went on to win the Ivy League championship. The school authorities, however, were not amused. They hauled Shaun Teevens before the college disciplinary committee and suspended him from school. The charge against him, now get this, was "emotional violence." Now, I know this sounds unbelievable. But, listen to the statement that was issued by the chairman of the college disciplinary committee and I think you'll begin to get an insight into how the *ethos* really works.

The members of the committee suspended the skaters because we believe that they have violated the rights of Native American students who had come to this college expecting to thrive and grow as individuals without having to live with stereotypic attitudes imposed on them. When they, (the Indians) received their letter of acceptance to Dartmouth, they were not told that, because of their backgrounds, they would be the victim of emotional violence. The long deliberated decision to suspend, represented an institutional stance that such victimization is not tolerated.

So read the statement and my friend was suspended. He was in the end let back into the school because a group of alumni raised a war chest of money and threatened legal action on the grounds that Teevens' First Amendment rights and academic freedom had been violated. But the school did not drop the matter. The college instituted, instead, the most bizarre disciplinary program that I have ever heard of. Shaun Teevens, the Indian Skater, was ordered to take an Indian to lunch once a week for a year.

Now think about that for a moment. It seems hardly flattering to the Indians to be used as part of a weekly punishment. This program was actually difficult to enforce statistically since there were only forty Indians on the entire campus. The fight over the Indian symbol probably seems trivial to anyone not associated directly with Dartmouth College. But the *ethos*, remember, is primarily concerned with symbols. Take another issue which is also symbolic, such as the issue of South Africa. It's abstract. It's in Africa somewhere. And most Americans do not really care about South Africa. They don't know much about it and most students don't really care much about South Africa either. But the left (i.e. the *ethos*) is passionately concerned about South Africa. Let's look at what happened to a Dartmouth freshman who did not tow the orthodox line regarding sanctions against South Africa.

157

The freshman happened to be black. He is also a conservative black. In fact, he was on the staff of *The Dartmouth Review*. His name is Les Grant. His crime against the *ethos* was to help dismantle three shanties that had been built on the central common illegally in protest of corporate investment in South Africa. Les Grant thought the shacks were an eyesore as he passed them everyday on the way to class. They looked like piles of garbage to him. People were sleeping in them, playing guitars, smoking pot, and they had been there for three months in violation of both college rules and local zoning laws. Les Grant thought the shanties were acceptable for, perhaps, three days. But they had been there for three months. And there seemed to be no sign that they would ever be removed. Grant petitioned the college to do something about this. After all, the college common was the property of all students, not just the organized campus Left. But his complaints fell on deaf ears and nothing was done. Finally, he and several other students decided to take matters into their own hands. They went out one night and dismantled these shacks with sledgehammers. These shacks did not actually look much different dismantled than they had intact.

What happened to Les Grant following this incident is almost beyond belief. Having a black student opposing disinvestment in South Africa was bad symbolizism, insofar as the campus *ethos* was concerned. So the *ethos* retaliated against Les Grant. First, the militantly left Afro-American student organization hung and burnt Les Grant in effigy. It then held a mock trial and found him guilty of "racism" calling him, of all things, a "nigger". Les Grant, a black student, a conservative, was then hauled before the College Disciplinary Committee. This took place in a campus atmosphere in which Les Grant was called a "nazi," a "brownshirt," a "fascist," a "bigot," an "Uncle Tom," and a "klansman," all in print. He was then suspended for two terms. His crime, ostensibly, was the destruction of those shacks. His real crime was holding opinions contrary to the prevailing liberal *ethos* that permeates America's academic establishment.

This was how Dartmouth College chose to welcome to the campus someone who happened to be black, and happened also to be a conservative. That he was black, in fact, made his conservative opinions all the more outrageous.

After Les Grant was kicked off the campus, the town of Hanover finally ordered the shanties removed, pointing out that they were an eyesore and were in violation of local zoning laws. The town also informed the college that if the shacks were not removed from the common, Dartmouth would be fined $100 a day. Eighteen left-wing protesters were subsequently arrested by town police for preventing the removal of the shacks. This incident received national attention. One of the left-wing students actually punched a police officer. The college did nothing to these students. The President of Dartmouth College, David McLaughlin, even wrote the police pleading with them not to prosecute these left-wing law breakers. He said, "They did not realize the gravity of their offense." He didn't write the same letter about Les Grant to the College Disciplinary Committee. In the midst of this entire episode, 150 left-wing protesters occupied the administration building in protest of Les Grant's attempt at garbage removal. The occupation was, of course, also against the law and in violation of college rules. But nothing was done. In fact, the occupation was encouraged by the Dartmouth president himself. At one point, a black militant berated the college president, David McLaughlin, for being out of town on Martin Luther King's birthday. The militant told McLaughlin that this proved, beyond a doubt, that McLaughlin was a racist. The Dartmouth president apologized. He said he would try to do better in the future. He was then seen on the CBS Evening News that evening marching out of the college administration building arm in arm with the Dean of the college singing "We shall overcome." Overcome what?, one might ask. Overcome whom? Everyone assumed that they meant that conservative black freshman. Les Grant was another victim of the *ethos*.

I have one personal anecdote that also demonstrates this pervasive *ethos*. It is a story, in fact, that I hesitate to tell at all, because it is so outrageous that it's almost beyond belief. One morning in the month of May, 1982, I was delivering copies of *The Dartmouth Review* to various administration offices of Dartmouth College. On the way out of one of the buildings I was suddenly confronted by a middle-aged, upper-level college official. No words were exchanged. He was completely unprovoked. But suddenly, he charged. Fists waving, feet kicking. I found myself under physical attack by this Dartmouth College official. He delivered several punches while my arms were full of newspapers. And he actually tried to push me through a plate-glass door. I didn't punch back at all, knowing that if I did I would be expelled immediately since I was a fairly well-known conservative on the campus at the time.

So I restrained the official by using a headlock and waited for people to arrive. Unfortunately, this college administrator had sunk his teeth into me, penetrating four layers of clothing and causing a four inch gash in the chest area. Needless to say I was shocked by this behavior, as were the dozen or so college employees who ran out of their offices to subdue this berserk administrator. Afterwards, I had to go to the college infirmary for a tetanus shot. The administrator, Sam Smith, pleaded guilty of assault in a local court which fined him $250 and placed him on probation.

It's obvious, said the *Manchester Union Leader* in a story on the episode, that "Dartmouth College administrator Sam Smith's bite is worse than his bark." But this story gets even stranger. Three days after the biting incident the Dartmouth faculty assembled and voted 113 to 5 to censure not the assailant, but the conservative newspaper I was distributing, *The Dartmouth Review*. The faculty resolution blamed *The Dartmouth Review* for printing material that was so offensive that it had evidently unhinged this administrator and caused him to go berserk. Smith's physical assault, in the eyes of the Dartmouth faculty, was defensible given the content of my newspaper. Smith is still working in the college and since has received a promotion.

The Dartmouth Review is once again in the national news. Three students have been suspended from school for periods of up to six terms. The President of Dartmouth College, in a recent address, accused *Dartmouth Review* staffers of being "ideological provocateurs posing as journalists." President James Freedman said the College "must not stand by silently when a newspaper recklessly sets out to create a climate of intimidation that destroys our mutual sense of community and inhibits the reasoned examination of the widest possible range of ideas." And what exactly did *The Dartmouth Review* do to provoke this unprecedented outburst? Well, it published a number of articles criticizing the way some professors have conducted themselves in class. The first article was critical of Professor Richard Corum's rather lax requirements in a freshman English composition course. Ordinarily, students in this course are required to read Joseph Conrad's *Heart of Darkness* and John Milton's *Paradise Lost*, and then write essays about the books. But Professor Corum never included these books on his reading list or the required essays, and instead took his students to see the movie "Broadcast News." As it turns out, *The Dartmouth Review* article had a salutary effect on Professor Corum's course. He has since reintroduced *Paradise Lost* and *Heart of Darkness* to his list of required reading and has requested that his students actually write papers.

Another article was sharply critical of Professor William Cole. Cole is chairman of Dartmouth's music department. *The*

160

Review article included a transcript from a class when professor Cole said that sexism keeps women out of jazz, discussed the problem of nuclear waste and said "all you guys are honkies." Cole also used a string of obscene words that I would not repeat publicly, or privately for that matter. *The Review* article posited the thesis that Professor Cole's class did not meet Dartmouth's standards either. Professor Cole once sued *The Review* for printing another article on his teaching methods. The suit was dropped.

Fearing another possible lawsuit, *The Dartmouth Review*, upon advice of counsel, invited Cole to respond to the article. *The Review* offered to provide as much space as Cole needed for his response. Four *Review* staffers carried a letter containing this offer to Cole's class. They waited for the class to finish, and then handed the letter to Cole. Cole immediately grabbed the student's camera and smashed a $300 flash attachment on the ground. That was the extent of the violence according to all accounts.

Three of the *Review* students were subsequently charged by the college Disciplinary Committee and found guilty of harassment, violation of Professor Cole's privacy, disorderly conduct and violating "the principle of discourse." As evidence, the disciplinary committee cited the *Review* student's "vexatious oral exchange" with Professor Cole.

What does President Freedman mean when he accuses *The Dartmouth Review* of "dangerously affecting — in fact poisoning — the intellectual environment of our campus." One assumes here that President Freedman is talking about the *Review's* opinions, since no one is accusing the *Review* of any violence whatsoever. Indeed, it was Professor Cole who engaged in violence, verbally as well as physically. And what does President Freedman mean when he calls the *Review* kids "ideological provocateurs posing as journalists?" I thought the college campus was supposed to be a place of robust debate, which would seem to include even "ideological provocateurs." Well, the "ideological provocateurs" have filed suit against President Freedman, Dartmouth College and William Cole for violation for their right to speak and publish freely. Enough is enough.

So what does all this add up to? You would think, after all, that adults, (i.e those running the universities) would have better things to do than chase after students for dressing up as Indians, expel students for removing garbage from the common, expel students for offering responsible criticisms of their professors, and harass students for distributing a conservative campus newspaper.

To demonstrate that Dartmouth is not the exception, let's take another Ivy League school where the *ethos* is just as prevalent — Yale.

Wayne Dick, a student at Yale University, had the audacity to distribute a flyer parodying Yale's fifth annual Gay and Lesbian Awareness Days (GLAD). There was nothing obscene or crude in his flyer, certainly nothing as obscene as the films that were shown during the GLAD festival. But Wayne Dick, who posted flyers, was put on two years probation, jeopardizing his chances of getting into a top law school. Like Dartmouth and other academic institutions, Yale has clear protections for freedom of expression. As Yale Associate Dean Patricia Pierce put it however, these protections do not extend to "worthless speech."

Worthless speech? Who decided what worthless speech is at Yale? Yale University's Executive Committee, in Kafkaesque fashion, meets in secret and does not issue written opinions explaining the basis of its decisions. The committee did meet over the matter and judged that "BAD Week" [Dick's parody of Yale's GLAD Week] poster produced by Mr. Dick "constituted an act of harassment and intimidation toward the gay and lesbian community." Keep in mind that the student was not found guilty of cheating, stealing or assaulting anyone. He was found guilty of bad thoughts, which the liberals, in twisted fashion, called harassment and intimidation in order to justify the draconian nature of the punishment. Dick offended the *ethos* and so it fired back at him. No appeal was allowed, unless the Yale Executive Committee itself granted it. So on May 16, 1988, Wayne Dick wrote a letter to Bartlett Giamatti, then President of Yale, and made his case. He wrote:

> I have been told that my poster is not protected by [Yale's] free-dom of expression regulations because it is worthless and offensive, but I respect others' right to express their views... I most often express my views on the defensive since I still find myself in the conservative minority. To avoid heated arguments and to avoid hard feelings, I have often kept silent... I am of the opinion that homosexuality is not an absolute good...
>
> I ask that my sentence be overturned if the free expression regulation is in force or that the sentence be reduced because of my ignorance of the special status of the debate on homosexuality... If my sentence is not overturned, please advise me as to other views that I am also not allowed to criticize, so that I won't knowingly violate my probation and the standards of Yale University.

Dick's outrageous sentence was eventually overturned about a year later but only after enormous media pressure and a change of university presidents.

So what's really happened to the college campuses in recent years? My thesis is this: All major liberal ideas have proved a colossal failure over the course of the past decade or so. Lyndon Johnson's war on poverty actually made poverty worse. This has been demonstrated by George Gilder, Charles Murray and others. Even Lyndon Johnson's former press secretary, Bill Moyers, hosted a CBS documentary on how poverty programs have created an entire class of people dependent for their existence on the benevolence of the welfare state bureaucrat. He showed how this has destroyed the black family unit in the inner cities and has undermined its sense of self-worth. No one, Republican or Democrat, is seriously talking about expanding "The Great Society" anymore. Everyone is talking about welfare reform, meaning encouraging private sector involvement. No one is saying we need more economic redistribution.

In addition, all those national liberation movements the left championed during the sixties went awry. Their heroes, when they got into power, turned out to be tyrants. Look what happened to Vietnam and Cambodia — virtual prison camps. And look what happened to Ethopia and Mozambique, both of which were food exporting countries before the Marxists took over. Today, millions starve.

Given these results, the Communists in recent years have suffered some setbacks. The Communists took a terrific drubbing in recent elections in Italy. Margaret Thatcher today is riding high in England and has just announced the most radical policy shift in the direction of free enterprise that anyone has seen since 1920. Collectivism is dead intellectually, spiritually and, I believe, politically. In addition, it is young America that is the most conservative age group.

The students, in large part, are in revolt against the stale sixties' *ethos*. That's the meaning of the 80 or so conservative students newspapers that have sprung up on campuses across the country. These are students of western civilization. They want to be equipped to enter the world and compete with the Japanese.

But those running the universities are less interested in education than in political indoctrination. The left-wing academy, having lost intellectually and politically on every important issue, now clings desperately to its icons and to its symbols. The left is so intellectually and spiritually bankrupt, (and I think they know it), that all it can do is defend some of its symbolic gains such as the shanties, the abolition of the Dartmouth Indian and the harassment of the conservative newspaper. Symbols are all it has and it clings to them with tenacity. It makes them feel good to call Ronald Reagan and Margaret Thatcher "fascists" and "nazis," even though they know those words do not accurately describe them. To call them such names makes the left feel virtuous. Its entire political agenda has been reduced to posturing and name-calling because it is so void of ideas. Its frustrations are being taken out on its students as its world is imploding around it. The students, of course, being now predominately conservative, young, energetic and full of enthusiasm, represent everything it hates most.

The last hope for the sixties left — for the feel good *ethos* that pervades the corridors of academe — is Daniel Ortega, that little dictator in green fatigues and designer sunglasses. Even its hero Fidel Castro is deserting it by putting homosexuals in jail and quarantining AIDS victims, a program that obviously does not conform to the *ethos*.

What's a leftist to do these days, except desperately hold to its symbols? Meanwhile Communist China continues to privatize and move in the direction of free-market capitalism. The academy will eventually follow the rest of the world. But because of the tenure system, which tends to entrench people who have long since outlived his or her usefulness, the university establishment lags about a quarter century behind the rest of the country. It always has and probably always will, as long as the tenure system is in place.

My predication, however, is that we are going to see a major shift in the academic environment in less than ten years. I know a lot of people who are now enrolled in Ph.D. programs and vying for jobs in the academic world, and they are not liberals. They are interested in serious scholarship, not women's studies or special interest curricula. But we need more conservatives to enter the academy.

I am hopeful that the university will soon become a place of serious learning and not just a platform for malcontents, where people are accepted or ostracized according with some political litmus test. Education must return to what Matthew Arnold said it should be, the study of the best that has been thought and said.

Students should be encouraged to read Shakespeare, Dante, Chaucer and Hemingway. Malcolm X should be an elective, not a requirement. Students should be told that in order to be an educated person, they ought to be familiar with Aristotle, Aquinas, and the history of how the American Republic came into existence. And reading the classics of literature and philosophy is of far greater importance than forming an opinion of Oliver Tambo.

I think we are eventually going to do away with the politicized curriculum because that's what the students want these days and I believe that the free-market in the end does work. Black students are coming to understand that a black studies major does not take them very far, but competence in reading and writing will take them wherever they want to go.

We shouldn't despair too much about the college campus. Abbie Hoffman and Amy Carter may be grabbing some headlines, but they are not winning the hearts and minds of the students. Margaret Thatcher is. ROTC is more popular today than ever. CIA recruitment is up. And the deadbeats of the sixties are getting old even as they sit in their academic chairs.

The market for bankrupt leftist platitudes is shrinking while the market for quality education is growing, which is precisely why William Bennett is among the most popular speakers in America today. The left no longer really has a coherent program to advance. They have been reduced to a peculiar ill-defined set of feelings, which in *Poisoned Ivy* I call the *ethos* for lack of a better term. It is an *ethos* that manifests itself in administrators biting students and witchhunts for Indian Skaters. The campus left is extremely intolerant, but I imagine it is very difficult for them to maintain a rational state of mind as their assumptions are daily refuted, their doctrines proven false, and their world in mid-collapse. My inclination is to sit back, watch the Left panic, and continue to read Accuracy in Academia's *Campus Report*.

Benjamin Hart is the author of three books, Poisoned Ivy, The Third Generation: Young Conservatives Look to the Future, *and* Faith and Freedom: The Christian Roots of American Liberty. *Mr. Hart graduated* cum laude *from Dartmouth College where he founded* The Dartmouth Review. *He presently serves as the director of lectures and seminars at the Heritage Foundation in Washington D.C.*

CHAPTER ELEVEN

FIRST PRINCIPLES:
A PRIMER OF IDEAS FOR THE COLLEGE-BOUND STUDENT
by HUGH HEWITT

The central challenge is not reforming faculties. It is opening minds. The thrust of people concerned with the preservation of academic freedom should not be extinguishing the freedom to be ridiculously wrong, but preserving the opportunity of students to judge for themselves the merits of opposing views.

IT IS A REAL tragedy, I think, to insert into an otherwise interesting and provocative book a contribution by a lawyer. For those of you, who, for whatever reason, have been attendees at a conference arranged, run and largely populated by lawyers, this remark will require no explanation. The bar has the uncanny ability, an unmatched skill really, at making the lively dull, the controversial mundane, and the polemic merely indecipherable. Perhaps I was invited to the Accuracy in Academia conference as a sort of innoculation, a vaccine that will protect the rest of the conference from lapsing into discussions of Supreme Court cases, legislative history and the overriding importance of footnotes. If I served that purpose, the trip over was worthwhile.

The ostensible reason behind my being invited is because I have written a little book — *First Principles: A Primer of Ideas for the College-Bound Student*. It is an odd, indeed almost squirrely, book — odd in its intended audience, odd in its message, odd in the very fact that it and others like it need to be written and read, and odd in the fact that a lawyer — not an academic — wrote it. A word or two about each of these oddities.

First Principles is written for 17 to 20 year olds, young men and women either on the verge of applying to, entering or continuing college. Not many serious books are written for this audience. I know of only one other recent text — Ben Hart's *Poisoned Ivy*. Publishers like to say that this audience is not a book-buying audience. Regnery-Gateway has decided with *First Principles* to engage in a little supply-side publishing. We shall see the result.

The message of *First Principles* is also unusual. In its particulars it is not particularly conservative with a capital C. The short chapters are introductions to recurring issues, most of them political — things like defense, race, Communism, poverty and money. It is not a polemic. I did not think that a polemic was necessary. It is an introduction, an alert that on all of these issues and others there are vigorous debates underway on what the nation's policy ought to be, and that all of these debates have two if not more sides. It is a warning that academic elites have lost interest in balance, in objectivity, that academic elites have become advocates. This will not surprise you. Joseph Epstein, writing in the September 1986 issue of *C o m m e n t a r y* on the case of Professor Foley, remarked:

> A difference that never fails to astonish me between under-graduate education now and then — then being roughly thirty years ago, when I was an undergraduate at the University of Chicago — is that now university teachers who have strong political views feel no need to suppress them in the name of fairness or disinterestedness or a higher allegience to the subject being taught.

Far from fairness or objectivity, Epstein concluded, advocacy had become standard operating procedure. He concluded:

> University academic departments nowadays seek out feminists, Marxists, and others in whom the political impulse runs stronger than any other, to teach their bias — and to do so in the name of intellectual diversity.

My book neither challenges Epstein's assertion, nor does it disregard it. I accept his view as fact. Many of the participants in AIA's conference on academic freedom accept his view as fact. What *First Principles* tries to do is answer the question: "Okay, political bias in university teaching is a fact. What should be done?" The answer in my view is quite simple. Make the vulnerable enrollee less vulnerable. Steal the impressionable mind. Focus the younger student on the fact that debate exists and that it is a violent, partisan, and — this is key — largely covert battle.

I doubt that it is difficult for many here to recall the awe which accompanies an undergraduate to campus, the feeling that learning from that day forward was going to be conducted on a higher plane. This awe almost automatically translates into an enormous respect for the professor behind the podium. It is — especially for students pursuing course work that treats political subjects — an indiscriminate awe. How can it be otherwise? This or that faculty member is degreed, for goodness sake, has written articles, has perhaps authored a book. The indicia of intellectual candlepower are all over the place.

In the hands of the objective, or as Epstein puts it, disinterested teacher, this awe is a wonderful thing. The student will be receptive to new ideas, to difficult reading, to the lengthy process of opening the mind. In the hands of a committed partisan it is an extremely dangerous commodity, for reasons obvious to all of us.

Some critics of the academy will argue that this danger must be combatted by dueling against the partisan. Perhaps, but there is an alternative. Dispose of the awe. Take the impressionable young mind and introduce a healthy dose of skepticism. Teach younger students that the debate is ongoing, and they will be far less likely to end up prematurely in one camp or the other.

Let me be clear. I am not arguing, nor does my book argue, that all incoming students should believe that, for example, the nation's defense should be the number one priority of the federal government and that a modern and balanced nuclear arsenal is a necessary though not sufficient component of that defense. Far from it, in fact. *First Principles* instead argues that a vast number of learned people have concluded just that fact, that others believe otherwise, and that the college freshman has got to know the rudiments of both views before he begins studying the wisdom of the derailed SALT II Treaty. Another example. A high school senior, *First Principles* argues, does not have to arrive at the university's doors committed to support of the contras. He or she must, I believe, arrive equipped with the outlines of the history of avowedly Communist governments — the means by which those governments seized power, their development, the human cost of that course, and the relationship between Communist governments and internal and external opposition — before he or she sits down in a three hour a week lecture course devoted to a critique of American foreign policy in Central America.

The message of *First Principles* is simply this: Hey kid, you are vulnerable. Modern secondary education in America is abyssmal when it comes to history and government and chances are you know damned little about anything. Watch out, the book says, there are people on campus who will take advantage of your ignorance.

I mentioned at the outset that it was odd that a book like *First Principles* had to be written, and that others like it need to be written. It is odd, but it is also tragic. When I worked at the National Endowment for the Humanities, the preliminary results of a study of what high school students know were becoming available. They are astonishing. Two-thirds do not know when the Civil War was fought, and three-quarters do not know when Lincoln served as president. FDR does a little better. Half of our high school population know when he was president.

If it was just chronology about which the high school population is confused, I suppose it would not be so alarming. The values of the American experience might still be closely held and understood even in the absence of a passing acquaintance with history. But an appreciation of those values is also missing. Across the river in Alexandria, Virginia, the seniors at one of the commonwealth's showcase schools, by a vote of 51 to 2, agreed with the proposition that there was no moral difference between the United States and the Soviet Union.

Only an idiot or an editorial writer for *The Nation* would not be appalled by such a state of affairs. It is so terrible a state, that even if Secretary Bennett were tomorrow vested with the authority to hire and fire faculty at all universities, and he did a thorough job replacing intellectual frauds with objective scholars, still the legions of ill-informed and unprepared college students would not diminish significantly. There would remain a vast reservoir of ignorance which could be used and abused by the advocates of moronic political adventuring.

The defense of the educated mind, and necessarily the defense of the western ideal, does not depend on reforming the university or reforming the media, though those are certainly important steps. That defense — abdicated for nearly two decades now — begins with and depends upon a serious commitment to educate serious students about serious issues when they are in high school and even before.

Unfortunately, and here's the rub, there is no money to be made there. There is no money in teaching. Believe me, there is no money in writing books for this audience. There is no tenure track, no glamour, no round of interviews on talk shows.

The incentives, in fact, lie in the opposite direction. There is money, and fame and careers to be had in Peace Studies. There is an instant audience for those who write or teach shortcuts to cultural literacy. There is, manifestly, a tenure track waiting for the professor who will align him or herself with the new and novel theory of this or that.

This array of incentives, or disincentives, to joining the battle of ideas at the level where victories would be enduring explains the last oddity about *First Principles* that I mentioned — that it was written by a lawyer.

As a practicing lawyer, my livelihood does not depend upon the applause of fellow faculty members, on the student evaluations handed in at the end of the term, or upon the judgment of the editors at the local press. Free of the cultural pressures of the university, I am not obliged to make the simple complex, or assault the accepted wisdom solely to forge a reputation. *First Principles* can be accused of being less than comprehensive. So what, I reply, there's an excellent chance that a 19 year old will read, understand, and God forbid, enjoy it.

There are precedents for this approach, or course. The books of Eric Hoffer always seemed to me to be appeals to the common sense of the American public. There was a market for such appeals. I believe it persists.

Reformers should be encouraged, I think, to be market-makers for teachers, books and articles addressed to repairing the huge holes in the public's grasp of public policy debates. In particular, I think we all ought to be concerned with providing campus populations not with "the right answers" but with an honest menu of choices. The temptation will exist — and it ought to be resisted, strongly — to turn the battle for balance into an ideological war. The demand for balance must not be itself a covert campaign for ideological correctness. There is no such thing. The idea of the university must accomodate obnoxious thinking, indeed, it must accomodate evil thinking. The demand for balance must be seen and understood to be the demand to oppose the obnoxious and the evil without fear of retribution or ridicule.

As that demand grows more visible, as it picks up momentum and success, it should be on guard against zealotry. Because the crusade on the left has proven so overwhelmingly successful, the demand ought not to be seen as incompletely met if it itself does not become a triumphant crusade. I would be as unhappy with an academy dominated by the right as I am with the one dominated by the left. Nor do I think such dominance is necessary. The West did not become the West as a result of an iron rule of a particular dogma. It is the opponents of the Western ideal who demand the dogma, who seek to shout down opposing views or to close the faculties to membership from traditionalists. The re-opening of the universities is an important and urgent task, but its success will be measured by the ability to stand back at some point and say, balance has been restored. Many may view this request for caution as suspicious, echoing the plea of advisors to the Austrian Crown for mercy towards the revolutionaries of 1848. "Mercy by all means," replied Prince Schwartzenberg. "Mercy is a very good thing. But first let us have a little hanging." Many will want a little hanging. We should commit now, when the task is large, to seek only, and to be satisfied with, a return to balance, to fairness, to objectivity, in short to sound and professional teaching.

In sum, I would like to return to the main point of my remarks and the main point of my book. The central challenge is not reforming faculties. It is opening minds. The thrust of people concerned with the preservation of true academic freedom should not be extinguishing the freedom to be ridiculously wrong, but preserving the opportunity of students to judge for themselves the merits of opposing views. The first step in that process rests in conversation with the students themselves, a conversation that should not be delayed until the customs of the university have carried them so far away from objective analysis as to make reclamation almost impossible, but should begin at the time they begin to think about political and moral issues, a time that begins, I believe, years before they set foot on campus.

Hugh Hewitt is the author of First Principles: A Primer of Ideas for the College Bound Student. *A graduate of Harvard University and the University of Michigan Law School, Mr. Hewitt was an editorial assistant to former President Richard Nixon during the writing of* The Real War. *Mr. Hewitt, who was a White House Assistant Counsel and General Counsel for the National Endowment for the Humanities, is presently serving as the Deputy Director for the U.S. Office of Personnel Management.*

PART THREE

The Assault on Academic Freedom and Free Speech

CHAPTER TWELVE

EXPLORING ACADEMIC FREEDOM
by LES CSORBA, III.

Academic Freedom traditionally refers to the freedom of scholars...to teach, publish and engage in research unhindered by others. Those protected by academic freedom in turn, have the responsibility to conduct research honestly, to report their findings accurately, and to teach without bias. In democratic societies, academic freedom is respected as a right. In totalitarian societies, where education is partly directed toward indoctrination, it is rejected.

- Academic American Encyclopedia

SINCE REED IRVINE founded Accuracy in Academia to publicize cases of academic misinformation, political imbalances, examples of intolerance, and incidents of attempted indoctrination, there has been an uproar in academia not heard since William F. Buckley completed his celebrated book, *God and Man at Yale*, subtitled "The Superstitutions of Academic Freedom." Before AIA even released its first publication, we heard all the usual cries, threats and denunciations. "McCarthyism," "Fascism," "Censorship," and our old friend, the "chilling effect," all made their expected appearences. Now the first rule in scholarship, as I understand it, is to gather your facts. It is a rule that applies in most every other profession as well. But what of these scholarly critics — where were their facts? On what were they basing their criticism? Had they waited a few weeks, they might have had the opportunity to read over the first newsletter or *Campus Report*. Surely that would have been the more scholarly approach. Surely that would have been the responsible manner in which to offer criticism.

Now the simple truth of the matter is this. Accuracy in Academia was founded to encourage debate in the classroom, not to stifle or restrain it. Anybody who thinks the founder, Reed Irvine, does not like confrontation and debate does not know Reed Irvine. He is a fiesty patriot, a modern day Patrick Henry who elicits remarkable responses from his critics, such as this from Benjamin Bradlee, the executive editor of *The Washington Post:*

> You have revealed yourself as a miserable, carping, retromingent vigilante, and I for one am sick of wasting my time in communication with you.

Accuracy in Academia raised an idea — that teaching is not indoctrinating — and the only people who truly objected to AIA's founding and its philosophical premise were the professors who most feared public criticism. Instead of dealing with its questions in serious debate, they wanted to do battle with the caricature — with the jack-booted brownshirts they see running up and down the halls, crashing down lecterns and hauling innocent scholars like themselves out for interrogation. They have as many illusions about their critics as they do about themselves.

As Hoover Institution fellow Thomas Sowell wrote: "Parents, students, taxpayers have a right to know what's going on. Accuracy in Academia has no power to do anything more than tell them." He concluded by observing that "Deep thinkers are worried about the confrontation — not about the cancerous problem that requires it." (See Appendix D, "Campus Battlefields," Dr. Thomas Sowell.)

So the confronting began. Students assaulted their professors with well-researched questions. *Campus Report* distributors and reporters began publicizing events that took place in classrooms and on the college campuses. AIA staffers began investigating reports and invited the campus intellectuals to respond. Once again, debate on college campuses was lively and thought-provoking. And, as their principle defense, professors, deans, and university presidents desperately reached for this right they call "academic freedom," a presumed shield against incoming fire.

Now let's consider "academic freedom". Its obsessive usage has effectively clouded some of the more pressing problems in academia, problems that should trouble the men and women of the academy themselves. The "right" has been an effective defense for academics claiming immunization from exposure and criticism. But "academic freedom" has also been a powerful offensive weapon that some intellectuals have employed in order to perform their various ideological dramas in the classrooms; lecture halls converted into political theaters.

Offer professors the privilege of exercising this right, and scholars of this sort come rushing up with all the restraint, dignity and erudition of hogs charging the morning trough. And just try pulling the trough away once their heads are buried in it. They don't just enjoy this right; they consume it until there's nothing left, and then oink for more. Some professors may turn up their snouts when any of our country's other rights and privileges are offered them, but here's one they can really wrap their jowls around.

I know, I've been told that cheap barnyard imagery is not very kind or elegant, but how else do you convey the immoderation of these people in exercising what after all can be a very useful right? To put it in such terms brings us back to the basic proposition: we have some professors in academia today who clearly are out of hand. They become our concern, society's concern, only when they take to acting out their inner turmoil in the classroom. What they think is their business. What they teach is the business of the community which supports them.

But listen to Richard Berendzen, the President of American University in Washington D.C., who was one of the first scholars to use that devilish little term "McCarthyism" in response to AIA's founding.

"With respect to teaching," he announced, "that's a much more private enterprise. It's an intimate interaction of the teacher with the student." Ah, but as Boston University President John Silber argued, "teaching is oral publication." There's no "private enterprise" here. "Anybody who wants to turn teaching into a mystery religion or into a sacred communication between the lawyer and his client is talking nonsense. What the professsor decides to talk to the student about in the privacy of his office is one thing, but what he professes is for public knowledge."

Now here comes the point about academic freedom, and let us see if we cannot think clearly about the whole business.

Academic freedom is simply not the same right as free speech. To act as though they are identical is an evasion, a rhetorical ruse. Free speech is not the issue at all, because no one is arguing that these visionaries cannot go outside the classroom and say anything they like.

As Max Weber wrote in *Science as a Vocation*, if a professor "feels called upon to intervene in the struggles of world views and party opinions, he may do so outside, in the marketplace, in the press, in meetings, in associations, wherever he wishes." However, "it is somewhat too convenient to demonstrate one's courage in taking a stand where the audience and possible opponents are condemned to silence."

It is instructive to read the definition of "academic freedom" as defined by the *Academic American Encyclopedia.*

Academic freedom traditionally refers to the freedom of scholars...to teach, publish and engage in research unhindered by others. Those protected by academic freedom in turn, have the responsibility to conduct research honestly, to report their findings accurately, and to teach without bias.

We give this particular responsibility the name "academic freedom" to denote its academic function. The first word, academic, qualifies the second, freedom. It only confuses the issue, to invoke the right of free speech or "freedom of conscience" or "intellectual freedom," as so many academics attempt to do. These are personal liberties which we all enjoy and they are not in question. But academic freedom by definition is a professional right that one exercises only in the course of carrying out certain professional responsibilities.

We must ask ourselves whether professors are defending a scholarly right, or protecting ideological privileges — *academic freedom or academic license?*

One professor at Arizona State University passed his days in class teaching about all the dangers and horrors of nuclear power. Now whatever you may think of this man's cause, the point is that he was advancing that cause day in and day out, in a class entitled "Political Ideologies 101." Surely, we could agree that, whatever our political faith or creed, if you are going to call a course "political ideologies," then it ought to be about "political ideologies." That's not a political proposition but rather, it seems to me, a point of common sense.

The same professor has a book which he assigns to his class each year called *Atom's Eve: Ending the Nuclear Age.* I highly recommend it as an example of the new brand of scholarship we are discussing. Midway through the text you hit upon a chronology of the rise and spread of the nuclear age. The major events, good and bad, are all listed in weary succession for 39 pages — everything from Hiroshima to the founding of the Clamshall Alliance. But some events were deemed unsuitable for inclusion in the list, such as the Baruch Plan, advanced in 1946 to place the development of atomic technology under international supervision. Along with omissions of Soviet treaty violations, this bit of history was apparently of no relevance — unlike, of course, the Clamshall Alliance.

Yes, right away let us agree, such professors have a right to their views. That right has never been in question. The question is simply whether apart from all the rights and privileges these professors enjoy, are there not a few responsibilities that come with the vocation? We all know what their rights are, what we need to clarify, I think, are their responsibilities.

Horrific material has been taught on college campuses in the name of academic freedom. Take Owen Morgan, a human sexuality professor at Arizona State University, who shows slides that graphically depict males and females engaging in various sexual acts. The professor's presentation includes several closeup shots of a couple engaged in oral sex.

One student, who complained to the Board of Regents, described the slides: "While the first slide was on the screen, Dr. Morgan made the following comments: 'I sure hope that she doesn't sneeze. Imagine if she got a cramp in her jaw now.'" The student said that when the next slide appeared, the professor commented, "Now that's a little toothy for me." On another he cried, "Hey now, there she goes, Linda Lovelace style," a reference to the actress in the notorious hard core porn film, "Deep Throat."

Another female student, disgusted with the class, reported that Morgan had told her she could make up a missed exam by writing a ten page report on her sexual experiences, an offer she declined. While a number of other students at ASU, including the student body president, argued that the presentations were "inappropriate," Dr. Morgan and the university countered, claiming the professor's "academic freedom" should not be abridged.

Another human sexuality class, this time at San Francisco State University, which shows beastiality films, caused quite a stir on campus in spring of 1988. "You're awfully nervous today. It must be the beastiality that's making you nervous," said Professor John Elie to students during the films, according to the campus daily, the *Golden Gator*. "Gasping and groaning, the audience witnessed the men and women engaged in sex acts with dogs, a pig and a boar," wrote Michelle Guido of the *Golden Gator*.

The course, "Variations in Human Sexuality," has 640 students enrolled. Most students in the class agree that one film, rather than three, would have served the purpose, wrote Guido. Elie admits the films stretched academic freedom to the limit, but nonetheless, not offensive enough to prevent their showing.

There is much debate as to what the limits of academic freedom are, if it has any limits at all. The only way to determine the limits of any right is to ask yourself what its purpose is.

179

We do not question the right of any professor to his views, and the right to offer his views in the classroom. But teachers enjoy the right of academic freedom to teach. And if they are not using it for that purpose, then the right simply does not apply. Professors are granted this right supposedly because at some point they earned it, by having some concrete knowledge of his subject or discipline which makes him worth listening to, and not just another man or woman with an opinion sounding off like the rest of us. These two human sexuality professors, it seems, are trying to do something more than teach, something a little more than provocative. Their bizarre teachings are possible manifestations of their own personal sexual biases, which are irrelevant. They have nothing to do with their particular expertise, or the description of the class in the course catalogue. The material, it appears, is unnecessary and inappropriate, and should not be protected by one's "academic freedom." But frequently, such material is. Academic freedom has become an unfortunate, but rather useful device for *license* which allows a professor to introduce material that is personally offensive to his students. He exercises his academic freedom at the expense of his students.

Academic freedom serves an academic purpose, and not an ideological one. In his book *Academic Freedom*, Russell Kirk asked the question, to what truths ought the Academy be dedicated? His answer: "...To the proposition that tolerance is wiser than ideology."

Teachers enjoy this right so that they can teach freely. And if they are not using it for that purpose, then the right simply does not apply. Yes, a professor is just as entitled as the rest of us to engage in political activism. He can even have a hidden agenda; we should expect that. But he's not entitled to call his activism "scholarship." And neither, I'm sorry to say, is he immune from public criticism once he has decided to mix those two vocations. He can't vent his grievances in the classroom, and then insulate himself against any criticism that returns his way.

The question is whether in advancing their doctrines — liberation theology, Marxist utopianism, peace at any price, moral equivalence, relativism and so on — do professors engage in scholarship or ideological polemics? The familiar proposition "I have a right to profess my opinions" does not lead logically to "and you must hire me to do so."

The only way to determine the limits of any right is to ask yourself what its purpose is. Why are teachers granted this right?

Surely, it was not for their own benefit alone. Universities were not set up around the country merely to provide malcontents with a means of registering their grievances against society. There are others involved here; their students for instance. Some educators have got the idea that academic freedom is simply a means we use to protect and nurture such valuable national assets as themselves. And indeed, they can be assets, but only in so far as they perform the service of *education*.

Professors have argued that "we are teaching as we see fit. Our subjects have to do with values, which after all are subjective. We give our interpretation, and that's all we can do."

This is not only a sophism, but an admission of professional incompetence. If it's all a matter of interpretation, why then we are all equally qualified to teach a college course. The argument destroys its own credentials. Yes, of course a professor will inevitably have his own opinions, and of course some things can be taught only by one's own interpretation. But his or her mere opinions are presumably not what got him the job in the first place, or what qualifies him to keep his position.

A narrow but useful formulation might be this: whatever it is that a scholar and a college professor is uniquely suited to do — that is what he ought to do. And given the demands of those tasks, very little else.

Academic freedom is a vital right on college campuses, and indeed it is threatened. But the worse threat to any right is the one who abuses it. And it has been abused. The victims have been the students. They have suffered from the apparent lack of openness on college campuses which has closed the minds of so many young Americans as Professor Bloom forcefully argues. But the ultimate victim is society and the vitality of the great experiment we know as America. The American public, seemingly more and more disenchanted with higher education, seem to agree.

CHAPTER THIRTEEN

ACADEMIC FREEDOM: WHAT IT MEANS AND WHAT IT DOESN'T MEAN

by S. I. HAYAKAWA

Academic freedom is not a civil right, like the right to vote. You don't do anything to earn your civil rights. They are automatically yours by virtue of citizenship in a democratic society. Academic freedom, on the other hand, has to be earned. It doesn't come automatically with your job as a college or university teacher...you must first earn an advanced degree in your field of knowledge or have in your record some equivalent intellectual or artistic achievement.

THE AMERICAN ASSOCIATION of University Professors has the following to say about the relation between a professor's duties as a scholar and teacher and his obligations as a citizen:

> It is the teacher's mastering of his subject and his own scholarship which entitle him to freedom in the presentation of his subject. Thus, it is improper for an instructor persistently to intrude material which has no relation to his subject, or to fail to present his course as announced.

> Because academic freedom has traditionally included the instructor's full freedom as a citizen, most faculty members face no insoluble conflicts between the claims of politics... If such conflict becomes acute and the instructor's obligation as a citizen and moral agent precludes the fulfillment of his academic obligations, he should either request a leave of absence or resign.

But of course many activist professors, under the waves of emotion generated by events in Vietnam or Nicaragua or South Africa, neither resign nor take leaves of absence as they abandon their academic duties to convert their classes into political rallies.

In the face of this abandonment of professional responsibilities, I have maintained that those who are paid to teach literature or mathematics must continue to do so, whatever political activities they might want to engage in outside of class hours. For saying this when I was President of San Francisco State College, I was duly censured by a faculty meeting for "interfering with academic freedom."

But academic freedom, far from meaning professional irresponsiblity, means precisely the opposite. Academic freedom is not a civil right, like the right to vote. You don't do anything to earn your civil rights. They are automatically yours by virtue of citizenship in a democratic society.

Academic freedom, on the other hand, has to be earned. it doesn't come automatically with your job as a college or university teacher. In order to be entitled to full academic freedom, you must first earn an advanced degree in your field of knowledge or have in your record some equivalent intellectual or artistic achievement. Next, you must as a rule serve as a junior faculty member for a year or two or more. Finally, a committee of your faculty seniors will go over your record and decide, subject to the approval of the Dean or the President, whether to grant you tenure — and the full academic freedom that goes with it.

It is no accident that academic freedom and tenure go together. Before you have tenure you are essentially a professor on trial. You enjoy much freedom, of course, but your ideas and actions are still subject to the censure of non-reappointment. When you are granted tenure, however, you are by definition a fully-qualified professional in your field, whether in geology or literature or physical education or philosophy. You are certified as not being an amateur, a dilettante or a crackpot. Your intellectual competence has been established.

But what of a professor's right to have strongly-held views on matters that have nothing to do with his area of expertise; views on the wickedness of trade unions or the errors of the foreign policy of the Reagan administration? Here we are concerned not with the professor's academic freedom, but with his civil rights. Like the stockbroker's or the milkman's views on such matters, the professor's views may be those of a wise man or a crackpot, but he is entitled to espouse them as a professor. In this context, he is just another vote.

The dismissal of a professor of uncertain scholarly attainments but of quite definite pro-Communist sympathies was demanded by a Lion's Club in a small city in California. The response of the professor's department colleagues was to grant him immediate tenure, not because they admired him or agreed with him, but principally because they didn't want to seem to be yielding to pressure from the Lions. (They didn't seem to notice that they were yielding to pressure from the Communists.)

This incident points to the problem for many professors. The Lion's Club of course is profoundly of the middle class. But professors in some departments — most notably in the humanities and the social sciences — believe it to be almost a religious duty to hold the middle class in contempt. According to them, the middle class is smug, vulgar, anti-intellectual, anti-artistic, materialistic. You must, as an educated person, hold middle-class values in scorn.

However, a contradiction arises from the fact that universities are profoundly middle-class institutions. Middle-class parents send their sons and daughters to college to affirm and strengthen their middle-class status. Working class people go to the university in order to join the middle class. Most American colleges and universities are basically designed for the middle-classification of everybody in America!

Professors who despise the middle class are essentially aristocratic in outlook. They are in a difficult position. Many of them are clearly unhappy when they find themselves in highly democratic institutions such as state universities and state colleges.

A typical example is a teacher of English literature at a state university in California — hereinafter referred to as the "Professor." He wrote an article in *The Nation* a few years ago to say that except for a few "younger and often more intellectually active faculty in the social sciences and the humanities," the California state universities are institutions in which "mediocrity is the end as well as the rule..."

The faculty, the Professor continued, is dominated by "a large anti-intellectual emphasis upon schools of education, business administration, industrial arts and other sub-academic services."

This, of course, is characteristic liberal arts arrogance, which, I am sorry to say, I shared as an English and Philosophy major for much of my early life.

According to this view, only in the liberal arts — and possibly in political science or anthropology — is there any genuine intellectual life. What goes on in schools of education, business administration, engineering, agriculture, industrial design and the like is "sub-academic." Education that is career-oriented is by definition illiberal — and therefore really not education at all.

"The state colleges," the Professor continues, "carry on the main work of technical training and indoctrination for submissive service in the middle ranges of corporate and state heirarchies."

In other words, state colleges, instead of training people to become gentlemen, connoisseurs of literature, critics of society, revolutionaries or philosopher kings, undertake the task of preparing young men and women for jobs in industry or government! How disgraceful!

The Professor must indeed be, if he is still in the state university system, a miserable man. He despises the very *raison d'etre* of the institution he works for. He views the trustees and the governor as busy manipulating the system so that "the economically privileged shall keep full power over education and withdraw its access from the socially and politically unsubmissive." He despises administrators, who are to him "the super janitors who run the colleges." He scorns most of his professorial colleagues and their "sub-academic" concerns. One wonders why he deigns to remain in such a miserable educational setting. Maybe he likes the pay and the security.

At a reception following the commencement exercises at San Francisco State in 1973 — my last commencement before my retirement from academic life — I was greeted by a man who introduced himself as a skycap at the San Francisco airport. "You don't know me," he said, "but I've often carried your baggage." He proudly introduced his wife, his younger children and his eldest son, who had just graduated with a degree in business administration and was on the threshold of a career very different from his father's.

I was proud of that graduate in business administration and of the fact that our state university had made possible this milestone in the history of his family.

No doubt the Professor will find the achievements of that graduate in business administration "sub-academic" and beneath contempt. What continues to puzzle me about some scholars in the liberal arts is that their own humanity and human sympathies appear to be diminished rather than broadened by their humanistic studies. One wonders what the humanities are for if their principal product is this kind of elitist snobbery.

The organization Accuracy in Academia is concerned about the serious attacks on academic freedom now rampant on the campuses of distinguished and elite colleges and universities throughout the United States: Harvard, Dartmouth, Wellesley, Yale, the University of California at Berkeley, the University of Southern California and others.

Among the many speakers whose speeches have been interrupted, disrupted or cancelled because of student demonstrations are people like Caspar Weinberger, Alexander Haig, Chief Justice William Rehnquist, and Jeane Kirkpatrick. They have been shouted down, heckled, pelted with red paint and eggs; some have had to be escorted out of the lecture hall by security officers because of the dangers of physical assault.

What is happening on such elite campuses is a direct continuation of what occured during the 1960s at the same or similar institutions. An undergraduate student at Harvard, Steven Kelman, wrote a book about the disturbances at that university, *Push Comes to Shove: The Escalation of Student Protest*, which contributes much to our understanding of student disorders, then and now. What he wrote then applies with equal force to what is happening now.

> Students are today's idle rich. Being idle, well fed, and generally satisfied.The first non-negotiable demand of the oppressed student class is therefore for a rapidly changing stream of sensations ...And the hostility...is directed against its oppressors, institutions which require routinized-behavior (such as going to classes every day) or which discourages experimentation with new sensations such as drugs. The three most serious oppressors: University, Law, Family.

Also inherent in student radicalism is elitism — a profound contempt for ordinary people — which Kelman calls the "rotten kernel" of student radicalism. Hence the tactics of confrontation.

If radical students respected their fellow citizens, they would reason with them. But no, they cannot be bothered by reasoning with anybody, because they know what is right — so they will shut down by force whatever and whomever they object to.

Elitism is certainly the curse of student political life. Actuated by moral arrogance, the liberal elitist gives assent to the radical elitist's rape of the democratic process. This is why the student movement is so much like Nazism.

"The elitists must be fought and fought hard," writes Kelman, "because...the bloody history of the twentieth century has taught us that democracy, majority rule, and civil liberties are not luxuries, but the alternatives to mass murder and suffering. They are the necessary preconditions for any decent society."

Let me wind up these remarks with some reminiscenses from my days at San Francisco State — a thoroughly non-elitist institution, formerly known as a "street-car college," where most of our students, perhaps three-quarters of them, have full or part-time jobs or children at home to take care of.

It must have been 1964 or thereabouts when we had as a speaker on our campus the late George Lincoln Rockwell, at the time the notorious head of the American Nazi Party. Student body officers discussed the coming event with many fellow-students and decided on a policy as to how to behave at Rockwell's speech. They agreed that there was to be no rude behavior, no demonstrations. Those who wished to express their disapproval of Rockwell's anti-Semitic views were to wear yellow arms-bands and remain silent. There was to be no applause.

At the end of his speech, which was never interrupted but listened to in silence, there was a faint scattering of applause, which quickly died down when it became clear that the rest of the audience was not joining in.

Thereupon Mr. Rockwell strode back to center stage and bowed stiffly. "Ladies and gentleman," he said. "This is the first time in my experience when a college audience has given me a fair hearing. Thank you," he said, and bowed stiffly and marched off the stage.

I was very proud of our student body at that moment, when more distinguished universities around the country, including Berkeley were being torn up by student protests. For a while I remained proud.

But not for long. We too had our elitists: students who didn't have to go back to work as clerks, taxi-drivers, waitresses, bartenders or baby-sitters the moment classes were over. With demonstrations, riots, classroom disruptions and vandalism, our elitists disrupted the college incessantly from then on.

In order to restore order at San Francisco State, the trustees appointed as a new president in 1966 a charming and thoughtful pyschologist. Student radicals, white and black, broke up his inauguration ceremonies.

Nevertheless, he tried to communicate with and be friends with the radicals. In May of 1968, he fled, calling the vice-president from New York to say he was resigning and was on his way to a new job in Ethiopia.

His successor, one of our own professors, was appointed at once, but resigned in November, his problems with both students and trustees having proved to be insoluble.

Therefore, a third professor had to be appointed in 1968. The trustees had really reached the bottom of the barrel. I was appointed to this job Thanksgiving week of that year. Life has never been the same since.

Dr. Hayakawa, a former U.S. senator from California, is President Emeritus of San Francisco State University. He is also a renowned semanticist, who serves has honorary chairman of U.S. English, a national organization whose goal is to make English the official language of the United States. Dr. Hayakawa has served as Special Advisor to the Secretary of State on East Asian and Pacific Affairs since 1983. He received his Ph.D. from the University of Wisconsin, has held a variety of teaching posts, including five years as a lecturer at the University of Chicago and 13 years as a Professor of English at San Francisco State College. He serves as national advisory board member of Accuracy in Academia.

CHAPTER FOURTEEN

FIRST MUZZLED, THEN JAILED:
THE TRIALS OF A STUDENT WHO DARED TO CHALLENGE HIS PROFESSOR.
by GERARD ARTHUS

The university is a place for testing philosophies and discussing the issues, not brainwashing or inculcating the values of a philosophy which is sick and dying. Collectivism everywhere has proven to be a miserable failure, yet the social science departments in many universities act as if some sort of utopia can exist in a socialist society if we only could find the right dictator to force the people to realize the virtues of coercion.

THE FOLLOWING IS an incident which occured at the State University of New York at Farmingdale. However, names and places could be changed with a similar relationship between what happened to me in this case and what is evidently a fundamental problem with modern higher education in general.

During the spring semester of 1986, I had enrolled and paid for a course entitled Humanities 103, "Philosophy, the Law and the Modern Citizen," taught by a Professor James Friel. The course description was as follows:

> This course is an introductory course which deals with leading ideas in the fields of philosophy, law and citizenship. The relationship among those topics is discussed. While theory is discussed, an effort is also made to apply some of these concepts through citizen apprenticeship. Leading thinkers in each field are considered and readings are taken from modern and earlier writers.

What the course description claimed the class was to cover and how the professor eventually conducted the class were soon found to be very different. The first day of class the professor walked in and announced that he would be absent for the next week as he was to attend a conference. We later learned that this same professor had been paid to speak at a conference at the College of William and Mary while he was also being paid to teach classes which he was not attending at Farmingdale University. He had surreptiously told the university that he had to attend a conference, not that he was being paid to participate in one. To my knowledge, such behavior, while it may not be illegal, demonstrates much about the character of James Friel as a person.

Also, on the first day of class, Friel directed the class to purchase a book which he had written and published entitled, *The Gospel According to Reagan*. Once again, while not illegal, the requirement by a professor that a class purchase a book written by that same professor amounts to him using his position to enrich himself. While I have had other professors who assigned books they had written, the proper procedure would have been for the professor to at least waive the portion of the cost of the purchase that would have been his profit.

It is apparent what this professor saw as the value of education — its value only to himself. The conflict began, however, when Professor Friel finally began to teach. After returning from the conference, Professor Friel notified the class that he had heard that the United States government was using radioactive waste to treat food in an effort to enhance its color. He chastised the Reagan administration for what he considered to be another example of insensitivity on its part. His statement had an adverse effect on many of the students in the class. After being recognized, I querried as to where he obtained such startling information. Friel claimed that he had heard this tidbit of information from a friend who had read an article in a newspaper published somewhere in California. When asked for the name of the paper, he said he did not know.

When I asked Professor Friel how he could make a statement based upon, at best, fourth-hand hearsay information, his comment was that it was his opinion, and that facts were not really that important. I then asked him if he was referring to the food irradiation process. After agreeing this was the case, he admitted having no knowledge of this food treatment process. When I pointed out to him that such treatment does not enhance the color of food but has the opposite effect, he told me to bring the information to the next class if I had it. When I brought several articles from medical and scientific journals to class he refused to either read the material or share it. I made copies and privately distributed them to the class.

The fundamental problem I had with this professor was his refusal to deal with facts in an intellectual manner and to insist on his right to inculcate the class with his opinions which, when he was questioned, could not be backed up with factual information, academic sources or professional publications. From the very beginning, I made it clear to this professor that my disagreement was not with his ideological persuasion but with the intellectual content of his opinions, particularly his refusal to cite sources for his frequently non-objective statements. He seemed to particularly relish dragging President Reagan into almost every discussion and almost always in a derogatory manner.

The title of his book, *The Gospel According to Reagan,* turned out to be a blatantly irreligious diatribe whose intellectual content was not in even a small way relevant to the proposed content of the course. The fact that the title of the course and what the professor brought into it were not remotely related left many students with the idea that they were being forced to pay for something which they had not voluntarily agreed to be part of. There were several other instances of this behavior on the part of Friel. One of the more interesting occured during a criticism he was conducting of President Nixon. He could not remember the name of the individual who opposed President Johnson in the 1964 election, the only election in that decade in which Richard Nixon did not run as the Republican nominee. I had to remind both the professor and the class that Johnson's opponent had been Barry Goldwater.

The disheartening effect such lack of competence has on the students is evident. Anyone who questions the professor gets penalized when grades are given, and students quickly learn how to take courses and receive grades by telling professors what they want to hear. What eventually led to my problems was a statement made by Professor Friel to the effect that "Man had reached the zenith of his intellectual development and whatever he did through science and technology only destroyed the environment." After being recognized, I asked Professor Friel what his basis were for such a claim. He responded that there was no basis for his claim, that it was his own opinion and everyone is entitled to his opinion. He then told me that if I continued to ask such questions he would ask me to leave the class. He then asked me, not once but three times, if I had anything further to say. After his incessant questioning, I told him that I would say nothing further and would sit there and observe the class. He then told me to leave and so I did.

Immediately I went to the administrative offices and met with several school officials. After several weeks of inactivity, the acting president of the university agreed to allow me to re-enter the class. He asked me to see the dean of students and make the proper arrangements. After speaking to the dean of students, I was issued a letter signed by him at the direction of the acting president of the university directing the professor to allow me to be present in the class.

The dean also notified the professor earlier on the morning of March 11, 1987, that I would be coming to class that day. When I did enter class that day, Professor Friel told me that I was not allowed to enter the class. I handed him the letter from the dean and told him it was a communication from the acting president of the college. I sat down at my desk. He then said he did not care if the letter was from the President of the United States, he did not want me in the class. Friel then left the room and returned with security officers. They asked me to leave and I told them to read the letter from the president of the college. They refused to do so. It was at that point that they attempted to remove me from the desk at which I was sitting by choking me and covering my mouth. This was later confirmed by security officials present in the classroom.

The officers also testified that the class was quiet and no disturbance was occuring before they entered the room. After they decided that they would use force to remove me from the class, they told the other students in class to leave. But three students stayed behind to witness the scene. The security guards started hitting me and the students in the class insisted that they halt their activity. The officers promptly removed the disturbed students from the room. One of the students, Paul O'Connell, then went to the office of the vice-president and complained about the unnecessary use of force by security officers. After speaking to several individuals in the administration, Mr. O'Connell left and attended his regularly scheduled classes. One week later, on March 18, 1987, this student was arrested for allegedly interfering with the officers who were arresting me on March 11. It was then implied that if he helped them out, the school would drop the charges against him. But, thankfully, he refused. His case has still not gone to trial.

In the meantime, while a judge has ordered the university to reinstate me into the class, my case is still pending. AIA has helped me out with a good part of the legal expenses to date, contributed by generous donors associated with the organization. However, the battle is not over and Paul O'Connell and I have already filed a civil suit which will proceed after we successfully defend ourselves against fraudulent charges instituted by the university.

It must be understood that the main conflict with this professor was not a difference of philosophy, but simply the refusal on his part to substantiate his biased and politically misdirected opinions with even the smallest shred of evidence. He not only felt the need to criticize the President of the United States in the classroom, together with religion and the free-market system in general, but he stood to profit by the sale of his own book to a captive audience.

The worst part of all this was what I would call the truth-in-packaging problem. Students sign up for a course and expect to receive instruction consistent with what was indicated in the college catalog, but receive instead a collectivist diatribe from an obviously incompetent instructor who could in almost all cases not even support his own opinions with substanitive factual evidence. To make matters worse, when confronted with facts which would repudiate his wild assertions, Professor Friel frequently launched a vicious attack on the speaker without bothering to examine evidence which contradicted his ineffectual utterings. The class simply became a forum for the opinions of a professor who would whip students into submission by the threat of lowered grades as a result of criticism.

This is the situation I found in this class of Philosophy and Law. It would have been easy to sit back, tell the professor what he wanted to hear and receive a nice A for class performance. I, however, chose to question his opinions posed as facts and suffer the consequences from an academic community which has two sets of standards. One standard is reserved for enlightened liberals of a collectivist bent, and the other is for anyone who does not go along with their game plan. Those who profess to support tolerance for groups of the left become extremely quiet when they are faced with tolerating those who disagree with their way of thinking.

The university is a place for testing philosophies and discussing the issues, not brainwashing or inculcating the values of a philosophy which are corrupt. Collectivism everywhere has proved to be a miserable failure, yet the social science departments in many universities act as if some sort of utopia can exist in a socialist society if we only could find the right dictator to force the people to realize the virtues of coercion. I believe Professor Friel has taught the class, which witnessed my arrest, a valuable lesson. Close your eyes, ears and mouth to what you see, agree with the authorities as long as their philosophy is the same as your professor's. Open your mouth and ask for truth, try to demand it, and suffer the consequences of assault, fabricated charges based on lies, public humiliation and incarceration. Does it sound familiar, the very Holocaust which Friel and his ilk are constantly bemoaning with accusations of Nazism hurled at the President of the United States and anyone else with whom Friel disagrees? It becomes part of the method used to inculcate the collectivist ideals of the Friels of the world.

These students learned first hand who the real "Nazis" are and, fortunately, the many students who volutarily testified at the trial on my behalf and the ones who could not because the judge refused to allow them, all know the real story. They were there.

I believe today's students are not as stupid as the Friels of the academic community believe they are. The existence of Accuracy in Academia, the Intercollegiate Studies Institute, Young Americans for Freedom and other conservative and libertarian groups on college campuses today indicates the direction they are heading. Perhaps this is what scares Friel and others of his ilk the most; the message of my challenge to him was that many of tomorrow's students will not accept a philosophy of collectivism and lowered expectations. Today's students desire a world where they get more than Friel; the world of a successful free-market economic system where, if an individual works diligently, the benefits increase proportionally. Friel constantly ridiculed President Reagan's "Trickle down" economic theory, but Friel's system would incure an equal distribution of misery for all especially those who disagree with him. I am thankful to Reed Irvine, AIA and all the others who have supported me in this struggle for objectivity and sanity at the university level. I am sure that good news will be forthcoming. Anyone familiar with the New York judicial procedure, however, realizes that time has no meaning and the system spares no expense when it comes to lawyer's fees and courts costs. But I will press on.

Gerry Arthus graduated magna cum laude from C.W. Post University with degrees in Philosophy and Political Science in 1987. While taking a class at the State University of New York, Farmingdale last year, Arthus challenged the accuracy of statements made by the professor. This resulted in his forcible ejection from the class by campus security guards and his being suspended, arrested and charged with felonies. Mr. Arthus successfully fought his suspension by the university, acting as his own attorney. He has filed a civil suit against the university.

CHAPTER FIFTEEN

FIGHTING FORDHAM
by PHYLLIS ZAGANO

I recognize that a tenured faculty member's decision to publish in Screw, *however personally offensive many of us might find it, could and would be defended as an exercise of academic freedom.*

- Fordham President Joseph A. O'Hare, S.J.

FORDHAM UNIVERSITY IS an institution founded in 1841 by the Archdiocese of New York as a seminary for its priests. The bishop of that day found he did not have sufficient priestly personnel to staff the new seminary, and so he recruited a religious order to teach his future priests. The fortunes of that first religious order were not good, and soon the bishop had to recruit another order, the Society of Jesus, better known as the Jesuits. As things would have it, the Archbishop of New York, John Hughes by name, soon became dissatisfied with the Jesuits at Fordham, and so he withdrew his support of the institution and established the archdiocesan seminary elsewhere. The Jesuits were left to their own devices in the Bronx.

Things have not changed that much. While Fordham once had some reputation as an institution of Catholic higher education, in 1968 it asked the New York State Department of Education to consider it a nondenominational institution. More recently, according to the New York State Division of Human Rights, it has exhibited marked hostility to at least one faithful Roman Catholic of the Archdiocese of New York. In March, 1986, after two and one half years of investigation on the part of the State of New York, the State Division of Human Rights found probable cause to believe that Fordham engaged in or is engaging in the unlawful discriminatory practices I complained of, that is, they did not reappoint me as an assistant professor of communications because of my sex and my religion, and they retaliated against me after I sought redress of my grievances from the proper state and federal agencies.

These are the facts of the matter. I was first unanimously appointed to the faculty of communications at Fordham University in 1980. I was unanimously reappointed to a second two year contract some time after. But in July, 1983 my department chairman, George N. Gordon, told me that the five tenured faculty had voted not to reappoint me again because, according to Gordon:

- I did not see the difference between productivity and activity.
- The department was overtenured and wanted to make room for younger people.
- I was not succeeding at general fund raising for the department.
- One committee member objected to my U.S. Navy reserve commission.
- I was in the middle of American liberalism, and should have had a "ban the bomb" poster on my office door.
- I was perceived to be very much involved in Catholic matters and affairs, and some did not like it.
- There was the "subconscious factor" that I am female.

It may calm your doubts to know that I took notes during this conversation. Shortly after this meeting concluded, I returned to Gordon's office to tell Gordon something. He said, regarding my non-reappointment: "You may as well lay back and enjoy it."

In March, 1987, *Crisis* magazine published an article by me entitled "Fighting Fordham: A Diary of Reminiscences." Here is that diary, a factual account of a story in which academic freedom becomes a twisted and badly abused principle of intellectual life.

June, 1983

You know, I really loved the place. And things were going so very well. I'd won a Faculty Research Grant. I'd been picked for summer teaching. I had been asked to develop a course for the honors program, and worked in its guided research division as well. I'd had some other research grants. I'd published *The Nuclear Arms Debate*. I was on the editorial board of *Catholicism in Crisis*. I was finished with my work on the media reaction to the Bishops' Letter and ready to begin writing, and I had a half completed major bibliography on the propaganda surrounding nuclear weapons and deterrence already in the computer. I'd met the requirements and more. A good year, all around. The summer, all of July and August, I'd write. But it did seem strange that I didn't get a Merit Raise. A senior faculty member from another department mentioned the grievance procedures and offered help, but I thought it's really better to let these things pass. I couldn't quite figure it but, well, onward.

July, 1983

The long Fourth of July weekend would be full of good beach days. House guests and drop-ins, a party on Saturday. I arrived Friday to find that a registered letter was waiting at the post office, but the post office was already closed. I signed for it Saturday and was stunned by the news. The Associate Vice President for Academic Affairs of Fordham was regretfully informing me I'd not been renewed. My contract would run out in August the next year, 1984. Of course, no one could believe it. I called my chairman at his home, but he would not discuss it over the phone. So I would meet him in his office Tuesday noon.

Are you taking notes? George asked. George N. Gordon, chairman of the department of communications at Fordham University, finished a few phone calls and directed his attention across his desk at me, there to find out what had happened. This must, after all, be some mistake. The five tenured faculty had voted me out: Ralph Dengler, SJ, George N. Gordon, Donald C. Matthews, SJ, John M. Phelan, and Edward M. Wakin.

What was their complaint? You do not see the difference between productivity and activity, he said. We are overtenured. We must make room for younger people. They questioned this, they questioned that. I did not bring in grants. Grants, I asked. The perception was that I was hired as a general fund raiser for the department and I had not succeeded as such. It was a mixed vote, he said. The question was not do we have evidence that she is a bad teacher, the question is do we have evidence she is a good teacher?

But what are you telling me, I asked. I think you have substantially misjudged me.· I was not hired as a fund raiser, although I have tried to help with sponsored research where I could. Does my Navy Reserve membership affect this? This is possible, he said. My veteran and Navy status? He agrees. What? He tells me one committee member made remarks about it. You are in the middle of American liberalism, he advises. You should have protested nuclear energy or had a ban the bomb poster on your office door. What else? Catholic?

You are perceived to be very much engaged in Catholic matters and affairs, he says, and some don't like it. What else, I ask. There is the subconscious factor that you are female, he says. I recapitulate what he has said and he agrees again. I leave and call a friend. We speak for some time; my friend thinks the whole thing's silly. They should fire those jerks and make you chairman, he says.

I return to tell George Gordon something. He says regarding the whole thing "You might as well lay back and enjoy it."

I stop in to see the Vice President for Academic Affairs, who tells me he is very surprised. He'd made no secret, he says, that he wanted me kept around here. The vote was 2 against, 3 abstain. Why don't you take a look at your department's publication record, he says. You'll be surprised.

Committees, plans, advice. Stick with the senior people who have had experience in these things. Don't involve the junior people. Get the students out on your side. No. I will not involve students. It is unprofessional. Meet. Talk again with your chairman. Did he really say those things to you? The President will hit the ceiling when he hears.

August, 1983

George Gordon and I have lunch on Fordham Road. It was a ping-pong match, he says. One said, we're finished with her, let's get rid of her, another immediately agreed. Besides, then there is no threat of a female tenure suit. There is precedent for a female tenure suit, but not for a female reappointment suit. We walk back, and I say I'd noticed that there was not much publication among the senior faculty. The dissertations were a little strange, too. There seemed to be a preoccupation with sex. I've sunk even lower, George says. I've written for *Screw*. Monday's issue.

Soon enough I find out what *Screw* magazine is.

September, 1983

The deadlines are upon me. I have 90 days to file my grievances.

I file with the Faculty Grievance Committee on the Merit Raise, with the Tenure and Reappointment Appeals Committee (TRAC) on Reappointment, and with the President on Academic Freedom. I wait. Once I actually see it in print, I tell the Vice President for Academic Affairs that Gordon has written in *Screw*. More than raunchy. And the book, *Erotic Communications*. It is all stunning. The Vice President says, tell the Catholic League. Or, better, tell this man who's at Morality in Media. He is an alumnus. He'll get it to the

President. And so I do, and so he did, but nothing happens. The President's aide meets with me, just to gather facts, he says. The statutory procedures will follow in due course. Or so he says.

October, 1983

Three letters will be enough. They go to the President from Frank Barnett, President of the National Strategy Information Center; Rear Admiral Bruce Newell, USN, the Navy's Chief of Legislative Affairs, and the Most Rev. John J. O'Connor, Bishop of Scranton. I'm not so sure they ever got an answer. And Gordon keeps on publishing in *Screw*.

November, 1983

TRAC turns me down. I've never found out why. I never got any report. Appeals? I begin to talk with more faculty. *Screw* magazine upsets me. How can they not do anything? I write to the U.S. Department of Labor to ask about Title 38 U.S. Code protection of my job. I'm a Naval reservist. Can they fire me because I am a member of the armed forces?

December, 1983

The Faculty Hearing Committee upholds my Merit Raise. No procedures for evaluating teaching, they find. My work compares favorably. But where's the raise?

The senior faculty outside the department start to get concerned. They will visit the President, and give him a copy of *Screw* magazine, and show him what Gordon has written, and ask for my reappointment. Fr. Lauer will lead them. Off they go: Rev. Richard Dillon, Associate Professor and Chairman of Theology; Rev. Joseph P. Fitzpatrick, SJ, Professor Emeritus of Sociology; Dr. Elizabeth Kraus, Professor of Philosophy; Rev. Quentin Lauer, SJ, Professor of Philosophy; Dr. Andrew Myers, Professor of English; Dr. Roger Wines, Associate Professor of History. They pass along my regrets on having to file a complaint with the Equal Employment Opportunity Commission, but the time is running out. I must preserve my rights, even if I do not exercise them. And nothing happens.

January, 1984

I meet with the President at my request to find out if he will act on the Academic Freedom Grievance. These things must be taken in order, he says. On *Screw* magazine: I've lifted up a corner of the carpet of the university and uncovered something disgusting. He gestures toward his rug. There is a committee of administrators to decide what to do. These things must be taken in order. The Faculty Hearing Committee deals with Academic Freedom, not me.

And nothing happens. They cancel my graduate course. They won't give me permission to apply for early tenure. Where is the Merit Raise? I go to see the people at EEOC, who tell me Fordham cannot retaliate against me. No Merit Raise, no "due process." The Merit Raise is overturned by the Administration.

February, 1984

The Vice President says he didn't want to do it, but he was told to overturn the Merit Raise. The Faculty Hearing Committee is suddenly re-constituted. Three of the five members are replaced for various reasons.

March, 1984

Conciliation. That is what should happen. The Navy assigns a Navy Reserve lawyer to monitor, investigate. He comes with me to meet with the Vice President for Academic Affairs and the Fordham lawyer. Dr. Zagano is in a rats' nest, the Navy lawyer says, she could not get a fair hearing from that crowd. What do you want, the Vice President asks. A fair hearing, a reappointment. They offer neither, not even a two-year contract in another school of the University. The Vice President and the lady lawyer seem happy to wait me out.

The statutes say that if I establish a *prima facie* case, I will have a formal hearing before the Faculty Hearing Committee. We meet informally.

April - June, 1984

I am invited to a formal hearing, I present more documents. The Committee said to argue from my strengths, why I am good. Pages from *Erotic Communications* show my chairman's values. He'd shown a pornographic film to a class at Hofstra University in 1978 and asked them questions: "...physically produce 'the itch' as you watched?" "Describe the scene or sections which you found repulsive." "which...best describes the dominant sexual activity in your life?" This man told me I was "too Catholic." My own work ought to speak enough for itself. Teaching, research and publications, university service.

July, 1984

The Faculty Hearing Committee finally meets. There is a University lawyer there, another one, who controls the meeting. My witnesses are not permitted to testify fully to my credentials. We are not here to determine the merit of your work, the lawyer says, only what facts you have to prove your academic freedom has been abrogated. But they did not give me the procedures for the meeting before it started. My department is meeting with the administration before the hearing, on a "department matter." They troop in one after another with the same story. Fr. Lauer is with me. And another Navy lawyer, again to monitor. Exhibits are handed in, and never seen again. We know we've lost. How foolish. So this is what a kangaroo court is.

August - December, 1984

Papers, filings. The State has taken over the EEOC charges. They are investigating. We meet for conciliation purposes, but no conciliation is offered. The Labor Department decides to take another look.

I file suit. Title VII of the Civil Rights Act of 1964. I have been discriminated against because of my sex and my religion, and therefore denied equal protection, terms and conditions of employment. I file *pro se*, by myself. This is so obvious, they'll understand they've lost before its begun. But they don't. They're going to fight.

Happily, at this point Charles T. Duncan and Harry A. Poth, Jr. from Reid & Priest, agree to take the case *pro bono*.

January - May, 1985

The papers go back and forth. The Vice President swears he never received the complaint. The process server swears he did.

We go to court. The Fordham lawyer complains bitterly about the documents and wants the whole thing under seal. She does not want Gordon's articles in the public record. Technicalities. The student newspaper covers the appearances. "I wrote them because of my personal relationship with Al Goldstein" Gordon tells *The Ram,* the student newspaper. "I would do it all over again if I could." The University defends his right to publish in *Screw*.

June - August, 1985

National Review arrives. There we are. "This whole case is cause to wonder about Fordham's attitudes toward women and Catholic values as well." Letters, back and forth. Cardinal O'Connor writes Fordham President O'Hare: "I have been unable to shake from my consciousness or my conscience, over the past two years, the question of the employment and retention of a writer for a pornographic magazine." President

O'Hare writes *National Review*: "At the same time, I recognize that a tenured faculty member's decision to publish in *Screw*, however personally offensive many of us might find it, could and would be defended as an exercise of academic freedom."

September, 1985 - February, 1986

Document discovery begins. We give them everything they ask for. They don't return the favor.

"The Les Kinsolving Show." *The Chronicle of Higher Education. The National Catholic Register. The Wanderer. Fidelity. American Education Report. National Catholic Register. Campus Report. Chronicles of Culture. The New York Post.*

March, 1986 - May, 1986

"After investigation, the Division of Human Rights has found PROBABLE CAUSE to believe that [Fordham] engaged in or is (are) engaging in the unlawful discriminatory practice complained of." Sex, religion, retaliation.

The Village Voice. Human Events. The Ram. Thomas Sowell's column. *The Ram* again. And again. The Wanderer again. *The Ram*, this time by an alumnus. *Catholicism in Crisis,* twice in a row.

Fordham files for a reopening of the State case. I answer, this is just obfuscation and delay; Fordham is attempting to adduce what ought to be adduced at the hearing. I am beginning to talk like Della Street.

Examination before trial begins. Depositions. Court reporters.

June, 1986 - January, 1987

Campus Report. The Chronicle of Higher Education. Eastern Oklahoma Catholic, another alumnus. The Center for Women and Religion.

Donations from Fordham alumni. "I hope you will see it as an indication of my unqualified support of your cause." Christmas greetings from strangers. "I want you to know that I fully support you in your efforts to seek justice in this situation." No hearing scheduled yet on the State case. The Labor Department is still investigating, Fordham's been promising them witnesses since June. More depositions. Seven-hour days. Thirteen of them so far, and two more scheduled.

I am a teacher. Doing nothing would have been far more destructive than doing something.

So ended the *Crisis* article. You should also know that the University Professors for Academic Order found in my behalf after investigating only the facts surrounding the abrogation of my academic freedom (that is, my claims that my Catholic beliefs and my political leanings helped lead to this non-reappointment). The UPAO finding reads in part: "the great weight of evidence makes it clear that Dr. Zagano's views were the major factor in denying her contract renewal." Too Catholic. The vote was 2 against, 3 abstain.

Where are we now? Twice the New York State Division of Human Rights attempted to hold a public hearing on this matter — on May 13, 1987 and again on June 29, 1987, but Fordham attorneys gained adjournments. Finally, on October 26, 1987, the hearing opened, after Fordham refused to make any offer of settlement even after such was suggested by the judge. In the Federal action, Fordham is not cooperating in discovery proceedings. And in the Labor Department's investigation, Fordham has delayed for 18 months now its production of witnesses. Is Fordham afraid to deal with the merits of my case?

Let me give you some idea of who I am. I counted the entries on my c.v. recently. In my cut-down, selected bibliographic listing I have 47 articles and reviews, 16 professional papers and public talks, and two books. I belong to four professional societies and am on the editorial boards of three journals. Ordinarily such a recitation would be at least irrelevant and at most pompous boasting. But many of you do not know me, and more of you do not know my academic work. Beyond, things have become so very muddled that we, all of us (myself included) tend to forget that this is in very large measure a convoluted situation which abrogates my own academic freedom while simultaneously attacking the foundations of the very notion of academic freedom.

As long as we are on the topic of academic freedom, remember that about a month after my chairman told me I was "too Catholic," he told me he was an editorial writer for *Screw* magazine, the weekly anti-Catholic tabloid of pornography published in New York.

Now, you should know that for a long time I tried to keep this story out of the press. The student newspaper was on to it while I was still at Fordham, but I believed very much in the academic process, in the judgment of professionals. I did not want to hurt the University, and I honestly believed that Fordham would do right by me. There were — and are — a number of faculty who supported me, including many I had never met.

My chairman had come to Fordham from Hofstra University at the recommendation of two senior communications faculty, including the Jesuit priest he replaced as chairman. I do not know if they were aware of the fact that in 1978 Chairman Gordon showed a pornographic film to a class of his at Hofstra University and then asked those undergraduate students to fill out a questionnaire about it.

Please remember that I did speak with Fordham's then out-going President Finlay on this matter. He told me that I had lifted up the corner of the carpet of the University and uncovered something disgusting. But two years ago when *National Review* ran a brief editorial about me, opining that "This whole case is cause to wonder about Fordham's attitudes toward women and Catholic values as well." Quite the opposite evaluation came from the new president of Fordham, the Jesuit priest who for 13 years had served as editor of the Jesuit weekly magazine, *America*. This new president, Joseph A. O'Hare, S.J. by name, wrote: "I recognize that a tenured faculty member's decision to publish in *Screw*, however personally offensive many of us might find it, could and would be defended as an exercise of academic freedom."

I need not rehearse for you the faults in his logic. The First Amendment does not protect obscene speech. *Screw* magazine is perhaps the only publication actually judged by a court of law to be obscene according to the standards established by the U. S. Supreme Court in *Miller v. California.* I join John Cardinal O'Connor, who has twice (as far as I know) written presidents of Fordham on my behalf, in saying that "I have been unable to shake from my consciousness or my conscience...the question of the employment and retention of a writer for a pornographic magazine" at Fordham. Indeed I would question it at any institution of higher learning, Catholic or non-Catholic, public or private.

One need not have "Catholic values" to recognize that you do not put a *Screw* magazine editorial writer into a classroom with students under any circumstances. One need not inquire of Solomon as to whether such a person ought be the chairman and deciding factor in the academic life of a Catholic woman.

It is no doubt astounding to recognize that an institution which is at least nominally "Catholic" would take such pains to fight one of its own for over four years now. Observers who know more about these things than I do see my own case as microcosm of the peculiar situation Catholic universities in the United States have gotten themselves into, and in fact a large part of the battle Fordham is waging against me may have very little to do with me at all.

There is some irony in the list of those who have supported me, and those who have not. Witness the fact of a letter written on the stationery of the University Center for Rational Alternatives in New York by a professor of philosophy whom I have never met, but whose clarity of vision and tenacity of heart can and must call forth respect, if not always agreement. Some may recall that there was a debate over Communism about 45 years ago — when Communism still had some respectability in academic circles — and this letter is from the man who saw that theory's nakedness. The letter is to Fordham President Joseph O'Hare, and it is from Professor Sidney Hook, and it reads in part:

> In all my many years of experience with cases of persons deprived of their posts, this seems the most bizarre case not only because Dr. Zagano is a practicing Catholic, but because among the alleged grounds for discontinuing her services is that she concerned herself *too much* with Catholic affairs. If true, this is rather surprising because of the impression, held until recently by many, that Fordham University was not hostile to religion and *a fortiori* not hostile to active Catholics unless their practices interfered with the performance of their professional duties or conflicted with accepted Catholic doctrine.

Thank you Dr. Hook. I am indeed a teacher, how could I not do this?

Phyllis Zagano is a founding member of the editorial board of Crisis *magazine, and a member of the editorial boards of* The New Scholasticism *and* American Journalism. *She earned her B.A. at Marymount College, Tarrytown, an M.S. at the Boston University School of Public Communication, an M.A. at Long Island University, and a Ph.D. at the State University of New York at Stony Brook. She is editor of* The Nuclear Arms Debate *(Hudson River Press: 1983), and of* Religion & Public Affairs: A Directory of Organizations & People *(The Rockford Institute: 1987). Her current research, "An Analysis of American Religious Debate on Peace, Freedom and Justice," is supported by a grant from the United States Institute of Peace.*

CHAPTER SIXTEEN

BATTLING STANFORD
by STEVEN W. MOSHER

Why would Stanford University, whose very reason for existence is to protect academic freedom and advance the cause of the truth, buckle to pressure from China, a country whose human rights record is one of the blackest in the world? First of all there is clear evidence that there was heavy pressure from China. Secondly, though I think it goes beyond simply buckling under political pressure, I think that there is among the liberal faculty at Stanford and especially among the members of the Anthropology department a great feeling of sympathy for China because China is, afterall, a Socialist country. We wouldn't want to call it a Communist country.

WHEN I WENT TO CHINA to study rural life there, I never suspected I was about to witness some of the most horrifying crimes of our age. I found women in their third trimester of pregnancy being coerced into abortions, and saw infanticide used by the government as a means of controlling population growth. My subsequent publication of this information so enraged Chinese officials that they denounced me as a spy and demanded of my university, Stanford, that I be punished. Stanford University obediently launched a four-year investigation of my research and publications, and in the end expelled me from the Ph.D. program.

Late in March 1979 I first arrived, elated yet diffident, in the Pearl River Delta commune that I hoped to study. The village that was to be my home for the next year housed 1000 families, but was scarcely larger than a city block. So crowded together were the homes that their tile roofs almost touched; each house was separated from the next by a gray-brick wall, broken only by a recessed entryway. I felt I was inhabiting a catacomb, an effect enhanced by the stone slabs underfoot and the total absence of greenery.

As an anthropologist whose goal it was to penetrate the private world of the villagers, I saw that getting through to the Chinese as people was the main challenge of the coming year. I was an outsider, neither Chinese nor Communist, and I wondered how long it would take to make contacts with local peasants and cadres, and worried that it might not be possible at all.

My acceptance into the plain-spoken world of the peasant began two days after I moved into the village when I was feted by my neighbors. My Cantonese proved passable, but my efforts to imitate the local dialect produced gales of laughter. They were pleased at the attempt, however, and were so patient when my speech came out garbled that I was glad I had chosen not to use an interpreter.

The longer I stayed in China, the more I came to realize how anomalously advantageous my situation was. While most foreigners resided in Beijing, the taut political nerve center of China, I spent my time in the relatively relaxed countryside of Guangdong Province, half a continent away from the capital. While most foreigners are sequestered in hotels and deal only with officials who professionally manage foreigners, I lived in a village farmhouse and spent my time with peasants and rural cadres. While foreigners are normally restricted to the cities, visiting the countryside only for short periods under the escort of officials and guides, I worked unaccompanied and unobserved. A Beijing directive instructing local officials to cooperate fully with my research opened all doors.

In retrospect, it is clear that the main hurdle I had to overcome in the course of my research came not from without, but from within. I arrived in the village favorably disposed towards the Communist revolution, primarily because of the benefits that it had supposedly bestowed upon the peasantry. Living in communes, where their basic needs were taken care of by the state, I believed that China's rural millions were better fed, better dressed and better housed than ever before in Chinese history.

These idyllic images of life in the PRC, which had been inculcated in me at Stanford University, were almost totally false. Yet so strongly had they been etched onto my consciousness that it took me literally months to see through them to the reality of village life. Through long conversations with practical, down-to-earth peasants I was able to see the programs of the new regime through their eyes. The commune meant not land to the tiller but forced collectivization and famine. The politicization of all life meant corruption and incessant political campaigns. The revolution had meant not full rice bowls, but tyranny.

For my village friends one of the most disturbing political campaigns was that to limit childbirths. In March of 1980 a directive came down from the Guangdong provincial government ordering all communes to ensure that their population increase rate for that year did not exceed one percent. All women pregnant with second or higher order children were to report to "reeducation centers" until they agreed to abortions.

In my village some eighteen women pregnant with their second or third children were singled out for "reeducation." These were ordered to the "reeducation center," a commune dormitory located in the local seat of government 10 miles distant. There they were told that they would not be allowed to return home until they submitted to an abortion. All of them were in the late second or third trimester of pregnancy when their period of incarceration began.

I visited them often during their days of imprisonment, and witnessed the tremendous pressures to which they were subjected. They were roused at first light and, following a hurried morning meal of rice gruel, their reeducation began. Throughout the day, until late at night, teams of party officials took turns haranguing them about submitting to an abortion.

Although the officials tried to keep up the pretense that they were merely using persuasion on their captives, their ultimate argument was always force. At least once a day the women were presented with the following Hobson's choice: Either submit to an abortion now, or see your unborn child put to death during labor.

One official, in particular, was brutally explicit about this. Singling out one of the women in the group who was only weeks away from giving birth, he would say, "You, there, who are eight months pregnant. You should not think that you can simply sit through these meetings until you give birth to your child. We will not allow this. If you go into labor before you agree to an abortion, you will not be allowed to give birth."

Not only did this official threaten women with infanticide, he actually followed through with his threat. When a woman went into labor during the course of a meeting, she was taken immediately to the hospital. The doctor, under orders to terminate this "over-quota" child, waited until the cervix was fully dilated and the child had begun its descent into the birth canal. Then he took a hypodermic, filled it with formaldehyde, and injected this substance directly into the child's brain through the fontanel, or soft spot, of the skull. The child expired instantly, and was born dead a few minutes later.

During a subsequent visit to China in May 1987, I found that this procedure had become common. Medical doctors, under orders to terminate all "over-quota" children at birth, frequently resort to such injections.

I had not expected, when I arrived in a village in South China for a year-long stay, to be an eyewitness to women in their third trimester of pregnancy being coerced into abortions. Nor had I expected to find infanticide used by the government as a means of controlling the number of births. If I was profoundly shocked by what I had seen, I was also perplexed by the question of what to do with this explosive information.

I quickly saw that nothing would be served by going public while I was still in China. Not only would premature publication provide Peking with a ready-made excuse to expel me from the country, it would put my principle sources in considerable danger. The Ministry of State Security would spare no effort to determine how I had come by such sensitive information. Prudence dictated silence.

So it was that for the remaining three months of my time in China I published nothing on the topic of China's population control program. I even tried, after finishing my research in this area, to put the entire appalling business out of my mind.

In July 1980, after a lengthy trip by van into the interior, I left China. Before publishing my findings, however, I decided to contact the central government. It was at least possible that responsible officials in Peking were unaware of what was happening in the far southern province of Guangdong. I would write to the woman in charge of China's population control program, a Vice-Premier named Chen Muhua. "Guangdong province's own population control regulations," my letter read in part, "which forbid abortion after the sixth month of pregnancy, prohibit the use of coercion in abortion, and outlaw infanticide, are being widely and systematically violated in the Pearl River Delta."

I was bending over backwards to give Peking the benefit of the doubt. Yet what was in doubt? Peking was almost certainly aware of what was happening in Canton. After all, the coercive campaign against births that I had witnessed was not restricted just to the 80,000 member commune in which I had lived. The procedures drawn up by the committee's population control group — including the threat against the lives of "over-quota" children — had a followed a directive issued by the prefecture, itself an extension of the provincial government. What the provinces do openly in China, they do with the knowledge and approval of the central authorities. What I had observed in the Canton countryside was part and parcel of the national plan, directed from Peking.

Vice-Premier Chen never answered my letter. But I did receive a response of sorts. Before the summer was out, a campaign of slander against my research and my reputation was in full swing. Peking had decided that here was a foreigner who had found out far too much about conditions in the countryside. At least that's what I concluded after hearing that the Ministry of Public Security — Peking's KGB — had declared me to be an "international spy."

Several months later my first article on the coercive population control program was published. Its appearance unleashed a storm of criticism from academic circles in the United States — not against Peking, but against me. Angry sinologists predicted that my article would have a negative impact on US-China relations, specifically that it would endanger the scholarly exchange program between the two countries. Professors at Stanford University, where I was completing a doctorate, put the matter in more personal terms, complaining that my article might cause them to lose opportunities to do research in China.

Others made reference to domestic political considerations. Clifford Bennett, the former chairman of Stanford's Anthropology Department, was the most explicit. "What will happen when the pro-Life movement in this country becomes aware of what is happening in China?" he asked rhetorically, as if he could imagine no greater calamity. I was dismayed at what I took to be the suggestion that I should deliberately withhold legitimate research findings because of their possible domestic political impact.

Amidst all this hue and cry about the political consequences of publication, the substance of my reports was greeted with silence. I had not expected Stanford professors to be concerned about the abortion issue *per se*, since most of them supported it as a "women's choice." But I had looked for some indication that they found infanticide repugnant, not to mention some display of concern that women in China were being denied a choice. Only Professor G. William Skinner of the anthropology faculty even mentioned this issue, and his throwaway comment revealed "moral standards" that make mockery of the phrase. He drew a parallel between China's coerced abortions in the third trimester of pregnancy and the Reagan administration's efforts to stop the federal funding of abortions. Both of these actions were, in his phrase, "equally reprehensible," as if the forcible taking of an unborn child's life could be equated with its preservation.

Advancing arguments that had more to do with ideology and self-interest than scholarship, academics at Stanford and elsewhere one after another urged me to cover up the reality of what was taking place in China. The old adage linking scholarly advancement to publication was turned on its head. Instead of "publish or perish," the message to me was publish and perish. After a long period of time spent agonizing over my responsibilities as a scholar to the truth and my personal commitment to human rights, I decided that I could not in good conscience remain silent, whatever the cost.

In retrospect, I believe matters would probably have ended with these kinds of veiled threats and informal censure had not two things happened. First, I determined to continue to publish. My refusal to participate in the suggested conspiracy of silence led the anthropology department to launch a punitive investigation into my China research. Second, my articles describing forced abortions in the countryside came to Peking's attention. The Chinese Academy of Social Sciences (CASS), an agency of the government, responded by sending a confidential document to Stanford University in which they listed a number of "crimes against the people" that I had allegedly committed. The most serious of these involved the population control article. CASS did not question the facts reported in the article, rather they criticized my motive in writing such an "attack" on China. I was also accused of violating research, travel and customs regulations, lesser charges which the anthropology department did not at first take seriously.

This confidential document was nothing more than hearsay. It was signed by a high-ranking Party official whom I had never met. It included no statements from first-hand witnesses of the alleged research, travel or customs violations, and was vague in many specifics. Nevertheless, that short document — about two pages long in Chinese, three pages in translation — played a crucial role in the departmental investigation into my research and publications. This investigation was not only long underway when the committee in charge came to the embarrassing conclusion that the principle charge against me — that I had published an article "attacking China" — had to be dropped, but the mere fact of investigating my writings on China hinted of a medieval inquisition. To actually find me guilty of "attacking China," under whatever guise the charge may be described ("jeopardizing US-China relations," etc.), would be a grave violation of academic freedom. Academic institutions exist to protect their members right to publish freely, not to punish them for doing so. The charge was dropped.

The investigation then went under cover, and was pursued doggedly for 19 months. So convinced was the anthropology department of the truth of China's allegations that at one point they refused to allow individuals to testify on my behalf.

In February 1983 the Stanford University Department of Anthropology expelled me from its Ph.D. program, issuing a vague statement that I had engaged in unspecified "illegal and seriously unethical activities" during my 1979-1980 research in China. I then appealed to University President Donald Kennedy to reverse this decision. After an investigation lasting nearly two years, Kennedy in turn rejected my appeal, this despite having come to have "doubts" about the original evidence and charges.

In an attempt to publicly justify his action, Kennedy reversed Stanford's earlier policy of secrecy. On October 1, 1985, he released a thirty-five page letter with a forty page appendix of material which reveals the specific allegations and findings of the original Confidential Report of the Anthropology Department as well as several new allegations. I quote the allegations in Kennedy's public report below, and follow each with a refutation. I believe that my rebuttal proves beyond a reasonable doubt that I had been falsely accused and wrongly denied the Ph.D.

ALLEGATION 1. "The Committee [from the Anthropology Department that investigated my research in China] believes that Mosher lawfully imported the van, and lawfully donated it to the brigade [an administrative unit larger than a village, smaller than a commune] at the end of this stay. His major purpose in bringing the van to [the brigade] was to enhance his access to information by creating incentives and, later, obligations to local officials. The Committee cannot conclude that this purpose was clearly improper. However, in obtaining only oral permission at the provincial level to import the van, Mosher acted imprudently in light of the warning he had to clear moves of this kind with the Ministry of Education in Beijing." (Confidential Report [herinafter CR], p.31; see also Kennedy to Mosher, September 30, 1985 [hereinafter Kennedy], p.16.)

REBUTTAL: Anthropologists customarily give gifts to their informants in return for their cooperation, and to say that my gift of the van to the brigade was only "not ...clearly improper," slights accepted practise. I was more circumspect than most researchers. Not only did I inform the Chinese government at the time I imported the van how I intended to dispose of it, I even donated it to the community as a whole rather than to an individual or group of individuals.

It is not true, as the Anthropology Department and Kennedy contend, that I received from the Committee on Scholarly Communication with the People's Republic of China (CSCPRC) a "warning...to clear moves of this kind with the Ministry of Education in Peking." This claim does not even square with the Anthropology Department's own report, which states that the CSCPRC "does not mention telling Mosher to inform Ministry of Education officials of Beijing of all arrangements made with local officials." (CR, p.34) The CSCPRC did suggest that I contact the Guangdong provincial branch of the Chinese Academy of Social Sciences (CASS) and the provincial department of foreign affairs with my van request. This I did. My request was forwarded to the Ministry of Education and the national office of the CASS. A month later I received word from the provincial foreign affairs department that it had been approved by these departments.

In arguing that I was wrong to obtain "only oral permission" to import the van, Stanford betrays its ignorance of the way China works. The Chinese bureaucracy relies primarily on oral communication, not written directives. (See Michael Oksenberg. "Methods of Communication within the Chinese Bureaucracy," *The China Quarterly* 57:1-39) This unreasonable demand for written proof of probity is typical of the guilty-until-proven-innocent approach taken by Stanford throughout the investigation.

ALLEGATION 2. "The Committee cannot say that there was any illegality or serious impropriety in the nature of the documents Mosher collected in China. The Chinese Academy of Social Science (CASS) had, in the end, not complained of the data he gathered, though they clearly know of its nature. They had earlier informally signaled through [the CSCPRC representative in Beijing] to Mosher, that the class status registers were "sensitive," but this characterization is too vague for us to base a determination of misconduct on it." (CR, p. 32; Kennedy, p.16)

REBUTTAL: The obsession with secrecy of totalitarian regimes such as the PRC is well-known. Yet Stanford accepted at face value Peking's allegations that I collected "sensitive" documents. Apparently only the vagueness of this accusation prevented the faculty from basing charges upon it. Were

Peking to have used a more specific term — "secret documents" for example — I presumably would have been found guilty of misconduct.

There were several occasions when Chinese officials stated their allegations of spying with great specificity. One China scholar reported to Stanford that "[Mosher] obtained state secrets, particularly about the work of the public security forces and the Communist Party, which caused Chinese officials in Peking to believe [he] was an intelligence agent." If precision is the only operant criterion, why was I not found by a credulous Stanford faculty to have been an "intelligence agent" collecting "state secrets?"

ALLEGATION 3. "The Committee believes that Mosher deliberately lied to the Committee acting in this role as representative of the department in attempting to determine the facts surrounding his research in China. The Committee considers this a serious breach of the norms governing the relations between graduate student and department on matters concerning the student's professional life." (CR, p. 32; Kennedy, P.16)

REBUTTAL: At no point during the four years that I was under investigation by Stanford have I been untruthful. But I have consistently and adamantly resisted pressure to give false testimony by "confessing" to alleged actions that I did not commit. For refusing to (falsely) incriminate myself, I have been accused of lying.

ALLEGATION 4: "Because we have no reason to doubt that Mosher obtained permission from provincial officials to have his Hong Kong research assistant remain with him in the village, we cannot conclude that his action of bringing her into the PRC was clearly improper. In this instance, however, we conclude as we concluded in the case of his importing the van that, in obtaining only oral permission from provinicial officials, Mosher acted imprudently in the light of the warning he had to clear his local arrangements with Ministry of Education officials in Beijing. In fact, we believe Mr. Mosher was even more imprudent in the case of his research assistant than he was in the case of the van because he was on notice from (CSCPRC) that Beijing officials had turned down his request to have her work for him." (CR, p.40; Kennedy, p.20)

REBUTTAL: Not only did Stanford ignore evidence I submitted showing that my research assistant legally entered and worked in China, they chose to disregard expert testimony by a senior State Department official given on my behalf, "Ethnic

Chinese," the official wrote to Stanford, "usually travel to China not with a passport and visa but rather with a 'return to the country permit' (huixiangzheng). These are quickly and easily obtained in Hong Kong: Guangdong tourist authorities told me that in 1980 nearly two million were issued to people coming just to Guangdong province. In other words, this is a mass movement which essentially takes place unmonitored. Under the circumstances, the Guangdong customs authorities would not in all probability have asked what Mosher's assistant intended to do in Guangdong, nor would there have been any deception involved such as going back to visit her kin." But Stanford's most fantastic error here is the claim that, prior to the beginning of my field work, "Beijing officials had turned down [my] request" for an assistant. No such request was ever made. The secret Chinese document, which Stanford so highly prizes, is emphatic on this point: "As far as Mr. Mosher's need for a secretary is concerned, neither Mr. Mosher himself nor the CSCPRC ever raised the issue in advance, and we certainly did not agree to it."

ALLEGATION 5: "With regard to Mosher's aborted trip [into the Chinese interior] we conclude the following: Even if Mosher did have oral permission to visit Kweiyang City and to travel by private motor vehicle, we believe he was imprudent to make the trip without such permission being specified in writing on his travel permit. By making the trip, he was testing the limits of the Chinese security system, an act that, as an exchange scholar with the obligation to protect the reputation of the program, he should not have contemplated." (CR. p.40; Kennedy, p.21)

REBUTTAL: I applied for permission to travel by motor vehicle on my original travel application form, as attested to by the senior department official in his statement to Stanford. My request was granted in writing. I was issued a travel permit giving the "means of transportation" as "che," or "small passenger vehicle." I am at a loss to understand how those at Stanford who judged my case can simply ignore documentary evidence.

ALLEGATION 6: "Because the trip was a risky one, we believe that by taking his local driver with him on the trip, Mosher showed a lack of concern for the safety and future of this villager." (CR. p.40; Kennedy, p.21)

REBUTTAL: The Chinese authorities had made it a rule that I have a driver for trips outside the commune. This trip, which I had written permission to make, was no exception.

ALLEGATION 7: "We on the committee feel that Mosher violated anthropological ethics by publishing pictures without masking the identity of subjects. This violation is all the more serious because Mosher was given adequate warning to scrutinize everything he published with the problem of protecting his research subjects in mind." (CR, p. 44; Kennedy, p. 23)

REBUTTAL: I do not regret having published these pictures, which show doctors, themselves unwilling participants in this drama, performing forced abortions and sterilizations on women in the third trimester of pregnancy. For Stanford to narrowly focus on the issue of these women's identity without reference to the crime which is being perpetrated on their bodies is sheer hypocrisy.

Anthropologists have a professional responsibility to speak out on behalf of the largely inarticulate and sometimes oppressed peoples that they study. I saw the human rights of Chinese villagers being violated by a brutal population control campaign. I had not only a right, but a duty, to speak out. Forced abortion was found to be a crime against humanity by the Nuremburg Trials, and later international bodies have consistently reaffirmed this position. By publishing graphic evidence of forced abortions in Chinese women, I acted in the best interests of my research subjects, and in the best traditions of anthropological ethics. Nor was my effort quixotic. The recent successful moves in the U.S. Congress to cut off indirect aid to China's coercive population control programs came about in part because of my reportage.

Even Kennedy now admits that during the course of his investigation he was threatened by the Peking regime not to grant my Ph.D. "During and after his stay in China," a Chinese official wrote Kennedy, "Mosher's behavior seriously damaged the cultural and scholastic exchange between China and the United States. We believe that you are just as concerned as we are for the future normal and beneficial exchange between our two countries. I trust that you will make a correct judgment, based on the facts, and properly handle this matter." (Kennedy, p.39) In this context, the phrase "properly handle this matter" is unquestionably a euphemism for "deny Stephen Mosher's appeal for the Ph.D." This, of course, is precisely what Kennedy did.

Despite Stanford's claim that its decision was unrelated to my research reports, at several points Kennedy and the Anthropology Department criticized what they see as my alleged "failure to protect the reputation of the [academic] exchange program." (e.g., SECTION C, ALLEGATION 2,4) As

The Wall Street Journal editorialized, "We read this as confirming, rather than refuting, the essential charge that Stanford's actions were linked to Mr. Mosher's disquieting revelations about China." (October 28, 1985)

ALLEGATION 8: "Although we believe that Mosher was unwise to publish his article in a popular Taiwanese weekly where this would be read as a political attack on the PRC, we cannot judge this act to be misconduct, both because we are not convinced that Mosher fully understood the implications of his choice of publishing medium and because we believe the (sic) Mosher's right to publish where he chooses is protected by the right to freedom of speech." (CR, p. 44; Kennedy, p.23)

REBUTTAL: My report on China's coercive population control campaign was the reason my principal advisor gave for resigning from my dissertation committee. It was also one of the main charges leveled against me during the Anthropology Department's investigation. The Anthropology Department's claim that my report played no part in my dismissal is, in my opinion, a self-serving falsehood. Were Stanford to admit to expelling me on this ground, it would call into question the University's commitment to academic freedom.

Exercising my right of freedom of speech, I have published a series of articles in the popular press concerning recent events in the People's Republic of China which compliment my more scholarly articles. These have been published in English and Chinese, in Hong Kong, the Republic of China, Taiwan and the United States, and have been factually correct and objectively written.

For the Anthropology faculty to suggest that such articles may be read as political attacks on the PRC is to enslave scholarship to ideology and practical politics. It is hard to imagine similar allegations being leveled against me had I done field research in East Germany and published my results in West Germany which, unlike The Republic of China or Taiwan, is larger and more powerful than its Communist competitor. In finding me to have been politically "unwise" to have published the truth, the Anthropology Department falls into the totalitarian error.

ALLEGATION 9: "Although [the Chair of the Anthropology Department] wrote Mosher that "Receiving payment for the pictures and/or the article would clearly be unethical under the terms of the Statement of Ethics," we on the Committee are not persuaded that Mosher would have been wrong to accept payment. We found it impossible to draw a clear line between

Mosher's receiving royalties for ethnographic books." (CR, p.44; Kennedy, p.23)

REBUTTAL: I believe that receiving income from the sale of books, articles, or photographs relating to one's field research is not unethical. But it is revealing that the Anthropology Department was divided on this fundamental point of ethics, with the Chairman of the Department taking the position that receiving payment was wrong, and the Committee dissenting. If the faculty itself cannot agree on what the ethical standards of professional behavior in anthropology are, then how could I, as a graduate student, be expected to have known what these "standards" are, much less be expelled for "violating them?"

ALLEGATION 10: "We do, however, feel that Mosher violated the norms governing relations between graduate student and faculty members by concealing from faculty members the details surrounding payment for pictures (that appeared in the article on coercive abortion in China). In particular Mosher was not candid about the very relevant fact that he and the 'translator' are now married." (CR, p. 23; Kennedy, p.45)

REBUTTAL: As the editor of the journal that published the pictures testified, payment went to the person who translated the accompanying article into Chinese, Huang Huiya. At that time (February 1980), Huang Huiya and I were friends. We were later married in a civil ceremony on October 30, 1981, but that marriage was unfortunately annulled on technical grounds immediately thereafter.

When asked by the Committee in November 1981 what my current relationship with Huang Huiya was, I explained what had happened. I further said that I hoped to remarry Huiya in the near future, and in fact did so on January 21, 1982. The Anthropology Department's allegation, which Kennedy accepted without question, that I deliberately concealed the nature of my relationship with Huang Huiya is false.

Concerning my activities in the village, I believe that my research assistant, who worked with me there on a daily basis for seven months, and not my distraught, vengeful former spouse, who was there for only two weeks, is the most credible witness. My research assistant testifies that "[Mr. Mosher] worked unceasingly towards his goals of conducting research... His relationship with officials were based on 'Openness and mutual respect...' No illegal activities occurred. It would have been impossible for them to." (Appendix A, p.3)

Now the investigation by Stanford University, begun in October 1981, continued for a year and a half. By the time it ended I had completed my dissertation. This dissertation was not about China, but Taiwan. One might well ask why Stanford investigated my research in China, since it was unrelated to my doctoral dissertation. I was expelled from the Ph.D. program on February 23, 1987, for reasons that had nothing to do with my dissertation research.

I next appealed to the President of Stanford University to reverse this unfair decision. The president was then Donald Kennedy, a former head of the Food and Drug Administration in the Carter Administration. Under Stanford regulations, he was required to rule on my appeal within 30 days. In fact, it was only after a three month delay that he decided to launch yet another investigation. This second investigation took two years, lasting from the end of 1983 until the end of 1985.

Despite the two years of additional investigation, involving private detectives and handwriting experts in Hong Kong and the United States, Kennedy was unable to sustain the original allegations of illegal and unethical behavior in China in 1979-1980.

The correct position for Kennedy to have taken at this point would have been to award me the doctorate. Instead, under pressure from the Chinese government and presumably also the Anthropology faculty not to do so, he levied several new charges against me under the guise of examining my "candor."

The impropriety of introducing new allegations during the course of an appellant procedure — while ignoring the fact that the original charges have been refuted — is self-evident. Why the Stanford administration shifted grounds is just as readily understood. As the Chinese classic Tso Chuan instructs us: "If you are determined to find someone guilty, you need not be troubled by a lack of evidence."

Kennedy's first new allegation is that I tried to "foist off" a thesis on China to a dissertation committee constituted to supervise research on Taiwan. In fact the dissertation committee that I had organized in March 1979 before leaving for Taiwan was defunct, two of its three members having resigned in October 1981 at the outset of the Anthropology Department's investigation. My sole remaining advisor was a young assistant professor, who let it be known that he reserved the right to withdraw at any time from that capacity. Six months later I formed another committee, consisting of two professors and the one young assistant professor, and submitted a manuscript on China. While the two professors responded constructively, the assistant professor wrote back that he did not feel qualified to read a thesis on China. He resigned from my committee, whereupon another Anthropology Department professor volunteered to take his place. If, as Kennedy implies, the submission of a manuscript on China was such a serious academic failing, why did only one of the three members of my second committee resign? Moreover, at that time the Anthropology Department was claiming jurisdiction over — and investigating — my research activities in China. If it is proper for the Anthropology Department to punish me for alleged "illegal and seriously unethical acts" in China, then why is it not also proper for me to submit a manuscript on that country?

Kennedy's second new allegation is that in 1977, a year after I resigned my commission in the Navy and transferred into the inactive reserves, I took a military flight from California to Japan. Now I have never denied this, though I have denied that it has the slightest relevance to my Ph.D. work at Stanford. Kennedy's position is that this trip is indeed irrelevant to my studies at Stanford except insofar as it contributes to his contention about my alleged "lack of candor." Kennedy might as well have said, in my opinion, that he is publicizing this matter for the express purpose of attacking my character.

Kennedy's third new allegation concerns a Nikon camera that I purchased near the end of my fieldwork. I unfortunately lost the original receipt, was unable to obtain a duplicate and wrote out a second receipt in my own hand. This accounting error, which I have never denied, is cited by Kennedy as another example of my alleged "lack of candor." Kennedy's argument for depriving me of the scholarly career of my choice has degenerated from "illegal and seriously unethical activities in China" to what I read as character assassination.

But Kennedy is not content merely to impune my character. He also launches a gratuitous and completely unjustified attack on my integrity as a researcher and scholar. In anthropology, he writes, "there is an extremely high responsibility for the welfare of those being studied (and) a critical need for fair and objective reporting of events." The basic reason why he is unwilling to allow me to continue on the Ph.D., he goes on, is because he does not believe I have met these requirements. (Kennedy, October 1, p.38)

Now I have to date published two books and a number of articles which have received favorable reviews in both the scholarly and popular press. With the exception of the Chinese regime, which has tried to discredit publications, which for the most part reflect unfavorably on aspects of its rule, my work has been widely lauded as fair, accurate and objective. Nick Eberstadt of Harvard University, for example, wrote of *Journey to the Forbidden China* that it is "a powerful, interesting, and beautifully written book. Mosher-watchers will note that this is his best book to date...Mr. Mosher's academic tribulations clearly have not killed him: *Journey to the Forbidden China* suggests that, to the contrary, they have served to make him stronger." Of my first book Martin Whyte of the University of Michigan had this to say: "*Broken Earth* is a lively and thought-provoking work that should not be simply dismissed by the scholarly community...The result is a critical view of rural life that may serve as a useful corrective to some of the overly benign accounts of the Chinese countryside... This work can only regret that...a fieldworker of clear potential may now be lost from the field." If it is my books that Kennedy believes lack fairness and objectivity, then I am afraid that he hasn't been reading the reviews.

If, on the other hand, Kennedy is referring to my reports on China's coercive population control campaign, then he is equally in error. A number of recent studies by well-known China demographers have fully vindicated the analysis I first presented in *Broken Earth* in 1983. For example, John Aird of the U.S. Bureau of the Census has written, "To overcome the resistance [of the people to the one-child-per-family policy], the authorities maintain extreme pressures both on the cadres and on couples of childbearing age...People who get pregnant without permission are lectured, harassed, publicly humiliated, fined, deprived of contract land, denied food, water, and electricity, and 'mobilized' to have abortions." Judith Banister, a Stanford Ph.D. and Chief of the China Branch at the U.S. Bureau of the Census, has carefully documented the evidence on coercion. She demonstrates that it is not an isolated activity, not limited to remote provinces, but is an intrinsic part of the enforcement mechanism of the program. Referring to the 1981 UN Symposium on Population and Human Rights conclusion that compulsory abortion is a violation of human rights and to other UN declarations in favor of voluntarism, she concludes "China's family planning program is in violation of these oft-stated principles." Nick Eberstadt, of Harvard University's Center for Population Studies, appalled by what is happening in China, has publicly called upon the Reagan Administration to urge "China's highest officials to desist from this terrible campaign against their own people." Responding to reports by myself and others, on July 10, 1987, the House of Representatives, by a substantial 289 to 130 majority,

223

condemned China's "coercive abortion and coercive sterilization" practices as "crimes against humanity."

Nor would anyone familiar with my case — as Kennedy should be after reviewing it for two years — doubt my concern for the welfare of the Chinese villagers I studied. It was precisely because I felt so deeply a responsibility for their well-being that I reported on the excesses of the Chinese birth control campaign. How many other researchers would have jeopardized their careers by making such information public in the face of threats from the Peking regime, and pressure from their colleagues?

Despite the fact that Kennedy has little or no expertise in the area of Chinese studies (he was originally trained as a bio-chemist), his leading role in the US academic community ensures that his mistaken views will be widely circulated. Even more serious, in my view, is that a university president should stoop to a public attack, accurate or not, on the scholarship of a young academic. Such an action strikes at the heart of academic freedom. Kennedy's role as Stanford University's President is to guard against precisely that kind of unwarranted intrusion of bureaucratic and political authority into the scholarly debate that he has now committed.

One of Kennedy's first actions in the course of his investigation was to write to China and plead for more evidence. "You have made allegations of smuggling, and bribery and so forth" he said in effect. "But we need to have evidence. We need you to provide statements from witnesses and other documents."

Peking took a couple of months to reply to this extraordinary request. When they finally did, their reply must have dismayed Donald Kennedy. The Chinese said, "We have provided you with all of the evidence you need to make a correct and proper decision with regard to Steven Mosher's appeal." They went on to assert that "We feel sure for the sake of US-China relations and for the future of the scholarly exchange program that you will make the right decision." This veiled threat left President Kennedy in a dilemma. The Chinese were not willing to provide (read: manufacture) evidence to back up the allegations they were making. What was Kennedy to do? In his final report he backed off from the charges of smuggling and bribing officials that had earlier been leveled. But he raised another allegation in their place. He prefaces his new allegation by asserting that there has been a gradual erosion of trust between myself and the Anthropology Department at the University which made it impossible for him to reinstate me in the doctoral program.

(After being investigated for four years, it is true that I did not much trust the people in the Anthropology Department at Stanford University.) Then he alleges that the reason for this lack of trust was a "lack of candor" on my part. Because of this "lack of candor," Kennedy argues that he has no choice but to deny my appeal for reinstatement in the Ph.D. program.

Of course Stanford has matters backward. My problems with the university arose not from a lack of candor, but from too much candor. Had I not been candid about what I had seen in China, had I not been candid in writing about forced abortions and sterilizations, I would never have gotten myself in academic hot water in the first place. But President Kennedy and Stanford professors are not referring to my work when they accuse me of a lack of candor, but to my response to the allegation: I lack candor because I have never confessed to the crimes for which I have been accused.

What's going on here? Why would Stanford University, whose very reason for existence is to ensure academic freedom to its scholars, buckle to pressure from China, a country whose human rights record is one of the blackest in the world? The answer, I think, is twofold. First, there is clear evidence that there was heavy pressure from China, and not only in the form of the two documents I mentioned. Pressure was also applied during informal meetings between Stanford professors and Chinese officials. Stanford was put on notice that no one from that university would be welcome in China unless I was dealt with severely. But this issue transcends mere political pressure. There is among the liberal faculty at Stanford, and especially among the members of the Anthropology Department, a great feeling of sympathy for China as a country of the Left. As evidence I submit the case of Philippe Bourgois.

Mr. Bourgois was, like myself, a candidate for the Ph.D. in anthropology at Stanford. In 1981 he proposed research on the class backgrounds of the guerrillas in the Communist-controlled area of El Salvador. His dissertation committee told him in no uncertain terms that they could never approve his proposal, because to do his research would be violating El Salvadoran law and to publish his research would endanger his informants. Mr. Bourgois, however, chose to disregard this advice. Travelling first to Honduras, he was able, with the help of Communist guerrillas, to cross the border into El Salvador. He had spent two weeks at a Communist base camp when it was assaulted by government troops. Bourgois fled, escaping back across the border to Honduras, from where he returned to Washington, D.C.

There he published in *The Washington Post* an account of his escapade entitled "Running for My Life in El Salvador," (February 14, 1982) in which he took a virulently anti-government position. His account of the attack on the Communist base included allegations of government atrocities. A congressional committee invited Mr. Bourgois to testify about what he saw, but did not reach any conclusions concerning the veracity of his tale.

At that point Mr. Bourgois was recalled to Stanford to explain to his dissertation committee why he had violated the committee's explicit instructions not to attempt research in El Salvador. He was also asked to explain how he had entered El Salvador and why he had publicized this episode given the risk to his informants. These allegations were all of a graver nature than those of which I was accused. But the consequences for Mr. Bourgois were much less severe. After a brief, informal meeting with his dissertation committee and the department chairman, he was suspended for one quarter. This brief hiatus did not prevent him from receiving his Ph.D. in 1985.

Contrast this with the treatment I received. For lesser — and false — allegations, I was subjected to a formal investigation lasting eighteen months, which resulted in my public expulsion from the doctoral program. Had I attempted to investigate the base camps of Tibetan freedom fighters resisting Han rule in China and been involved in a military action — the rough equivalent to Mr. Bourgois' actions in El Salvador — who knows what punishments Stanford would have devised?

When members of the Anthropology Department were recently asked by a *Washington Post* reporter to explain why the two cases had been handled so differently, they answered that Mr. Bourgois had contritely apologized for his escapade. I, on the other hand, had refused to confess or apologize. The possibility that I may not have anything to confess or apologize for seems not to have occured to them. In a striking reversal of American justice, I was presumed guilty at the outset. This explains why I, unlike Bourgois, was never given the opportunity for an informal meeting with my committee. Rather, without any advance warning, I was simply informed that the anthropology faculty had voted to launch a formal investigation into my research. When I refused to confess to my wrongly presumed guilt, this became a further charge against me ("lack of candor").

The very different ways in which these two cases were handled shows the bias that is at work in the Anthropology faculty

226

at Stanford. From their point of view, it is acceptable, even laudable, to criticize authoritarian or democratic governments, especially of small and weak states. But they frown on criticism of socialist countries, especially when these are large, powerful states with whom your institution has an ongoing exchange program. So much for academic freedom and due process.

Imagine what the reaction at Stanford University would have been like had my research been done in South Africa. What if the white government of South Africa was forcing black women to undergo late-term abortions and that some black infants were being put to death at birth. Where do you think I would be now? I think we can all agree that, at the very least, I would have my Ph.D. from Stanford in hand by now. In addition, I would probably have five or six honorary degrees from other institutions as well. And perhaps tenure at Harvard.

In October 1986, Melvin Belli filed suit against Stanford University on my behalf. In my suit I ask for three things: a public apology, a Ph.D. and an unspecified amount of compensation. The lawsuits in the U.S. are very expensive and time consuming. But I will pursue this matter to the end.

In the last year, after three years of wandering in the academic wilderness, my circumstances have changed somewhat for the better. I have joined The Claremont Institute in Southern California where I serve as Director of Asian Studies.

I have received an honor of a different sort from the PRC. Peking has declared me to be an "international spy." I take this as something of a distinction. "International spy" is a title that only the best researchers and journalists, like Fox Butterfield of *The New York Times*, are awarded.

Stephen Mosher, who earned one M.A. from Stanford in East Asian Studies and another in Anthropology, became a Ph.D. candidate in 1979, the same year he discovered the childbearing practises in China. His articles have appeared in Reader's Digest, The Washington Post *and numerous other publications. He is the author of* Broken Earth *and* Journey into the Forbidden China. *Mr. Mosher is currently the director of the Asian Studies Center at the Claremont Institute in Southern California.*

CHAPTER SEVENTEEN

ACADEMIC INTOLERANCE AT USC:
THE WILLIAM VAN CLEAVE STORY
by JACK CROUCH

It has come to my attention Dr. William Van Cleave may be leaving your faculty, resulting in USC's loss of his Defense and Strategic Studies program. The purpose of this letter is to express to you my strong admiration for the contributions Bill Van Cleave has made to advancing understanding of the national security requirements, and in preparing students to assume important positions in the defense policy community both in government and in private and academic endeavors. I hope that reports of Bill's departure are premature, and that his unique program will continue at USC. Your university has a well-deserved reputation for excellence, and it is fitting that excellent programs, such as Bill's, remain a part of your curriculum.

- Congressman Jack Kemp
to USC President James Zumberge

PRESIDENT JAMES H. ZUMBERGE of the University of Southern California has a vision for his enclave: to promote what he refers to as the University's "corporate image." In a January 27, 1987 interview in the campus newspaper, the Daily Trojan, Zumberge elaborated a bit on his idea: "A lot of our schools and units have been highly ranked across the country and because of all the entrepreneurial energy within them they seek the betterment of those units first and their relationship with the university becomes secondary. Until we reverse that, and get them to put the university's name first and the school or college second, you'll never generate the kind of corporate respectability that I think you deserve."

In creating this distinction President Zumberge puts the cart before the horse. The greatness and integrity of a university depend entirely upon the credibility of its individual components or colleges and units. If specific units of a university begin to attract national esteem, they can only contribute to the overall reputation of the university, not detract from it. Would it not be far more sensible, therefore, to foster and stoke the "entrepreneurial energy" within those units, encourage their development, and reinforce their strength so that the university at large can benefit from their operation and performance? Is that not, in fact, the *duty* of a university administration to its board of trustees, its faculty, its students and its alumni?

Clearly, President Zumberge does not think so. He seems to believe that the individual unit is expendable for the unity of the whole. This idea of placing the interests of the "university" before the interests of its individual components is purely self-defeating, for the very existence of the former depends upon the prosperity of the latter.

President Zumberge recently faced an intradepartmental crisis that proved the practical futility of his administrative philosophy. The situation was that of a departmental faculty becoming so politically imbalanced, and academically homogeneous, that it sought consciously or unconsciously to purge from that department all non-conforming elements. Without regard for any comparative measures of excellence or success, but based instead on intolerance of academic approach and political perspective, USC's School of International Relations (SIR) faculty used every bureaucratic artifice it could fathom in order to render one of its units, the Defense and Strategic Studies Program (DSSP), inoperable. The DSSP was forced into choosing either to conform to the SIR's narrow and singularly liberal-leftist academic and ideological standards, or to close its doors at USC and relocate.

The fact that this situation was allowed to develop and culminate in the first place is in itself perfidious of the tenets of academic freedom and integrity. The fact that virtually no steps were taken by the university adminstration to ameliorate the situation is simply inexcusable. By refusing to protect the Defense and Strategic Studies Program from what even the former Provost termed "faculty tyranny," President Zumberge lost one of USC's most distinguished professors, and allowed the dissolution of one of the most vital, prosperous and respected strategic studies programs in the country. Moreover, it unwittingly assisted in the growing national trend of purging conservative ideas, principles and values from the academy.

In a letter to President Zumberge, former Undersecretary of Defense for Policy, Fred C. Ikle, wrote: "For the long-term health of our national security policies, it is essential to have a new generation of well-trained scholars who are capable and willing to take important positions in government. If we didn't have the Defense and Strategic Studies Program, we would have to invent it."

It was precisely for that stated purpose that the Program was created almost twenty years ago. The Defense and Strategic Studies Program was the brainchild of Professor William Van Cleave. It was his answer to the pressing need for level-headed, practical, yet academically rigorous defense analysts in the national security community. For young men and women who desired careers in the area of defense and foreign policy, Van Cleave designed one of the most comprehensive, realistic and professional curriculum ever to be offered in the field of strategic studies.

Its policy-oriented approach was the Program's hallmark. In DSSP classes, theory was studied in the context of its applicability to real world defense analysis and policy making. Emphasis was placed on U.S. nuclear policies, programs, and options in the face of the Soviet military threat, as well as other threats to U.S. security. Empirical observation and the historical record were used to determine Soviet geopolitical objectives and military capabilities; the negotiating record, compliance and non-compliance with existing treaties were the references used to assess probable Soviet behavior toward future arms control agreements; the theory and practical application of strategy were examined for the wisdom they might provide in meeting today's military challenges; and so on.

Professor Van Cleave successfully bridged the gap between the theoretical aspects of international affairs with the practical requirements of national security by maintaining in his own career a balance between thorough scholarship and extensive policy experience. This professionalism, plus Van Cleave's enthusiasm and devotion to teaching, are what lent distinction to the DSSP.

To supplement his own teaching, Van Cleave invited many of his distinguished colleagues from both the policy and academic worlds to conduct guest seminars and to teach part of the Program's regular curriculum.

Every resource was exploited that could maximize the students' education outside the classroom as well. Expenses were paid by the Program to allow students to travel to field-related conferences and seminars around the country and abroad. Regular paid summer internships and paid research projects were arranged at such places as the Hoover Institution, the Department of Defense, Arms Control and Disarmament Agency, International Institute for Strategic Studies, London.

By the end of their formal education, DSSP graduates were thoroughly prepared in terms of the necessary knowledge, skills and experience to enter the career of their choice. In fact, there is a constant professional demand within the national security community for Program graduates. Van Cleave has perhaps been the nation's most successful single educator in placing his graduates in high-level professional positions in the national security field.

When Professor Van Cleave joined the faculty in 1967, the School of International Relations had a solid reputation for academic quality, and maintained a balance between the traditional and behavioral approaches to the study of international affairs. There was a rich and growing menu of specialized fields of study around which M.A. and Ph.D. candidates could tailor their degrees. There were two post-degree career paths that were considered equally legitimate and desirable: that of research and teaching, and that of practical policy making. Most of the faculty had experience in both. The SIR of the 1960s and 1970s was willing and able to accommodate students interested in either.

Degree flexibility was one of the most attractive features of the School in those days. There were distinct fields for the Soviet, European, Middle Eastern, African, Asian/Pacific and Latin American regions. Other fields included Foreign Policy Analysis, International Political Diplomacy, International Political Economy, and Defense and Strategic Studies. If a student could not fulfill every aspect of his personal degree objectives within this framework, he was allowed, indeed encouraged, to draw upon the resources of an outside department or university.

It was within that School of International Relations that the Defense and Strategic Studies Program flourished.

Today's School of International Relations is a shadow of its former self. Within today's SIR, political balance, academic diversity and degree flexibility are lacking; there has not been one faculty hire in the last ten years with any practical policy experience. All that remains is a rapidly fading and highly misleading reputation.

The first attempt to redirect SIR away from academic diversity was made as early as the mid-seventies under the directorship of Professor James N. Rosenau. Rosenau sought to replace the more traditional and academically diverse approaches to the study of international relations with a single, narrowly defined and highly theoretical approach. He sought faculty who shared his commitment to this narrow approach to this field and, incidentally, his liberal political views. The other long-standing approaches and viewpoints were disparaged, and their proponents were denied effective voices in the future of the School. Rosenau had some limited success, but his primary accomplishment was to stir up tremendous animosity among the faculty, who felt the integrity of their respective fields threatened. Rosenau was forced to resign as Director in 1979.

A new Director, Michael G. Fry, was hired in 1981 for the express purpose of quelling the faculty unrest and ensuring the strengthening and continued prosperity of the School's various programs.

Fry began to restructure the School around what he called the "generic" interpretation of international relations and foreign policy. This meant that academic specialization and specific areas of study were to be supplanted by a uniformly methodological approach.

This generic approach in practice whittled the Ph.D. degree field options down to essentially three highly abstract areas based on theoretical assumptions and methodological skills: theory (or what the SIR now refers to as its "core" curriculum), international political economy (IPE), and foreign policy analysis (FPA). These fields ignore much of the necessary substantive knowledge of particular policy subjects, actual political systems, geography, geopolitics, and history, and instead rely primarily on models based on the hypothetical interaction of international "actors" for the analysis of foreign policy and decision making.

This approach encourages the treatment of all nations, in the study of international relations, with political and moral equivalency. Indeed, when coupled with the decidedly liberal-left political views of the new faculty under Fry's directorship, it is an approach that can be fairly characterized as blaming U.S. policy for the international conflict with Communism. Cold war revisionist interpretations began to be emphasized in most SIR courses.

Since regional and policy studies would thoroughly undermine this generic view of international affairs, they had to somehow be eliminated from the curriculum of the School.

The current SIR catalogue boasts a curriculum that has been "completely reorganized since 1982." The school restructured that curriculum by default, using the tactic of homogeneous faculty hires. The character of the faculty was changed as senior faculty retired and resigned (under pressure) and as new faculty were hired in the fields of theory, IPE and FPA. Since faculty voting rules gave each member equal voice, even on issues outside his expertise, and regardless of lack of accomplishment, a tyranny of the majority was established. This tyranny was exercised on professors and programs that dared to remain "different," particularly the Defense and Strategic Studies Program.

The next attack on academic diversity, then, was to restructure the School's graduate guidelines. The new majority changed the School's graduate study rules and requirements to reduce even further the academic choices for students interested in area, policy and national security. The faculty decided that for an area or subject to qualify as a field of concentration, that field had to be represented by at least two full-time tenured or tenure-track SIR faculty members. That meant fields that had previously been represented by one regular faculty person — all of the regional studies programs — had to be either eliminated or incorporated into another field. As a consequence, the European and Middle Eastern fields were simply eliminated, and African, Latin American and Asian/Pacific studies were folded into the fields of IPE and FPA.

Soviet studies has been retained but reduced in emphasis more as a courtesy to its distinguished and longstanding faculty representative, Professor Rodger Swearingen, than for any other apparent reason, but little effort has been made to strengthen the field, nor to assure its continuance as a distinct field of study after Swearingen's retirement. The field of International Political Diplomacy has been largely stripped of its historical perspective and what is left is now indistinguishable from the core/theory field.

By 1984-1985, all that remained of the past was the thriving Defense and Strategic Studies Program.

The DSSP made it through the School's "reorganization" relatively unscathed thanks to its strength, visibility and success in raising financial support from national foundations. Many philanthropists shared Van Cleave's concern over the deficit of knowledgable defense professionals and were willing to issue generous grants to USC expressly to support the Defense and Strategic Studies Program. The University Administration initially agreed to the stipulations of the grants, which were: 1) that the funds would be spent only on the DSSP, primarily for student support and academic enrichment, and solely by Van Cleave's authorization, and 2) that the University Administration would do its part to ensure the strengthening and continued prosperity of the Program. Beginning in the mid-seventies, Van Cleave raised some $1.5 million from several reputable private foundations from which the University had been seeking funding for other activities.

The foundation funding enabled the Program to be virtually self-supporting, and allowed it to operate fiscally on a semi-autonomous basis from the School. In accordance with its primary obligation, the Program spent on the order of $120,000 per year, during its most active period, just on student financial support (fellowships, tuition credits, research and teaching assistant stipends) and on augmenting its research facilities. The Program also paid the salaries of second and third faculty members who had to be brought in from outside the university to teach the regular Program curriculum. In addition, Van Cleave was expected to pay for all of his own administrative and secretarial staff, all equipment, material and supplies, telephones, reproduction, postage, and even repairs and maintenance for the Program's physical facility.

There was a three year period when the School covered one-third of a second DSSP faculty salary. That money came not from the SIR budget, but from a U.S. Department of Education (DOE) grant to the School. Starting in 1981, the SIR received grants from the DOE to support something called the "USC Center for International Studies." Since neither Van Cleave nor any of the DSSP students had ever heard of such a "Center" at USC, Van Cleave investigated. He discovered in the proposals and progress reports submitted to the DOE that Fry had listed all of the DSSP assets and activities — including Van Cleave's internship program, the undergraduate honors certificate program in national security, post-graduate professional job placement and so on — as assets and activities of this non-existent "Center." Yet the grant financed none of these activities.

At the same time, the Program was producing more M.A.s and Ph.D.s than all other SIR fields combined. Enrollment and tuition credits for those students, upon which annual departmental budget allocations are determined, went to the School of International Relations, not to the Program.

234

The situation, though far from ideal, was at least tolerable. Van Cleave's prudent use of the Foundation funding enabled the Program to operate smoothly as he had designed it. Despite the SIR hostility and intolerance, the DSSP was buffered from the radical academic and ideological upheaval going on in the rest of the School.

By 1984-1985, however, it was impossible for the Program to remain unaffected. Within the "new" faculty Van Cleave found himself losing votes, on the order of 15 to 2 on issues that directly affected his own field and the DSSP. The rewritten graduate guidelines and the imposed graduate degree uniformity made it more and more difficult to construct attractive Ph.D. programs for students interested in defense policy. Also, it was increasingly difficult to sustain the strength, let alone ensure the growth of the defense and strategic studies field, without the addition of one or two permanent faculty appointments (as opposed to having to import visiting faculty on a semester-to-semester basis), and those appointments were not forthcoming.

Having successfully emasculated the other policy-oriented fields, the SIR faculty went along with efforts to change the nature of the Program to reflect the School's new academic approach and ideological perspective. Some of the faculty even launched a campaign of public denigration against the Program and its students, academic encroachment into the DSSP field of study, and direct interference with the Program's traditional activities and practices.

One argument — indeed the basis of the SIR's "official" opposition to the Program — was that the DSSP needed balance. The faculty complained that the Program curriculum was too narrow in terms of conceptual approach and subject matter, and that it needed to be broadened to include theory. In truth, the DSSP curriculum, with fourteen regular lectures and seminars, had breadth and depth in both conceptual and practical areas of study. Some seminars were dedicated entirely to theory and how it is applied in practice. Furthermore, Program students were taking their degrees within the SIR, where they were required to take core courses in theory, and other subjects in which theory was the primary emphasis. Finally, one would have thought that if the faculty had been so committed to "balancing" the DSSP field, they would have been just as enthusiastic about doing the same in the other SIR fields as well. Since no attempt had ever been made, however, at recruiting anyone with even semi-conservative or traditional views for those fields, one tended to question the faculty's true intentions for the Progam.

Another assertion made by a few influential faculty members and intended to discredit the Program was that the quality of its students and the teaching were substandard. An unfounded rumor was spread that DSSP students had the lowest GRE scores in the School. These faculty members could not understand, therefore, why Van Cleave "gave" those students such high grades in his seminars. Something had to be wrong. What was wrong, of course, was the assertion. A little research uncovered the fact that each generation of DSSP students had been among the highest in the School in terms of GRE scores. These students earned high grades not only in Van Cleave's classes, but in all of their SIR courses. In fact, more marks of distinction have been awarded over the years to Program graduates than to other SIR students for their overall performance on their degree qualifying examinations, not merely on the strategic studies portion. It should be pointed out that marks of distinction require the support of two or three faculty members who make up a student's degree committee. The ensuing professional success of many Program graduates is further testimony to the high quality of their academic and intellectual ability.

As to the insinuated slight against Professor Van Cleave's professional integrity, the faculty failed to dwell on the awards for teaching excellence that Van Cleave had received during his years at USC, or to mention the fact that he was consistently the highest-ranked professor in the School on student-teacher evaluations.

Another disquieting episode was an attempt by the SIR faculty to "invalidate" a set of Program Ph.D. candidates' qualifying examinations after they had been written and approved by the committees. One of the new (1983) rules that Van Cleave opposed was the elimination of the "take-home" written qualifying exam, and its replacement with "in-class," resourceless, three-hour-per-field written exams. Van Cleave's position was that a professor could better judge, and a student could better demonstrate his knowledge, competence, and analytical skills in a broad, thoughtful, well-structured take-home exam. Van Cleave did not seek to impose this testing approach on other faculty members, he only sought to retain the freedom to test students in his field in the manner of his choosing. He therefore sought and received Graduate School approval to continue his method of Ph.D. examination. Nevertheless, in Spring 1986, the SIR facutly moved to invalidate the five DSSP Ph.D. exams that had been taken and approved that semester on the basis that Van Cleave did not properly follow SIR examination procedures. The unethical and illegal motion failed in a faculty vote by a margin of only two votes.

In 1985, the director of SIR approved a special "one-time" seminar duplicating and encroaching upon the Program's established curricula. At the same time, some faculty members began to challenge the DSSP practice of enriching curriculum offerings by bringing to campus, with foundation money, distinguished professors to give program seminars. At this time, one such seminar, "Intelligence and National Security," guest-taught by a distinguished expert in the field, Dr. Angelo Codevilla, had already been endorsed by the Graduate Studies Committee. Nonetheless, the SIR faculty moved to cancel the seminar even though the class had a heavy enrollment, and had already been in session for three weeks! The motion failed by another slim margin. Due to the success and popularity of the seminar, the Program proposed to fund and offer it again the following semester. Again, Van Cleave received the approval of the Graduate Studies Committee, but this time the faculty succeeded in rejecting the course.

The faculty similarly voted to reject another Program guest-seminar taught by Professor Harold W. Rood for the Fall 1986 semester. Unlike Dr. Codevilla, Professor Rood, who holds the Keck Chair for International and Strategic Studies at th Claremont Colleges, was a long-time associate of the Program and the School of International Relations. He had taught for SIR's graduate program in West Germany, and had served, with Graduate School approval, on numerous SIR Ph.D. guidance committees over the years. He also taught, at Program expense, one or two SIR graduate seminars per year since the late 1970s. In fact, one of his guest-seminars, "Geo-politics in Theory and Practice," (a topic on which Rood has authored numerous articles and one book) had been adopted into the permanent SIR/DSSP curriculum. No other professor had ever taught it at USC. It was that course that the Program proposed Rood teach again in Fall 1986. Instead of the routine approval, however, the faculty red-flagged the request. Rood was required to submit a new and extensive course outline, along with his curriculum vitae and any other documentation that might "prove" his credentials. After reviewing these materials — which included his published works — the SIR faculty voted to reject the proposed seminar on the grounds that they could find no evidence that Professor Rood was qualified to teach a course in geopolitics!

The net effect of these actions threatened the operation and very existence of the Program. Van Cleave thus initiated discussions with members of the university administration about the future of the Program at USC.

In January and February 1985, Van Cleave met several times with the Vice President and Dean of USC's College of Letters, Arts and Sciences, to discuss the growing incompatibility and incongruity between the DSSP and the SIR. Van Cleave extensively outlined the history of the increasing leftward political and ideological imbalance within the SIR faculty, and gave a detailed account of the various forms of hostility that had been directed against the Program, its students and himself personally. He explained that the Program would not possibly be able to continue within the SIR under the one-man, one-vote system, which gave even to faculty who were inexperienced, untenured and unaccomplished an equal voice to his own in Program matters. The continuance of the Program, and of future foundation support, he concluded, depended entirely upon the protection and strengthening of the Program, which only the university administration had the power to ensure.

The USC officials initially expressed the Administration's unequivocal support for the Program, and as an indication of that support the Vice President approved a second hard-money, (that is, funded by the University and not the SIR or DSSP), tenured faculty appointment to strengthen the DSSP. Under existing university hiring regulations, however, such an appointment would be subjected to approval by the department faculty. Van Cleave warned the administration that given the unbalanced voting record and the unabashed intolerance of the current SIR faculty, the SIR would doubtlessly reject any candidate that Van Cleave might nominate for the second DSSP position, and instead use this as an opportunity to hire someone in line with its own ideological perspective. The Vice President assured Van Cleave that that would not be allowed to happen. Van Cleave was promised that if a selection were made by the faculty that did not meet his criteria for strengthening the Program, no hire would be made.

The criteria Van Cleave established for the second faculty appointment were: 1) extensive teaching, *and* government and policy experience, 2) ability to assist in raising foundation funding, 3) ability to assist in placing graduates professionally in government and defense related jobs and, of course, 4) competence to teach the seminars in the DSSP curriculum.

The candidates were narrowed to five. Of those five, four were nominated by the School, and one by the Program. Four of the candidates met scarcely any of the criteria. Given these criteria, Van Cleave's candidate was indisputably the most qualified. Van Cleave's candidate was rejected by a vote of 15-1, and one of the other four was selected instead.

Dr. Van Cleave immediately contacted the Dean and informed him that the SIR selection did not meet the criteria for strengthening the DSSP but instead represented further encroachment, and that he would have to claim his assurance that the hire would not be made. Despite the previous commitment, the Dean said that he could not override the faculty. The appointment was made.

Before deciding what to do Van Cleave talked with many students and alumni who were familiar both with the situation between the SIR and the DSSP, and with the person selected by the faculty to fill the second DSSP position. It was unanimous that this faculty action, given everything else that had occurred, could not be accepted.

Therefore, Professor Van Cleave informed the administration that if it was not prepared to protect the integrity of the Program from faculty tyranny, he would have to phase out the Program at USC, and leave at a time consistent with the educational schedules of his current graduate students.

Dr. Van Cleave submitted his resignation in February 1986, to be effective May 1987. Three Program Ph.D. candidates took it upon themselves to put those 15 months to good use to try to convince the university administration of the magnitude of USC's impending loss, and to devise a solution that would persuade Van Cleave to withdraw his resignation.

The students produced a lengthy memorandum to the Administration that outlined the history of the SIR/DSSP conflict, emphasizing the Program's qualitative superiority compared to other units in the School, and the value of the Program to SIR and the University. They suggested several feasible solutions for retaining Van Cleave and the Program, including the creation of an autonomous, interdisciplinary Defense and Strategic Studies Center, i.e. a degree granting entity with its own faculty and curriculum that would also draw upon the curriculum of several existing departments, including the School of International Relations.

In addition to the University Administration, the memo was mailed to all of the Program graduates and all of the Program's distinguished associates, many of them high ranking government officials. (President Zumberge's office refused to release the address list, otherwise the memo would have been sent to USC's Board of Trustees.) The authors of the memo urged the alumni and associates quietly to contact the

Administration with their support for the continuation of the DSSP at USC.

The response was overwhelming. Scores of letters poured into administration offices praising the Program, its high standards of academic rigor and excellence, its professionalism and its invaluable contributions to the nation. Each letterwriter emphasized that the DSSP was inseparable from its founder and Director — that without the knowledge, experience, talent, dedication and tenacity of Professor William R. Van Cleave, the Program could never have existed, much less flourished as it did.

The letterwriters also emphasized the ideological nature of the SIR faculty intolerance and hostility against the Program. As one alumnus wrote to the administration: "One of the important things at jeopardy in the current battle over the future of the DSSP is nothing less than USC's continued commitment to intellectual freedom. While I hate to interject the issue of ideology, since ideology is often the refuge of convenient excuses, the plain truth is that the current conflict with the SIR is primarily one of political ideology, and the attempt by the majority of the faculty to impose its political ideology on the minority."

Within the administration the situation was delegated to the new acting Vice President of the College of Letters, Arts and Sciences. The acting Vice President contacted Van Cleave in March 1986 and asked if he might be willing to withdraw his resignation if the administration could come up with an acceptable solution. Van Cleave said that he would be happy to consider any proposal by the administration. He explained, however, that the administration would have to move quickly, as Van Cleave had already begun to phase out the Program at USC. The acting Vice President said that he and the Provost would dedicate their highest priority to investigating the problems that led to the resignation, and in devising an acceptable solution.

In May, though he had not heard a word from the administration, Van Cleave wrote a memo to the Provost outlining the latest SIR attacks against the DSSP. In June, with still no communication from the administration, Van Cleave wrote again to the Provost and the Acting Vice President to inform them that, though his own optimism was dwindling, many of the letterwriters were anxious to hear what progress the administration was making toward the retention of the DSSP.

Finally, early in July, Van Cleave received a letter from the acting Vice President. The official acknowledged the receipt of all of the letters and said that he had responded to them with a "temporizing letter which served to...inform them that we were looking into the matter." He then explained that his investigation since March had consisted of discussions with the SIR Director, Michael Fry, and others on the School's faculty. The administration had failed to interview even one of the many senior members of the USC community who well understood the SIR situation. Not one of the letterwriters, all of whom were familiar both with the situation at the School and with Van Cleave's own professional success, and that of his alumni, had been contacted. Instead, the university administration confined its investigation solely to interviews with those who were the original and active source of the fundamental conflict.

Furthermore, no "solution" had been attempted by the administration at all. Instead the acting Vice President thought it "advisable to form an ad hoc faculty review committee charged to look into the difficulties, evaluate the situation and make recommendations to the College and Provost Offices." Van Cleave was then invited to recommend a suitable candidate to serve on this review committee.

Van Cleave responded to the acting Vice President with strong reservations about the utility, purpose and timeliness of such a review committee. Van Cleave could not understand the need to charge a committee to "look into the difficulties," when those difficulties had been explained to the administration in depth —first by Van Cleave himself, then by the student memorandum, and finally by every one of the letterwriters. All that remained, Van Cleave pointed out, was the decision by the administration as to whether it valued the Program and its contributions sufficiently to defend it against the SIR academic tyranny. Such a committee might have been useful two years earlier when Van Cleave first brought this situation to the attention of the administration, but by this point it was too late. Finally, Van Cleave questioned the seriousness of the administration's commitment to reach a constructive solution. He expressed concern that such review committees are most often formed to create the impression of constructive activity, while actually serving only to postpone a responsible decision, or hoping that the situation will resolve itself. Nevertheless, Van Cleave stated that, in consideration of these reservations, he would cooperate with the review committee. He contingently nominated a well-qualified person for the committee, the USC Dean. The nomination was rejected.

University officials seemed shocked that Van Cleave would question "the usual method used in academic institutions to resolve such differences." Furthermore, the acting Vice President suggested that if Van Cleave had to make professional decisions prior to the proposed committee report in December of 1986, then the administration would accept the February resignation as the final word.

After a few more exchanges of correspondence with the administration, including President Zumberge, Van Cleave's suspicion proved to be accurate: There had never really been any serious attempt by the administration to either understand the situation in the School of International Relations, or to come up with a workable solution that would retain Dr. Van Cleave and his Defense and Strategic Studies Program.

Within the School of International Relations, political ideology and narrow-mindedness triumphed over academic integrity and tolerance. The result was the destruction of its most productive and successful academic unit.

The University Administration became stultified by its own idealized image of a university based on a corporate model. As long as "collegial bonds" are maintained, President Zumberge explained in a letter to Van Cleave, the University at large will prosper. But there are other standards that are essential to the integrity of a university: academic balance and diversity and freedom of inquiry. When these begin to deteriorate, collegiality becomes enforced conformity, and education gives way to indoctrination. That is the price that President Zumberge has paid in his quest for "corporate respectability" for the University of Southern California.

Dr. Crouch received his Ph.D. from USC and served as a policy analyst at the Arms Control and Disarmament Agency. He is currently a National Security Assistant to Senator Malcolm Wallop of Wyoming.

Dr. Van Cleave relocated in 1987 and established the new Center for Defense and Strategic Studies at Southwest Missouri State University, Springfield, Missouri. All of the DSSP alumni and associates, and the national foundations that contributed to the Program at USC, are united in their support for the new Center, and to the maintenance of its national prestige. Dr. Van Cleave and the Center are committed to the continued contribution to the security of the nation through a program of academic excellence and professional training of future national security policy-makers.

CHAPTER EIGHTEEN

THE PLIGHT OF
CONSERVATIVE ACADEMICS

A CONSERVATIVE AT
GEORGE WASHINGTON UNIVERSITY
by CHARLES MOSER

In a curious way it turns out that there is greater freedom of speech within our society at large than there is inside the academy. It is up to those of us who are conservative academics to make our voices heard.

HAVING TAUGHT AT both Yale (1960-67) and George Washington University since then, I have the feeling that the more prestigious the university, the less likely there are to be decent conservatives on its faculty. At least I have been relatively more comfortable at George Washington than at Yale, even though I am an alumnus of Yale.

One may be conservative on a university faculty so long as you keep quiet. Especially if you teach courses in a less popular area like Russian Literature, when you have fifteen or at most twenty students in a class, your colleagues decide that what you have to say makes little difference. But if you offer statements on larger issues or try to reach a larger audience within the university, then you encounter considerable difficulties.

I might offer the example of the Faculty Senate at the George Washington University. The Senate has a fair amount of prestige among the faculty, and people generally are pleased to be elected to it. I have a certain number of supporters on the faculty who insist on nominating me to the Faculty Senate, so I have been a candidate for election probably six to eight times during my tenure at George Washington. But I have never been elected, because although I have a substantial minority with me, I can never gather a majority. If I am on the ballot

244

with someone nobody ever heard of, the votes will shift to him primarily because I am the alternative, and I am publicly known as a strong conservative.

This doesn't mean that I can't win on certain issues with which I am openly associated within the university. Indeed, on one occasion I was very active in a successful effort to save the Faculty Senate itself, which was in danger of being absorbed into a conglomerate All-University Assembly, which would have represented all constituencies within the university, including secretarial staff and maintenance personnel. So I helped to save the Faculty Senate, but I cannot be elected to it. That does not mean, however, that conservatives cannot be elected to the Faculty Senate, if only they keep a low profile. Indeed right now the Faculty Senate is headed by an excellent woman, an art historian, whose political views are very similar to mine. The difference between us is that by and large she does not take public positions on political matters, or join overtly political organizations.

Let me offer you another example of the difficulties open conservatives face on campus. My academic field is Russian language and literature, but I have long wished to teach a course on Twentieth Century American conservatism. There is a program at George Washington which allows faculty members to give experimental courses not necessarily within their field of specialization. So I proposed a course on the history and doctrine of American conservatism from 1945 to 1985, a course in which we would read works by such conservatives as Russell Kirk, Richard Weaver, Frank Meyer, Willmore Kendall, Joseph Sobran and — in economic theory — Henry Hazlitt, Milton Friedman and Paul Craig Roberts. In other words, it was to be an interdisciplinary course on the entire development of American conservatism since World War II.

The main difficulty with the course, it turned out, was finding a department which would accept it even as an experimental one-time offering. Since it was totally illogical to give it within my department, the Slavic department, I had to find another department willing to list the course. I approached Political Science, but they were not interested. I tried the Economics department, but they had no interest either. When I approached the History department, they did not say no, but dragged out a decision on the matter to the point where it was clear they really did not want the course. Finally I asked the American Studies department, the most logical place for the course to be situated. At first they refused, but when I then appealed to the curriculum committee of the entire liberal arts college at George Washington, the chairman of American Studies — a former Ripon Society activist — had a change of heart and permitted me to give the course under American Studies in the spring semester 1987.

I do not know this for certain, but I suspect the chairman of American Studies made that decision on his own, and when his colleagues found out about it, they protested. He probably said to them: "I have already told Moser he can teach the course this semester, but that will be it." For after I gave the course and it proved reasonably successful, I raised the question of repeating it, only to be told that American Studies did not wish the course to be given again. The conclusion to all this is that a course in American conservatism is not only not welcomed, but distinctly resisted at George Washington. At Yale the situation would probably have been even worse.

In a curious way it turns out that there is greater freedom of speech within our society at large than there is inside the academy. A Jesse Helms can speak before non-university audiences across the country and get his point of view across freely. But it is not possible for him to appear at many universities and be heard freely and seriously. So the basic complaint of the conservatives is that the available variety of opinion within the university is much narrower than within the society at large.

It is up to those of us who are conservative academics to make our voices heard. I am concerned that many conservatives — especially those who accepted positions with the Reagan administration — have left the academy, and are not welcomed back. Some are simply tired of the uneven battle and are pursuing other occupations. That is a disturbing development which I hope will be reversed.

On the positive side, I might mention the response to Allan Bloom's *The Closing of the American Mind*, which has been taken much more seriously than one would ever have expected both within the academy and by the general public. Its critique of American higher education in most essentials resembles the critique conservative academics have tried to make. If such a book can become a bestseller, then there must be an unease in the American spirit which responds to its argument.

Dr. Charles Moser is Chairman of the Department of Slavic Languages at George Washington University where he has held teaching posts since 1967. He received his M.A. and Ph.D. from Columbia University and taught at Yale for seven years before coming to Washington. His published works include Antinihilism in the Russian Novel in the 1860s, Denis Fonvizin, A History of Bulgarian Literature *and* Dimitrov of Bulgaria. *Dr. Moser also edited and co-authored* Combat on Communist Territory, *published in 1985.*

UNIVERSITY PROFESSORS FOR
ACADEMIC ORDER
by HOWARD HURWITZ

I believe that conservatives feel outnumbered and surrounded. Sometimes I feel like George Armstrong Custer, left with a single man and surrounded at the battle of Little Big Horn. As the enemy rode in for the kill, he is said to have shouted, 'Don't take any prisoners.' The optimism, apocryphally attributed to General Custer, might change the long face of conservatives on campus.

UNIVERSITY PROFESSORS FOR Academic Order was founded in 1970 and from the beginning it has sought to intervene on behalf of conservative academics who have been discriminated against. In 1970 conservatives were a small minority on campus. They were a small minority long before 1970 and they remain a small minority today. It may even be that they are an endangered species on campuses.

At least half of the academics who have sought UPAO's intervention have tried unsuccessfully to obtain help from the American Association of University Professors and other organizations. For conservative academics, we seem to be a court of last resort although UPAO tries to stay out of the courts.

In almost all cases we have tried to talk to deans and administrators of colleges in the hope of bringing about an amicable settlement of grievances. We undertake such intervention only after our Academic Freedom Committee has studied materials presented to us by a member, and we are satisfied that the evidence warrants our investigation and action.

In 1986, for example, a young assistant professor at a small eastern liberal arts college was denied tenure. He presented to us abundant evidence of his professional contributions,

248

including published articles — one on Russell Kirk — and campus activity. He alleged that his professional record was superior to that of most department members and that he had been denied tenure because of his ideology, unpopular with department members and the dean.

To make a long story very short, because academic freedom cases are invariably long, we wrote and spoke to college officials and brought about a change of mind. Tenure has been granted to the assistant professor.

Most have now heard about Dr. Phyllis Zagano and her complaint that she was denied academic freedom by Fordham University. UPAO entered that case at the request of Dr. Zagano. I was the on-site investigator for UPAO, but the president of Fordham refused to see me. I did speak to others and studied considerable materials in the case before making my recommendation to UPAO's Academic Freedom Committee. We reported that Fordham University had indeed violated Dr. Zagano's academic freedom. We sent the report to the president of Fordham and released our finding to the media. The president of Fordham was sufficiently perturbed by the report to phone and write me. The case is now being considered by the State Human Rights Division of the State of New York.

I estimate that we have been successful in about one-third of the cases we have entered during the past 18 years. It is a respectable average by baseball standards. We wish that it might be better, if only because of the suffering endured by colleagues who traverse hell during the time that elapses between the act of alleged discrimination and the final outcome. The scars remain no matter what happens.

There is one case that has a special fascination for me, because I may be the only UPAO member who knows anything about it. I shall disguise the names of the individuals and the college to protect the innocent, although I should very much like to lay low the guilty.

I had a long conversation with this UPAO member recently. The case began and ended in less than a year — a record performance in the history of academic freedom cases. First, there is the letter from the dean of instruction to the faculty member:

> Jim, I've approved your travel request to attend the Board of Directors meeting of University Professors for Academic Order, but I do so with misgivings.
>
> Both UPAO and its affiliate, National Council for Better Education, appear to be at least as political as they are educational. Also, UPAO approves of supporting Accuracy in Academia, an

organization which threatens academic freedom. I think funds from a public college should not be used in support of quasi-political organizations.

However, I recognized also that UPAO's political views vis-a-vis its educational views is a grey area and, in approving your travel request, am giving it and you the benefit of a large doubt. In the future, should you wish to attend UPAO happenings, I ask that you use your own funds.

P.S. UPAO was not the only group which 'stood to oppose the dangerous and unruly student riots of the 1960s' (from your 9/19/86 letter to me). Come to think of it, it couldn't have opposed the 1960s riots at all, since the organization was founded in 1970.

In reply, Jim wrote to the dean:

Thank you for your views on University Professors for Academic Order. I disagree that the organization is political and that its affiliations are less than honorable. If that were true I would resign.

I have asked the President of UPAO to send you a clarification of your viewpoints so you might fully understand the sound principles for which the organization stands. The facts should help.

Through this affiliation I have met enough honorable and respectable friends to say that it assists me in my profession. In addition, the organization has a positive impact on education. I'd like to invite you to attend the meetings...

In response to Jim's request that I write the dean, I drafted the following letter:

Jim G has sent me a copy of your note to him, dated October 2. In it you make a number of allegations about UPAO.

First, you state, "Both UPAO and its affiliate National Council for Better Education appear to be at least as political as they are educational."

UPAO is an entirely professional organization and is granted tax-exempt status by the IRS. It was founded by college and university faculty in 1970, including the late Senator John P. East, who, at the time, was a tenured professor of political science at East Carolina University.

Among our present members are Milton Friedman, Nobel prize-winning economist; Oscar Handlin, Pulitzer Prize-winning historian; former Senator S.I. Hayakawa; Ambassador Shelby Cullom Davis; several college presidents and distinguished scholars in diverse disciplines; and non-faculty people who subscribe to the purposes set forth in the enclosed brochure.

We affiliated with NCBE in December '85, and our agreement makes clear our complete independence of each other. NCBE confines its activity to the elementary and secondary schools; UPAO confines its activities to institutions of higher learning. Both UPAO and NCBE hold to traditional values in education — solid subject matter and firm requirements for graduation.

Second, you state, "...UPAO approves of supporting Accuracy in Academia, an organization which threatens academic freedom."

UPAO voted to support AIA at our Sixteenth Annual Meeting in Washington D.C., on December 7, 1985. AIA had been started up by Reed Irvine. Mr. Irvine addressed us and set forth in detail the objectives of AIA. He was questioned sharply by our directors. We were assured that at no time would AIA call for the removal of any faculty member no matter what the outcome of its investigations. UPAO has monitored AIA's activities, and we are convinced that no threat to academic freedom exists. Rather, AIA, as evidenced by its Campus Report, has expanded academic freedom to include students. For too long, too many students have been captives of some faculty members, who indoctrinate and discourage disagreement in class. AIA publicizes such faculty members, after investigation, including talks with any faculty member who responds to AIA's inquiry. The effect of AIA's on-going activity has been to reduce the incidence of severely biased lectures and unbalanced reading lists.

Third, you state, UPAO "couldn't have opposed the 1960s riots at all, since the organization was founded in 1970." The "riots" continued with undiminished force into the early 1970s. UPAO from its inception actively opposed the disorderly conduct that disrupted learning. At this moment, we oppose the politicization of campuses by disruptive students. In addition, we see "academic order" as encompassing respect and furtherance of traditional values.

Fourth, you state that in approving Mr. Jim G's "travel request," you are giving UPAO and him "the benefit of a large doubt." You add, "In the future, should you wish to attend UPAO happenings, I ask that you use your own funds."

UPAO sees your decision, based on your mistaken allegations about UPAO, as a violation of Mr. G's academic freedom. Clearly, you are discriminating against him because of his membership in an organization that does not reflect your views.

Finally, UPAO hopes and expects that on the basis of the foregoing clarification of our status as a professional organization, you will withdraw your caveat about Mr. G's future activity in UPAO.

UPAO is prepared to pursue this matter further. However, we prefer to settle academic freedom cases amicably. This will depend on your future relations with Mr. G, whom we know has served on the faculty of the college for four years and as many summers.

After a short interval, I called Jim G to ask how things were going and what additional help we might offer. He told me that he had received notice from the college that his contract to teach would not be renewed and that he had spoken to a lawyer who told him that contesting the college's notification was a long process with no assurance of success.

I had previously advised Jim G that he must exhaust the administrative processes and enter court only as a last resort. I told him that the dean's letter was, in effect, a *prima facie* case of discrimination; that UPAO would seek a meeting with the college president in the matter of academic freedom.

A few weeks passed and I called again. Jim had appeared before a college committee. He had introduced student statements as to his effectiveness as a teacher and the record of his activities in the furtherance of the college's role in the community. None of his colleagues had come forward to assist him; they feared retribution by the administration, and he had not wanted to place them in jeopardy.

Jim told me that he had decided not to challenge the college's decision to terminate him. He was starting his own business as a consultant. He already had his first client, whom he was advising on how to obtain credit for financing a business. If anyone can make a living off campus in a different line of work, it is Jim G. Surrender, however, is not my style. I wish that Jim G. had decided to fight back.

I believe that conservatives feel outnumbered and surrounded on the campuses. Sometimes I feel like George Armstrong Custer, left with a single man and surrounded at the battle of Little Big Horn. As the enemy rode in for the kill, he is said to have shouted, "Don't take any prisoners."

The optimism, apocryphally attributed to General Custer, might change the long face of conservatives on campus. We had better fight back — now and forever.

Dr. Hurwitz is the former President of University Professors for Academic Order. He is the author of 10 books in the social sciences, including An Encyclopedia of American History. *Dr. Hurwitz earned his Ph.D. from Columbia University in 1943. Dr. Hurwitz served for 10 years as Adjunct Associate Professor of Education at St. John's University. He is a nationally syndicated columnist, a radio and TV commentator, and has appeared on "60 minutes."*

DUKE: A TYPICAL AMERICAN UNIVERSITY IN EXILE
by MAGNUS KRYNSKI

To create a Marxist culture in this country, to make Marxism an unavoidable presence and a distinct, original, and unmistakable voice in American social, cultural, and intellectual life, in short to form a Marxist intelligentsia for the struggles of the future — this seems to me the supreme mission of a Marxist pedagogy.
- Professor Frederic Jameson, Duke University

MINE IS A REPORT from the field, from a Southern university which likes to call itself the "Harvard of the South." For some strange reason Duke still enjoys a reputation as "an ideologically and socially conservative place." Nothing could be further from the truth. Duke, to borrow Irving Kristol's compelling phrase, is a typical "American university in exile." In fact, Duke probably has the dubious distinction of being a pioneer in promoting leftist bias. I have no time here to give you a historical background, but I would like you to remember that Duke was for 15 years the personal fiefdom of Senator Terry Sanford, a McGovern-type Democrat. Mr. Sanford was responsible for the gross politicization of the university during his tenure as President from 1970 to 1985.

I am tempted to quote some gems of wisdom that have in recent years come out of the mouths of my colleagues at Duke, but I will quote only a statement by Professor Frederic Jameson, a literary Marxist celebrity with a salary in six figures. This is his conception of the duties of the classroom teacher as quoted by professors Stephen Balch and Herbert London in *Commentary* of October, 1986:

> To create a Marxist culture in this country, to make Marxism an unavoidable presence and a distinct, original, and unmistakable voice in American social, cultural, and intellectual life, in short to

form a Marxist intelligentsia for the struggles of the future — this seems to me the supreme mission of a Marxist pedagogy.

Stripped of turgid rhetoric, Professor Jameson proclaims that the duty of the classroom teacher is to prepare future revolutionaries. How differently did the German sociologist Max Weber conceive of the role of the teacher. Weber once wrote that the teacher "will beware of imposing from the platform any political positions upon the student, whether expressed or suggested...the prophet and the demagogue do not belong on the academic platform."

Now, Professor Jameson is not the only prominent literary Marxist at Duke. Other literary Marxist celebrities at Duke include Stanley Fish and his wife, Jane Tompkins. More Marxist celebrities joined Duke's faculty in the fall of 1987. As a matter of fact, Duke's concerted effort to buy the services of literary Marxist professors from all over the country has been the subject of a negative article in the July, 1986 *Chronicle of Higher Education* entitled "Duke's Faculty Hiring Spree is Talk of the Literary World." It emphasizes the feeling of many outside commentators that what Duke is doing is trendy, faddish, doctrinaire, academically unsound and rather absurd. One of those commentators thus characterized this development: "The whole situation is a kind of a joke, because on the one hand there's all this high-level talk about politics, but on the other hand what it's really all about is making money. They are the richest Marxists in the country."

I am dwelling on this incident of Marxist literary celebrities perhaps too long, but I have done it with malice aforethought — for I am going to make the point that a disastrous situation may occur and get out of hand as a result of *naivéte* or stupidity more than as a result of a dark conspiracy. The man who has embarked on this snobbish policy of celebrity-hiring is Duke Provost Philip Griffiths, who is not a Marxist, but who just lacks common sense or is easily manipulated. A moment like this, when a policy favoring Marxism becomes an object of ridicule and disaffection even among the majority of the liberal faculty members, is the time for conservatives to act.

Duke University has also become famous for discriminating against conservative speakers. Not only do the invitations show very clearly the bias of the university, but this is an area in which conservative pressure can be most effective. Combatting the entrenched tenured Marxist influence will be an ardous task of long duration, whereas success in achieving a certain balance in invitations is easier to accomplish.

Looking at one year in the life of a great American university, one notices that among the listed speakers, there is not a single Republican, not a single conservative Democrat, not a single Reaganite, not a single right-of-center speaker.

In 1986-1987, the major Speaker's Union invited Robert Mc-Namara, Gary Hart and Miss Makaziwe Mandela. The Public Policy Institute invited Senator Joe Biden; Ralph Nader had a joint invitation from the Political Science Department, the Public Policy Institute, the North Carolina Public Interest Research Group, and from the student government. In addition, the Public Policy Institute invited Mario Cuomo to speak in the spring of 1987 at the request of Senator Terry Sanford. Notice that Sanford, who retired from Duke in 1985, is still trying to exert his influence at Duke by remote control. Cuomo did not accept the invitation. If he had, Duke would have hosted three major Democratic political figures, three Democratic presidential candidates, and not a single Republican contender. The commencement speaker in 1986 was Lee Iacocca, a Democrat, and at that time, thought of as a potential presidential candidate.

Consider this question: Why, if the subject is the Strategic Defense Initiative, do we have to have the Christian pacifist Robert McNamara rather than a Kenneth Adelman or Zbigniew Brzezinski? *Why not have both points of view?* Why is it that only the Iacoccas, the Harts, the Bidens, the Cuomos are being invited, and not the Kemps, the Doles, the DuPonts? Why always a left-wing isolationist Democrat, and never a Republican or a conservative Democrat? Why commit the crime of depriving young men and women of their right to a clash of ideas, which is the basis of all education? Why is this censorship by omission practised all across the board, all the time? It is not a conspiracy; it is something worse: a consensus.

In 1986-1987, there were two Marxist conferences at Duke. In September 1986, the University sponsored a conference of authors and filmmakers from underdeveloped nations whose work was then evaluated by North American critics. The conference was entitled "The Challenge of the Third World Culture" and it was the brainchild of the Chilean leftist Ariel Dorfman, who is a visiting professor at Duke, Professor Charles Bergquist, Director of International Studies at Duke, who is known as a hard-core Marxist, and the previously mentioned Marxist Professor Frederic Jameson, Chairman of the Comparative Literature Program. Another prominent participant was radical poet Dennis Brutus of South Africa.

255

The conference engaged itself in America-bashing and denounced "neo-colonialism." The conference propounded the idea of using art to influence Western public opinion in favor of leftist movements in the Third World. The conference displayed blatant bias by not inviting a single anti-Marxist, anti-leftist. What made matters worse was the fact that the conference received a $10,000 grant from the National Endowment for the Humanities, taxpayer funds. Here are Professor Bergquist's lame excuses for this onesidedness as given to Les Csorba, editor of *Campus Report.*

1. "Most outstanding artists in the Third World are on the left," argued Bergquist. This may or may not be true, but we have in the United States a fabulous writer from Cuba, Armando Valladaras, who could have been invited. Failing that, a North American critic, for example, from the University of Miami, which has a fine Cuban Studies program, could have been invited.

2. Bergquist also contended that "the Conference's intent was a constructive exchange of scholarship rather than political debate. We wanted pluralism but we also wanted agreement on assumptions. Otherwise we end up talking past one another." I do not find this sophistry persuasive.

3. Accuracy in Academia lodged a protest with the NEH for funding this one-sided conference. But Bergquist asserted that the Endowment funds scholarly conferences, with both left and right wing outlooks, but does not require a balance in a single event. Bergquist also averred that Mr. Agresto of the NEH found nothing wrong with the conference. Mr. Agresto, it will be remembered, was under consideration for the position of Chief Archivist at the time, which required Senate confirmation. Perhaps he was inhibited in his response. Perhaps he wanted to placate the leftist Democrats on the confirmation committee.

The second leftist event was the conference held in March 1987, a conference of Marxist scholars from the Southeast in which 100 professors and graduate students participated. The conference was addressed by Malcolm Gillis, the Dean of the Graduate School, who thanked the conference for "helping us to increase the visibility of Marxist programs on this campus." Dr. Gillis, who, *horribile dictu*, is a Republican, added: "When I left this campus 20 years ago, there were very few Marxists here. When I returned in 1984, I saw Marxists in many parts of the social science faculty." I find this enthusiasm from a fellow Republican for a Marxist "scholars" conference rather bizarre.

The conference was organized by the Marxist Educational Press (MEP), based at the Anthropology Department at the University of Minnesota, and by Duke's own Program on Perspectives in Marxism. Professor Alan Zagarell, Professor of Anthropology at Duke, played a major role in organizing the conference. He is the brother of Mike Zagerell, editor of the *People's Daily World*, the official newspaper of the Communist Party, USA.

Both conferences were covered by *Campus Report*. I must admit that I did not even know of this second conference while it was in progress, and I learned of it sometime later from *Campus Report*. This emphasizes the significant role this publication plays in informing faculty of events even on their own campuses.

Were there any positive developments at Duke in 1986-1987? Yes, there were a few. Professor Zagerell was refused tenure at Duke. He protested and claimed persecution on political grounds, but Duke held firm. The commencement speaker was Ted Koppel, who delivered a surprisingly good address echoing Secretary Bennett's major themes, such as the necessity for high standards in education and a return to absolute moral values.

I also want to say in all fairness that the new President of the university, Dr. Keith Brodie, is a well-meaning and reasonable person who is no doubt aware that all is not well on his campus. In his inaugural address he pointed out that it is high time for academics to cease its mindless criticism of business. He also acted decisively to dismantle the shanties on campus but was prevented from continuing this firm policy by the emotionalism of the trustees, who supported the demonstrators. It is doubtful, however, that one individual can accomplish a great deal when he is surrounded by a leftist consensus among the faculty, the major student organizations, and certainly of the administrators, in particular, the provost.

The major event of the year was a referendum to re-establish a Public Interest Research Group (PIRG) chapter on the Duke campus. PIRG was kicked off campus in 1983, thanks to the campaigning of the College Republicans. Of those voting in April 1987, 55% or 1800 undergraduate students, opposed its re-establishment. The voter turnout was 3,285, or 53%, of the undergraduate enrollment.

There was a heavy involvement by the faculty, the student newspaper, and various left-wing student organizations, all of which supported coercive mandatory fees for the PIRG. The speaking invitation to Nader which I mentioned earlier was probably part of this campaign. I find the involvement of the faculty, particularly from the Public Policy Institute and Political Science Department, disturbing. I am old-fashioned enough to believe that this is an issue for students to decide, and faculty should have stayed out of the debate. What is even worse is that the faculty resorted to misrepresentations, if not outright lies, claiming the PIRG is an independent, nonpartisan group when it is obvious that PIRG is a national organization controlled by a professional, non-student staff; that it engages in legislative lobbying, and that it clearly demonstrates an ideological bent. This was the thrust of the decision by Judge Arlin Adams of the Third U.S. Circuit Court of Appeals in New York, in which he said: "These PIRG's are not non-partisan 'public interest' groups, but rather a political entity devoted to the attainment of certain fixed ideological objectives."

The faculty member most involved in supporting PIRG was professor of political science James David Barber, who several years ago won dubious fame by organizing an opposition to the Nixon library at Duke and more recently called for the impeachment of Ronald Reagan. The credit for this victory over PIRG goes to the College Republicans, rather than the faculty or the Administration.

How does one confront such difficulties at Duke? Perhaps a self-examination will extract some general lessons.

I did write letters to the President of the University, to the Provost, and to the Chairman of the Public Policy Institute. I appeared before the Academic Council protesting the invitation to Lee Iacocca as Commencement Speaker due to a lack of balance. I wrote "Dear Colleague" letters to fellow conservative faculty urging them to be vocal. And I did appeal, with some success, to the sense of fairness of some traditional liberals. I worked closely with the College Republicans and helped them with letter- writing campaigns.

What I did not do, and I regret it, was to criticize radical faculty members by name, and in print. The "chilling effect" that prevents criticism of certain leftists because of intimidation, was overpowering. I have promised myself to make amends for this omission in the future. I have started naming names. I feel better for it already.

I should have written more "Letters to the Editor" for reprint in both the student and local newspapers. And I should have contributed short notes to the national press, *Campus Report* and *National Review*. I advise everybody to eschew traditional inhibitions against criticizing fellow academics; the radical left does not deserve such courtesies for it poses too serious a threat to be treated with kid gloves. The best way of dealing with leftist excesses is to bring them into the bright sunlight.

My effectiveness would have been enhanced if a greater number of conservative faculty had supported me. I estimate that there are about 500 faculty in the Humanities and Social Sciences at Duke and that there are about 30 to 40 conservatives among them.

In one way the situation is better now than it was in the 60s; there are conservative students who are willing to take a stand, who write "Letters to the Editor," and who demonstrate both on campus and in the community. They deserve full faculty support.

We should mobilize conservative alumni and parents of conservative students on behalf of academic freedom, fairness and balance. We should suggest that students send copies of the college newspapers to their parents so that they will know what is actually taking place. We must also insist on the creation of a broadly based, campus-wide Committee to Coordinate Invitations to Visiting Speakers so that conservatives are assured that at least a few conservative speakers are invited each year.

We should also draw up a student "Bill of Rights" to help prevent the unfair treatment of students by radical professors. Finally, we should demand affirmative action in hiring faculty who will restore intellectual balance, establish diversity of viewpoints, and provide role models for students who lean toward a conservative philosophy.

Dr. Krynski is Professor of Slavic Languages and Chairman of the Slavic Department at Duke University. A native of Poland, Dr. Krynksi earned a B.A. from the University of Cincinnati and an M.A. in Spanish from Brown University. He also earned an M.A. and Ph.D. in Russian and Polish from Columbia University. Before coming to Duke in 1966, Dr. Krynski taught at the University of Pittsburgh, Kenyon College and Ohio State University. Dr. Krynski is an award winning translator of three major Polish poets and the author of numerous articles on politics, culture and literature in the U.S.S.R. and Eastern Europe.

CHAPTER NINETEEN

THE EDWARD ROZEK CASE:
PROFILE IN ACADEMIC COURAGE
by ANN DONNELLY

To Edward J. Rozek — embattled fighter for free men, free society, and the free university against fascism, Communism, and totalitarian liberalism.

- dedication by Sidney Hook
- Academic Freedom and
Academic Anarchy, (1969)

IN EARLY 1987, *Colorado Review*, a student newspaper at the University of Colorado at Boulder, published the results of an unusual study. Its editor-in-chief, Pat Taylor, researched public voter registration lists in the Boulder County Courthouse to determine the political affiliations of the school's faculty and administrators.

The *Colorado Review* revealed that there were virtually no Republicans among CU's top administrators, and that the overwhelming majority were Democrats. Among the 630-member faculty of the College of Arts and Sciences, only 41 (6%) were Republican. Of those 41, approximately half were scheduled to retire in five years. The data indicated little chance they would be replaced by Republicans since no Republicans had been hired to teach in the College for over ten years. Thirty-three university entities (institutes, departments and the like) had no Republicans at all, including ten of the most important humanities departments (Philosophy, English, Religious Studies, etc.). Even in the schools of Law, Engineering and Business, Republicans were an overwhelmingly outnumbered minority. The Law faculty, for example, included just one Republican teacher among 27 registered Democrats.

Secretary of Education William J. Bennett, who learned of the statistics during a 1987 visit to Boulder, commented: "If the statistics are correct, then you have a *putsch* (purge) of Republicans under way." The statistics were correct. *The Wall Street Journal*, in a July 1987 editorial, branded Boulder's Republicans an "endangered species."

Of the few dozen Republicans remaining of the faculty, only a handful could be considered philosophically conservative. Of that handful, only one professor was a persistent outspoken advocate of conservative beliefs within the academy and the surrounding community. This was Edward Rozek, who has served as a professor of political science at Boulder for over 32 years. Rozek's career provides a unique case study of the forces that have produced the leftward political and philosophical imbalance documented by the *Colorado Review* study.

ROZEK'S EARLY CAREER

A native of Poland, Edward Rozek escaped from his Nazi-occupied country during World War II and, in his early 20s, joined the Polish Tank Brigade under British command. He served as a reconnaissance officer in Montgomery's drive from Normandy across Europe, receiving the Cross of Valor three times, and the Purple Heart four times.

During the war, Rozek demonstrated the strength of will that seemingly enabled him to survive the pressures of his later life as an academic dissenter. After the war, Rozek spent many months in an English hospital. There he recovered from wounds and underwent a series of operations to restore his eyesight which he had lost in a tank explosion.

During the months of blindness, Rozek contemplated his future, finally deciding to emigrate to the United States. He arrived in New York in 1948, without family or financial resources, but determined to gain admission to Harvard University. After working for a year in a dairy and a gas station, Rozek entered Harvard in 1949 and quickly compiled an impressive academic record. In seven years, he earned a B.A. (*magna cum laude* and Phi Beta Kappa), an M.A. and a Ph.D in Soviet studies. He also authored a prize-winning book on allied diplomacy leading up the Yalta Agreements (*Allied Wartime Diplomacy*, 1958, Wiley). Walt Rostow called Rozek's book "a major contribution to modern diplomatic history and a morality tale whose lesson is still to be learned by Americans."

In 1956, Rozek accepted a teaching position in the Department of Political Science at the University of Colorado. In his first two years at Boulder, he was immediately recognized for teaching excellence, as the result of which he received the largest salary increases in his department.

After only one year at Boulder, Rozek's idealistic view of academic life had changed. University affairs were, he found, strongly influenced by politics. The prevailing viewpoint among those in power in Boulder was heavily weighted to the left.

Rozek first learned about the subtle but effective discrimination in 1957 when he was asked to serve as a member of a committee to select speakers for the annual World Affairs Conference, a university-sponsored five-day event. The committee and the event were chaired permanently by Professor of Sociology (now Emeritus) Howard Higman. Higman was one of the campus' most vocal and influential leftists. Hardly a "liberal", Higman once described himself to Rozek and others as a "Stalinist."

Rozek recanted his experiences as a member of Higman's committee:

> Our first task was to select the names of possible speakers who then were to be invited to the conference. Higman asked us all to suggest names. No restrictions or qualifications were imposed. Whenever a person was suggested as a possible speaker, the sponsor had to give a short biographical sketch of the candidate. All members of the committee were free to support or to oppose the candidate. If no vigorous opposition was encountered Higman would then put that name on a piece of paper which he was to keep for the final selection by the committee. Each time the committee met Higman had a new piece of paper, and he obligingly put down as many names as were suggested by the Committee members.

It was not until two months later that it became obvious that Higman would recall for more definite consideration only the names of those who shared his views. As a result of this procedure most of the speakers for the conference were dogmatic 'liberals' who had nothing but contempt for any view but their own. Higman would magnanimously invite four or five speakers (out of eighty or so) who were Republicans, military men, or of a more conservative persuasion, to mask the exceedingly lopsided, left slanted conference."

(In 1986, Higman was still directing the World Affairs Conference, paid for by public funds. A speaker that year, liberal investigative journalist Jonathon Kwitny, afterwards exclaimed: "I didn't know that many leftists existed in the whole country." The next year, Kwitny likened the 1987 event to a "1960's style SDS meeting.")

In 1957, Rozek's convictions impelled him to defend a colleague in a heated political controversy with Higman and friends. It was then that Rozek discovered that a deadly-serious ideological conflict was in progress but that only those on the left were organized for the struggle.

The controversy began when Professor of Sociology William Peterson, serving with Rozek as a member of the World Affairs Conference committee, questioned the wisdom of inviting former Communist Frank Oppenheimer as a speaker, without candidly explaining his background and credentials. Peterson, a former journalist and a registered Democrat, was aware that Oppenheimer had been a member of the Communist Party and that he still adhered to a leftist ideology. Oppenheimer indeed had testified that he had eventually broken with the American Communist movement, not because he disagreed with its goals, but because it didn't pursue them vigorously enough. However, his supporters in Boulder were misrepresenting Oppenheimer as a "liberal", to which Peterson strongly objected.

Oppenheimer's advocates, including Higman, were furious with Peterson for opposing them, though they did not dispute his facts. They proceeded to mount a drive to oust Peterson from the University, by seeing that he was denied tenure. Peterson turned to Rozek for support. Reluctant to take sides at first, since he had a family to support, Rozek inevitably agreed to help Peterson. After a struggle, Peterson was granted tenure but subsequently resigned to take a position at Berkeley. Later Oppenheimer received a permanent teaching position at Boulder and became a member of the "vocal left." (In 1980, the Regents awarded Oppenheimer, a mediocre scientist, the university's Distinguished Service Medal.)

An affidavit submitted by Peterson in 1964 indicated that the controversy had placed Rozek in a dangerous position within the academic community. Peterson wrote:

During the academic year 1957-58, when I was a member of the Department of Sociology at the University of Colorado, I was invited to join the faculty committee that was arranging the annual World Affairs Conference. I found after several meetings that most of the committee's members regarded this event as the personal province of one of my colleagues, Professor Howard Higman, and that he used his dominant influence to slant the program, behind a facade of neutrality, with pro-Communist speakers. I objected to a number of proposals made by him and others and the relations on the committee became somewhat strained. In particular, I objected to the proposal that the committee should invite to speak on campus Frank Oppenheimer. Higman transferred the sharp disagreements from this extracurricular activity to the Sociology Department, which then attempted to block my promotion to tenure rank. There was no pretense that my academic qualities were inadequate.

As a climax of the ensuing events, I was summoned to the office of Jacob Van Ek, then Dean of the college. (Van Ek was Higman's chief supporter). He also did not pretend that my academic work was in any way unsatisfactory, but told me that nevertheless he was determined to get me removed from the faculty. Since it was openly a political struggle, I asked the Dean whether he thought it would be helpful to the University to create headlines that a faculty member of a state university had been dismissed for his anti-Communist stand; and in the following week I received supporting statements from, among others, the American Civil Liberties Union in New York, and Dean Robert Fitch of the Pacific School of Religion in Berkeley, thus reinforcing my suggestion that my dismissal might became something of a *cause celebre*. I hired a lawyer, Mr. Charles Williams of Boulder, to defend me. Eventually I won and was given tenure rank; but in a different sense Higman and his friends won, for I left the University as soon as I could find another post.

While remonstrating with Dean Van Ek, I pointed out to him that he was accepting the word of certain members of the faculty against mine, without any systematic investigation of what had taken place. A few persons on the committee, I pointed out, both supported my point of view and would back my allegations concerning its activities. He invited me to name them. There were not many, for most of the few who agreed with me politically were frankly afraid to say so. There was, however, one member of the committee who had agreed to support me in spite of the danger that an anti-Communist stand might mean for him; and I told the Dean that Professor Edward Rozek would support all my charges and deny the counter charges of Higman and his friends. *Dean Van Ek's reply was that he knew about Rozek, and that after he had gotten rid of me, he would see that Rozek was also taken care of.* (emphasis added)

In 1957, students at Boulder petitioned for a philosophically balanced speakers' program, which due to Higman and others was skewed significantly to the left. Rozek knew from experience that the university-run programs were unlikely to be corrected. Thus, he founded the W. F. Dyde Forum, and later the Institute of Comparative Politics and Ideologies, and the Center for Science, Technology and Political Thought. These programs received only token university support, which was lavished on Higman's conference and other left-leaning programs. Rozek's programs were privately funded by philanthropic individuals and foundations such as the Coors Foundation. Rozek half-jokingly termed his programs "rescue operations" mounted to save students from the one-sided view of issues purveyed by Higman and others.

The Rozek program, over the years, brought to campus hundreds of leading professors from Harvard, Oxford, Cambridge, and many other prestigious institutions of learning. Rozek's guest speakers included eight Nobel laureates. They, and Rozek himself, were out of step with the prevailing liberalism and leftism. They irritated the ruling elite of the campus, typified by Higman, by defending capitalism and American democracy, while speaking factually about the grim history of various totalitarian systems, including Communism.

Though out of step with Van Ek and Higman, Rozek was never out of step with the majority of Boulder's students, who in most cases were seeking a sound education. Each year, Rozek's classes were (and still are) filled to overflowing. Students repeatedly recommended him for teaching awards. He received the Professor of the Year Award and the Distinguished Faculty Member Award. Many of Rozek's students went on to pursue careers in public service, or to become leaders in their communities, citing Rozek as having inspired them. Commonly, these were idealists who came to the university seeking not only scholarship but moral direction. The university's vocal leftists offered them a cynical, narrow, and largely inaccurate view of American society, which led to a philosophical "dead end street." In Rozek, who seemed the embodiment of scholarly decorum, students also found a passionate advocate for democracy and free enterprise. This persuasive combination posed a threat to the university's leftist elite.

During the 1960s, Boulder was a center for violent anti-war and leftist protests. Undeterred by the violence, Rozek continued to speak out as an opponent of Marxism as well as Nazism, and he persisted in bringing to campus speakers who dissented from the norm of the day.

In 1962, the visit to Boulder of Senator Barry Goldwater involved Rozek in a long and particularly bitter controversy with campus leftists. In Rozek's memoirs from the era, he records one of the most turbulent periods in his career as conservative dissenter *par excellence*.

As the spring semester (of 1962) began, the president of the Young Republicans came to my office to ask if I would be their faculty sponsor. Since I was the only Republican among the sixteen member of the Department of Political Science, it was obvious why I was asked. Then Pritchard informed me that the Club had invited Senator Barry Goldwater to speak and he had agreed to come on March 2. Pritchard asked me to introduce the Senator when he came. I replied that, as the President of the Club, he should do so. He insisted, saying he got nervous on the platform. I accepted the invitation to save him strain and embarrassment.

On the day of Goldwater's visit I collected several defaced posters announcing the speech, posters which the Young Republicans had displayed in different places on bulletin boards and elsewhere throughout the University.

There were bitter and sarcastic letters...and more vituperations of the Young People's Socialist League...I felt obliged to check this reckless character assassination. I took three successive issues of the *Colorado Daily*...a sample of the defaced posters, and three Soviet newspapers in which Goldwater was attacked in almost identical terms for possible use during my introduction of the Senator at 4pm.

Goldwater arrived at 3:40pm. After I was introduced to him we went to an adjacent room where I showed him the three Daily issues, the three posters I had with me, and asked him if he would object if I took those rowdies to task. The Senator said it would be all right with him. He was puzzled by the volume and bitterness of the attacks on him.

A few minutes before 4pm, we walked out onto the platform where several hundred people were seated because the auditorium was packed to the brim. When Goldwater entered the room, the audience warmly applauded this dignified man, as if to make up for the rudeness of his shouting detractors.

The program was to be broadcast live by radio, and promptly at four o'clock the Republican State and County chairman were introduced. After that I proceeded with my main task. The majority of the audience was wonderfully responsive. The Young Peoples' Socialist League began to shout and attempted to interrupt me. I had the microphone and never allowed myself to be intimidated.

Before introducing the Senator, I briefly recapitulated what was said in the *Daily* about him and then said, 'We believe that in a free society it is possible to listen to different men. We don't think it is necessary to intimidate them, to smear them. This university invited Norman Thomas to speak and no Young Republican was involved in smearing him, or obstructing him. We had the editor of the *Daily Worker* here, and no Republican made an issue of it. The secretary of Trotsky is coming next week and I urge all Republicans to respect the right of that person to speak here.'

After the Goldwater event, political factions on campus, led by the Young Socialists, erupted in a storm of protest against Rozek, aired at length in the campus newspaper. When word of the attacks on Rozek reached Goldwater, he promptly sent a telegram to Rozek:

Your introduction of me at the meeting last week was one of the most flattering I have ever experienced. I also want to thank you as an American for having so cogently brought to the attention of the students the marked similarity between attacks made by the Socialists at the University and the Communist press. I have nothing but respect for the dedicated service you gave in the cause of freedom in World War II and your carrying on of this crusade in your academic work.

The campus had become intensely politicized against Rozek. Leftist faculty members routinely equated his conservative, anti-Communist views, with Fascism and Nazism. Unfortunately, they influenced students to make the same error. And today that falsehood persists at Boulder, where outspoken conservatives are invariably labeled "Fascists" by vocal campus leftists.

Rozek recorded the following two incidents from the early 1960s, which illustrate the isolation and discrimination he endured during those years:

> Besides the unfair and bitter attack printed against me by the student paper, a number of faculty members criticized me openly in their classes, before their students. Mrs. Nell Wilson, an instructor in freshman English, after discussing me in her class, wrote on the blackboard the titles for their weekly assignment (theme). One of the subjects was 'Who is Dr. Rozek?' A student by the name of David Knop, a freshman called me to ask if I could answer several questions before he wrote a paper about me. I agreed to do so. The following week David was asked by Mrs. Wilson to read his paper. When David mentioned that I had fought in World War II and was wounded four times, Mrs. Wilson interrupted and asked in front of all the students, "on which side did he fight?" Her tone of voice and facial expression were interpreted by David and others to mean that she assumed I had fought on the Nazi or Fascist side. I had never met Mrs. Wilson.

And somewhat later Rozek wrote;

> At about 9:30 one night, the telephone rang. When I answered it, assistant professor Clifton M. Grubbs introduced himself and asked me if I would allow him to publish an article in the *Colorado Daily* entitled "In Defense of Professor Rozek." For a second I thought this was a joke or a trick, but I decided to act as if it were true. I asked him if he realized what might happen to him if he went through with such a plan. He answered that he did, but that he did not mind this and proceeded to explain this reason for his proposed action: 'You know, I am a left-winger, and today I attended a meeting of the American Civil Liberties Union branch in Boulder, where several of our colleagues, professors from the university, were discussing you. At one point they stated, 'we must and we will destroy Rozek.' I was shocked by this pronouncement by professors and members of the ACLU so I asked how they proposed to do that. They replied, 'We will isolate him, drive his students away from him, and destroy him. He will be finished.' I (Grubb) replied, 'You can't do that because before you destroy Rozek you will have to destroy me.' At first they thought I was not serious. I must have been blind before when I thought that these people were interested in civil liberties. From now on you won't be alone on this campus anymore.'

But there was little Grubb could do, and Rozek was largely alone. One day, he found a swastika painted on his doorstep. On another occasion, a faculty colleague confronted him with a Nazi salute. The analogy to Fascism was doubly unjust to Rozek, who had been imprisoned, wounded, and blinded by the Nazis, and whose face permanently bore the marks of Nazi shrapnel. Rozek's wife was warned to keep a close watch on the couple's two school-age children. One day, one of the two boys reported in tears to his parents that his schoolmates had called his father "informer." Later, when Rozek brought these painful incidents to the attention of CU President Quigg Newton, Newton publicly referred to Rozek as "paranoid." That it was Newton who was in error was indicated by Howard Higman's revealing statement in 1984 to the *Boulder Daily Camera*. Higman stated "those in opposition to his (Rozek's) politics have sought to stomp him out." As a member of the leftist establishment, Higman was in a position to speak authoritatively.

Though Rozek received little support from the university administration, he rarely lacked for defenders among his students, and former students. Over the years, Rozek's student advocates included both Republicans and Democrats. Their letters to various newspapers revealed that they had in common a strong sense of justice. One of the most articulate was former Miss America Marilyn Van Derbur (now Mrs. Lawrence Atler of Denver) who had graduated from Boulder Phi Beta Kappa. While at Boulder, Van Derbur had engaged in a highly publicized debate with Howard Higman, who often assailed the CIA and FBI in his "sociology" lectures. In 1962, Van Derbur, who was by then pursuing her career in New York, wrote to *The Rocky Mountain News* to defend her former professor, Rozek:

> Two years ago, when I was a senior at the University of Colorado, I had the rare privilege — and I consider it such — of studying with Dr. Rozek. He epitomizes to me what an American professor should be. I feel very deeply that Dr. Rozek's value to the university is inestimable and I have been shocked at the unfair and unprofessional attacks made against him by students, professors, and the administration. He is fighting for what so many of us believe in, but I'm sure none of us could ever begin to sympathize with him enough to be able to realize what a lonely battle it is for him at the university.

The controversy surrounding Rozek after Goldwater's speech was mild compared to the violence that met a later guest, Professor S.I. Hayakawa, who visited Boulder in March, 1969. Hayakawa, a distinguished semanticist, had recently been named President of San Francisco State University, where he had directly confronted lawless political factions similar to those on the Boulder campus.

The Hayakawa visit materialized after Rozek asked Boulder SDS (Student for a Democratic Society) member Jon Hillson if he believed in free speech strongly enough to support a speaking invitation to Hayakawa. Hillson agreed, provided

Rozek would invite a prominent Black Panther spokesman. They had a deal.

On the night of Hayakawa's speech in Boulder, Rozek began his introduction with the proclamation: "Welcome to the free marketplace of ideas." But the melee that followed indicated that the marketplace was far from free. In the auditorium (which was packed with over 3000 people), some 300 agitators were waiting to prevent Hayakawa from speaking. They began a noisy, violent demonstration, but they could intimidate neither Hayakawa nor Rozek. Metal chairs and bottles were hurled at the podium, narrowly missing the two professors. On this and other occasions, Rozek's students were given a vivid lesson in the distinction between democracy and mob rule.

In 1967, the Regents conducted an inquiry into allegations of discrimination against conservatives. They appointed a three man committee of independent scholars, known as the Dawson Commission, which consisted of a former Chief Justice of Colorado, a former president of Colorado School of Mines, and the president of Colorado Women's College.

Testifying before the Commission was professor of political science Frank Darling, who had a reputation as a brilliant scholar and teacher:

> The group which is promoting bad tenure practises...call them-selves 'the liberals'...these people tend toward a pacifistic point of view. With few exceptions, they are the least productive faculty members in scholarly publishing and research. They tend to be more interested in promoting their own political ideologies than in genuine education."

The Dawson Commission concluded that abuses of the academic freedom of conservatives *were* occuring but the university took no corrective measures. Realizing that no changes were forthcoming, Darling left the university in disgust to take another teaching position. He was one of a number of scholars who were unable to stomach Boulder's intolerance of their views. The departure of such professors accentuated the leftward tilt of faculty and administration that in 1987 would be documented by *Colorado Review*. Of the outspoken dissenters, only Rozek remained.

In 1969, American philosopher Sidney Hook, a social Democrat, devoted a chapter of his book *Academic Freedom and Academic Anarchy* to problems at Boulder. Conservatives, he wrote, were discriminated against by the administration "delaying their promotions, denying them salary increases commensurate with their achievements while rewarding colleagues disproportionately whose political views were more acceptable — and subjecting them to the galling tyrannies of academic vindictiveness."

To Boulder's leftists, Sidney Hook was a pariah, because he had abandoned his former pro-Marxist activism as soon as the brutality of the Soviet Union was revealed, hence becoming one of the most tireless anti-Soviet critics. Furthermore, Hook was one of the few liberals who championed the rights of conservatives to teach according to their beliefs.

One day, a research assistant to Joseph Cohen, Director of Boulder's honors program, came to Rozek highly agitated and obviously terrified. The assistant whispered that it had been learned that she was a former student and disciple of Sidney Hook. Cohen and his friends had said: "that filthy name (Hook) must never be mentioned in this office." When Rozek asked the assistant why, she told him "because he is opposed to Communism. If he were a Republican or a Democrat they would or could call him a Fascist. But he is a genuine socialist and they could not very well explain to those who had previously been told that only Fascists opposed Communism why Professor Hook opposed it also." The assistant stated that now that they had identifed her as an intellectual disciple and admirer of Hook, she was in danger and she kept repeating that she was very much afraid.

Rozek brought Sidney Hook to Boulder to speak the following year. Another of Hook's admirers, a student, drove him to the airport after the speech. The next day, the student found his gas tank filled with sugar and the engine of his car ruined. In 1984, Hook wrote to the *Boulder Daily Camera*, arguing that Rozek "ought to be respected and even treasured in the community. Yet there has been a consistent campaign against him. I have observed with astonishment the way in which he is a target."

One of the most famous of all historians of the Soviet Union, Bertram Wolfe, was a frequent visiting scholar at Rozek's Institute of Comparative Politics and Ideologies. Wolfe's visits to Boulder began in 1967 and continued until his death in 1977. Early in the century, Wolfe was himself an active participant in the American Communist movement. In the 1920s, he traveled to the Soviet Union and became acquainted with Stalin, Trotsky, Bukharin, and the other leading figures in the revolution. In 1928, Stalin expelled him and he returned to the United States. Wolfe eventually broke with Communism after Stalin concluded his pact with Hitler during World War II.

Wolfe's writings on the Soviet Union brought him invitations to teach at Oxford, Harvard, Stanford, Berkeley and other leading institutions. At the University of California, he was a Distinguished Visiting Professor and received an honorary doctorate.

Wolfe called Rozek a "genuine hero." Wolfe added that Rozek "has remained consistent in his dedication to freedom and has never missed an opportunity to oppose those endangering freedom. Rozek's civic courage is much more difficult than courage on the battlefield because it must be sustained over a much longer period of time against a shadowy enemy."

In the 1970's, violence on campus subsided, but the discrimination against Rozek did not. His salary increases, which early in his career had reflected his outstanding teaching, were kept to a minimum. When he protested, he was told to take his complaints through the appropriate channels. Presenting his academic record to the university's Affirmative Action Committee, Rozek received a favorable ruling. The committee recommended that his salary be raised $5000. But even after the Regents concurred with the recommendation, no adjustment was made. Rozek is currently the second lowest paid senior faculty member in his department, in terms of percentage increase in a ten year period. When he pointed this out to the Regents again in 1987, he was again told to take the matter through official channels, which for this outspoken conservative seemed to lead in a circle. In this case, Rozek would have been obliged to take his appeal before the university's Committee on Privilege and Tenure. That committee is currently chaired by an outspoken supporter of Soviet backed causes, Associate Professor Joel Edelstein. Rozek did not pursue the appeal believing such an effort fruitless.

Rozek's comparatively low salary in his department is puzzling considering his outstanding record of teaching, publications, and civic contributions. He has long been one of Boulder's acknowledged teachers of great distinction. His writings have maintained the highest standards of scholarship. His book *Allied Wartime Diplomacy* won the National Book Foundation Award in 1960. In 1964, he was co-author with Walt W. Rostow of the book *Dynamics of Soviet Society*. From 1958 to 1966, he was assistant editor of the prestigious *Journal of Central European Affairs*, and he has given hundreds of lectures to his peers in scholarship throughout the world. Within the academic community he is a leading advocate for the hiring of outstanding minority faculty. In effect, there is no area of academic life at which he has not excelled. Rozek never received an explanation for the administration's failure to comply with the recommendation of its own Affirmative Action Committee and of the Board of Regents, that his salary be raised.

In 1980, Colorado conservatives, including Rozek, were astounded by the Board of Regents' approval of two high awards for scholarships to two of the campus' most vocal leftists. They were activists, not scholars. The Regents approved the first-ever Distinguished Professorship for a philosophy professor (now Emeritus) David Hawkins and a Distinguished Service Medal for Physics Professor Frank Oppenheimer. The two men, Hawkins and Oppenheimer, had served together in the American Communist movement prior to taking positions on the Manhattan Project during World War II. After the war, they both obtained tenure at Boulder where they were among the most politically active of the left-leaning faculty members. David Hawkins, by his own testimony, had been an active member of the Communist Party in the early 1940's.

Directly thereafter he went to Los Alamos, where, his background apparently unknown, he served as Official Historian for the Manhattan Project. In the mid-1950's, he obtained a teaching position at Boulder. Over the years, Hawkins advocated a variety of political causes on campus, and was well known as a member of the ruling leftist elite. In 1986, for example, he organized the Boulder campus petition drive, which was largely successful to impose leftist opposition to classified research on the entire CU faculty. Later that year, he helped to organize protests against CIA recruitment, which were then repeated when the university suspended violent protesters. As a result of the opposition of Hawkins and other leftist faculty, the suspensions were lifted. "CU's administration never opposed Hawkins," Rozek has stated.

The 1980 Regent awards to Hawkins and Oppenheimer convinced Rozek of the need to bring the university's favoratism toward the campus left to public attention. Rozek entered the Republican primary for Regent against incumbent Regent David Sunderland, a Colorado Springs real estate developer who had voted for the two awards. The campaign climaxed several days before the September, 1980 primary election with an organized smear campaign against Rozek publicizing a deliberate fabrication — that Rozek had stolen contributions to his privately funded programs.

The well-timed smears, a windfall for Rozek's opponent in the election, are reported (by a reputable and experienced journalist) to have been arranged by a "well known Boulder liberal Democrat." This individual approached several major newspapers before finding a willing outlet for the obviously

272

fabricated story. The willing outlet was the campus newspaper *Colorado Daily*, which was edited by Timothy Lange, a self-proclaimed Communist. (Lange served as editor of the student funded newspaper for over a decade.) *The Daily*, apparently with Lange's full knowledge, printed the false accusations against Rozek, which were then reprinted throughout Colorado.

The success of the attack on Rozek was due in part to the complicity of a woman to whom Rozek was married in December, 1978, shortly after the devastating and sudden death of his wife of twenty six years of happy marriage. Rozek's second wife was Doris Buffett, an attractive, aggressive extrovert who is the sister of Warren Buffett. Doris Buffett became exceedingly vindictive toward Rozek when it became clear soon after their marriage that their lifestyles were ill-matched. Rozek sued for divorce, and the brief and unhappy marriage ended formally in 1980. Buffett, who had claimed to share Rozek's conservative philosophy, then apparently was exploited by his long-time opponents in Boulder in an elaborate and orchestrated scheme to destroy him.

Buffett became increasingly vindictive as the marriage ended. At one point, Rozek recalls that she poisoned fruit trees Rozek and his deceased wife had planted in their Boulder yard in honor of their two sons. On another occasion, Buffett let loose huge rats in Rozek's home, apparently as a reminder of his imprisonment in a rat-infested Nazi prison. Later, she demanded that Rozek hand over to her household items in exchange for personal belongings he cherished, which Buffett had in her possession without Rozek's knowledge or consent. These included photos of his deceased wife's funeral, which could have had no possible usefulness to Buffett.

CLIMAX OF THE CASE

In 1980, Buffett approached the Chairman of the Board of Regents and claimed that Rozek had misappropriated funds from his university programs. (The same fabrication was used several months later by Rozek's political opponents to end his Regent campaign.) The Regents responded to Buffett's charges by conducting a comprehensive investigation of Rozek's entire academic career, without his knowledge. After the investigation was complete, Secretary to the Regents "Bud" Arnold met with Rozek to inform him the investigation had taken place, that no evidence of wrongdoing had been found, and that the matter was closed. Arnold wrote: "the University, as the result of certain accusations, did have its auditors review University records and, as a result of the review, no charges or actions were brought against Professor Rozek as there was not evidence of wrongdoing."

The Regent investigation of 1980, which proved Rozek innocent of any wrongdoing throughout his entire academic career, should have ended the matter. Instead it marked the beginning of an unprecedented ordeal. There has never been any explanation from either the university or the Boulder District Attorney's office as to why a man shown to be innocent was subjected to prolonged and groundless investigations.

On November 7, 1980, Boulder County Judge Rex Scott appointed a special prosecutor in the case, at the request of Boulder District Attorney Alexander Hunter. Hunter did not reveal who filed the original complaint against Rozek. The special prosecutor was Deputy District Attorney in Arapahoe County John A. Topolnicki, an ambitious lawyer. Soon, Topolnicki was joined by the University of Colorado auditor and staff, and university detectives.

Topolnicki's official instructions were to investigate Doris Buffett as well as Rozek but he ignored those instructions, with surprising impunity. Instead, Topolonicki made Buffett an unofficial member of the investigating team. She was given an office next to Topolnicki's to allow her to actively assist in the persecution of her former husband. The four-room suite of offices occupied by Topolnicki and Buffett, which was filled with materials taken from Rozek's offices, was referred to as the "Rozek rooms" by Topolnicki and the other investigators. Doris Buffett, as a member of the investigating team, had access to all the materials Topolnicki had collected.

The Boulder law enforcement establishment, which was headed by District Attorney Alexander Hunter, apparently gave Topolnicki a free hand to do whatever he liked. Buffett's role in Topolnicki's investigation was a standing joke in the District Attorney's office. In 1984, Bob Miller, a Boulder attorney, stated that "some terrible, horrible abuse is going on, and no one seems to care. And its happening right here in hip, liberal Boulder."

In 1981, by which time the investigation of Rozek was well under way, Rozek met for the first time with his defense attorney, Harold A. Haddon. (Haddon later received the 1985 annual award of the Colorado Trial Lawyers Association for his defense of Rozek in the landmark civil-rights case.).

Also present at Rozek's first meeting with Haddon was distinguished attorney from Delaware Charles Maddock, Rozek's trusted friend and legal advisor throughout his ordeal. Rozek asked the two lawyers what action Topolnicki could be expected to take, and what rights Rozek had to defend himself. Haddon, who was familar with Topolnicki's reputation in the Colorado legal profession, presented Rozek with a terrifying prospect, that Topolnicki could arrest Rozek in his classroom, in front of his students.

Rozek later recalled his thoughts as Haddon tried to prepare him for such an eventuality.

Haddon knew that Topolnicki would stop at nothing. When I learned that he could come to search my home in the middle of the night, or appear in my classroom to arrest me as I was lecturing to students, I could not believe such a thing could happen in America. I knew that it happened in Nazi Germany or the Soviet Union, but not in a free country to a person who had not committed any crime.

When my attorney reconfirmed that such a thing was possible and that there was nothing he could do to protect me, my disbelief turned into horror and then into a sense of utter helplessness. Upon reflection, I reconciled myself to such a prospect and accepted it stoically. If such a ghastly thing happened, it would be a reflection not on me but on our legal system which allow a few unscrupulous 'lawmen' to terrorize their victims through abuse of police power.

For more than three years, I lived with the nightmare that I would be arrested in my classroom. I imagined the shock of my students if someone came to put handcuffs on me in front of them. I thought of all those students whom I had tried to inspire, and how their belief in me would be destroyed if they were to witness my arrest. One of the most terrible crimes is to destroy students' trust in a teacher. There are two virtues a teacher must have — honor and self-respect. Once those two virtues are destroyed, a teacher's life has no meaning. What was happening to me was a massive assault on those two prerequisites to effective teaching. I promised myself then that I would go to any lengths to show my students, and my own sons, that the accusations were false.

As an immigrant who arrived in the United States with no financial resources, Rozek often expresses his pride in the accomplishments of his two sons. Jonathon received a degree in Chinese Studies from Harvard. Christopher holds a degree in Classics from Christ Church, Oxford, and a law degree from Duke University.

The University of Colorado, which according to the laws of the Regents (Article 10)* should have protected Rozek, a faculty member, from outside pressures (since he had already been cleared of any wrongdoing), instead actively allied itself

---

*Laws of the Regents, Article X (Academic Freedom): "While (professors) fulfill this responsibility, their efforts should not be subjected to direct or indirect pressures or interference from within the University and the University will resist to the utmost such pressures or interference when exerted from without.

with Buffett and Topolnicki. On August 25, 1981, more than a dozen university officials searched Rozek's offices and home. Beth McParland, Rozek's secretary, later described the searches taking place that particular day.

Dr. Rozek was out of town and I, and his student assistant, were in his university office cleaning the storeroom as I ordinarily do before the fall term starts. Suddenly Topolnicki appeared accompanied by Larry Reisdorff (a university policeman) and a female police officer. Topolnicki served me with a search warrant and asked me, accusingly it seemed, what I was doing in the storeroom. I was treated like a criminal. They searched for about half an hour, and even took samples from our typewriter. Then they demanded that I meet them at the office of the Center (one of Rozek's privately funded programs) in downtown Boulder. But when I got there, it had been sealed by the police. When I arrived for school the next morning our university office was also sealed with pink police notices. I didn't know what to tell students who were arriving for registration.

Also on August 25, while Topolnicki and Reisdorff were searching the university office, they sent a large number of university police officers to search Dr. Rozek's home. The squad cars around the house alarmed his neighbors. Dr. Rozek had offered his home, while he was away, to a visiting scholar, a lady from Poland, Dr. Viktoria Kuna, who was there alone at the time. She had no choice but to let the police officers into his home and allow them to search whatever they wanted. After the search was over, she was quite understandably hysterical. It was hard to explain to her how such a thing was possible.

In all, twenty searches were conducted, none of which revealed any incriminating evidence. In 1982, nonetheless, Topolnicki had brought the FBI and IRS into the investigation. Still no irregularities were found. Despite repeated failure to find supporting evidence, Topolnicki filed 22 felony charges against Rozek (an extraordinary number considering they were later proved to be unfounded), including theft, forgery, and charitable fraud. Topolnicki had brought the combined weight of the university, the city of Boulder, and the Arapahoe County Police, the FBI and the IRS down upon one innocent citizen, Edward Rozek.

It was University of Colorado policeman who, in 1983, hand-cuffed and arrested Rozek. To Rozek, this profoundly painful moment was made all the more agonizing by the fact that officials of the university to which he had dedicated his career brought about his arrest.

Rozek described his arrest.

Topolnicki filed charges against me in the Boulder County Courthouse. All the press and television cameras were there. Topolnicki demanded $10,000 bail even though I had lived in

Boulder for 28 years without committing any crime. The judge, a new Richard Lamm appointee, agreed to the bail. As the press and cameras recorded the scene, two university detectives (one of whom was Larry Reisdorff) put handcuffs on me. The process of booking me went on for an abnormally long time, as Reisdorff stood chatting with the female official who was taking my fingerprints.

After the arrest and booking, Rozek was released. He later recalled that as he arrived home, the weight of the ordeal he had just passed through began to affect him. When Rozek turned on the television, he found that all channels were showing footage of his arrest and of the charges against him. The next morning, the Denver and Boulder newspapers also covered the story.

On the Boulder campus, the vocal advocates of academic freedom for the university's liberals and leftists were pointedly silent as Rozek was taken into custody. Among the groups that remained silent was the Boulder Chapter of the American Civil Liberties Union, members of which twenty years earlier had vowed to destroy Rozek.

Rozek's ordeal lasted four years. Each day, as he would arrive on campus for class (he maintained a heavy teaching load), he would be greeted with the devastating newspaper headlines describing the investigation of him. He would then go into classes where students had read the same headlines. He had been strictly warned not to discuss the case in class. "This was the hardest part — not being able to explain what was happening to my students," he has stated. At about the same time, several dozen of Rozek's most important contributors and friends around the world received anonymous letters stating that he had stolen contributions to his academic programs.

The negative publicity convinced most of Rozek's contributors to withhold funding from his programs. (It seems likely that this was one of the fundamental objectives of the attack on Rozek.) The university also withdrew its token funding. Ironically, then the university objected to the fact that his programs were incurring a deficit.

At the height of Rozek's ordeal, the tragedy claimed a second innocent victim. In June, 1982, his secretary, Beth McParland, was notified that her university position had been eliminated. Convinced that her termination was designed to complete the isolation of Rozek, whom she knew to be innocent, McParland decided to continue as Rozek's secretary. She paid a high price for her convictions. Her university seniority and benefits were gone and her pay was dependent upon the dwindling private contributions.

In February, 1985, McParland authored an article ("The Persecution of Edward Rozek", *National Review*), which has been an important source of information for this case. In August, 1987, McParland was reinstated to her university position [75% salary], following a university investigation.)

The plot against Rozek, as reportedly explained later by one of Topolnicki's assistants, was designed to drive the professor to take his own life. Such an objective would certainly explain the potentially crushing catalog of alleged felonies which Topolnicki assembled in his charges against Rozek. It would also explain the prolonged public humiliation to which Rozek was subjected for a period of four years. But Rozek, a devoutly religious man who had once considered entering the priesthood, was an unlikely candidate for suicide.

During this period, in addition to preparing his legal defense, Rozek undertook extra teaching to cover his mounting legal fees. Though the usual pay for a visiting faculty member to teach such courses was $3000, the university elected to pay Rozek just $135 per course, while paying his "undergraduate" on "student" assistant more than three times as much.

As the case dragged on, Rozek's secretary, Beth McParland, was present during many of the criminal court proceedings. McParland recorded her observations in a December, 1983, letter to Rozek's former student Mindy Franklin:

> Topolnicki, of course, made a royal ass of himself before, during, and after the hearing. In October (1983) Dr. Rozek and I went to see his lawyers in Denver. At that time, Topolnicki offered to plea bargain! Obviously he was worried that his case wouldn't stand up in court. Two days before the preliminary began, Topolnicki again offered a plea bargain. He said that, if Dr. Rozek would plead no contest to one charge of tampering with the evidence (a matter of a phone call amounting to $3.50), all other charges would be dropped and Dr. Rozek would be put on probation for a year. He also said that he had already arranged with the university that, if Dr. Rozek accepted this bargain, the university would not fire him. (It would appear that Topolnicki and the university have acted in concert in this case.) Dr. Rozek turned that offer down, too. He said it was as though he had been charged with first-degree murder, rape and armed robbery and was told that, if he pled no contest to jaywalking, all the other charges would be dropped.
>
> In addition to not having the proper witness roster, Topolnicki had failed to index his material. He entered over 300 documents into evidence over a three-day period, but he could never find what he wanted. Monday morning was taken up with testimony from the former university lawyer, Richard Tharpe, and the university auditor, Hugh Liddle. It is very strange, to say the least, that university officials were so deeply involved in this case. Liddle spent three

years dealing with the (non-university) Center's books as well as the university accounts controlled by Dr. Rozek.

Topolnicki had large charts detailing Dr. Rozek's alleged thefts and embezzlements. At one point during cross examination on the first day, Mr. Haddon asked Liddle just what amounts shown on the charts Dr. Rozek had put into his own pocket. He later asked Reisdorff the same question. In both instances, the answer was that Dr. Rozek had not put a penny into his own pocket.

Tuesday afternoon, the first witness was Gordon Jones who from 1976 until this past summer was the manager of the Adolph Coors Foundation. It came out during his testimony that Topolnicki's investigators had gone to the Coors Foundation last spring and told Mr. Jones that Dr. Rozek had stolen the Coors contribution over several years. They said the same thing to several other contributors, as a result of which some people who had been supporting the Institute for years stopped making donations. Mr. Jones was able to refute Topolnicki's allegations very nicely.

At one point. I went out into the hall for a cigarette. The reporter for *The Rocky Mountain News* came out for the same purpose. The reporters from all the newspapers and from Channel 4 had been hanging around off and on throughout the hearing. Even the reporters, who were so hostile last spring when the charges were filed, had changed their minds about the whole business once they saw Topolnicki in action. The reporter, Chance Connor, was in a state of shock. He said "This whole thing is a farce. I can't understand how it got this far."

After a lengthy and agonizing legal battle for Rozek, all charges against him were dropped. The day after his vindication in court, Rozek received a standing ovation from his students. He had survived a nearly superhuman test of will.

CONCLUSION

The costs of the vendetta had been high, for the victim, and for the taxpayers of Colorado. Rozek was physically and emotionally drained. He had exhausted his financial resources and owed $80,000 in legal fees. Nearly all his friends and contributors had fled. His splendid international reputation had been deliberately tarnished by officials of the university to which he had dedicated his career. Most painfully for Rozek, the teacher par excellence, his character had been falsely and deliberately blackened.

No one knows how much public money the university spent on the persecution of Rozek because, curiously, the Regents have never asked for any accounting of it. Former Regent Joseph Coors (a loyal and principled friend to Rozek throughout the ordeal) has estimated, based upon his familiarity with the Rozek case, that the university may have expended the equivalent of $400,000 on the investigation. It is known to have entailed the misappropriation of thousands of hours of labor and other resources by university auditors, detectives, and attorneys, over a four-year period.

Larry Reisdorff of the CU Police Department admitted to a reporter from the *Boulder Daily Camera* in 1984 that he had spent at least 80% of his time for three years on the investigation of Rozek. This was during a time when the incidents of rape and other crimes on the Boulder campus had tripled. Instead of protecting students, two CU detectives were assigned one night to spy on Rozek in a Boulder restaurant as he entertained historian John Lukacs, one of Rozek's guest speakers. The university's tactics would have embarassed even the late Senator Joseph McCarthy.

In May, 1985, Rozek filed a $10.3 million lawsuit against the university, university officials, Topolnicki, and Buffett, for maliciously prosecuting him and violating his civil and constitutional rights during the four-year ordeal. He is represented in the case by a brilliant and highly principled lawyer, Robert T. McAllister. The case is pending in Federal court.

The civil rights implications of the Rozek case were revealed in a conversation between Rozek and Boulder District Attorney Alex Hunter after the charges against Rozek had been dropped. Rozek asked Hunter who filed the original complaint leading to the appointment of the special prosecutor. Hunter replied "no one." Rozek asked "what, then is the difference between you and Yuri Andropov?" Hunter had no reply. The question of who filed the original complaint is still unanswered.

Hunter further acknowledged that neither he nor Special Prosecutor Topolnicki had the power to compel the university to order its police and auditors to cooperate in the investigation. The logical conclusion is, therefore, that University officials took part in the case willingly, though the Laws of the Regents of the University of Colorado specifically require the university to protect faculty members from the kinds of external pressures and interference directed at Rozek. The university's complicity in the attack on Rozek long after he had been emphatically cleared of wrongdoing could only be interpreted logically as an attempt by parties within the university to rid the academic community of his dissenting views and to discourage others from voicing similar views.

The role of high officials in CU's administration is unexplained. CU auditor Hugh Liddle and detective Larry Reisdorff, who directed the university's investigation, are unlikely to have acted in concert with Topolnicki on their own initiative. It is not known what administrator or administrators ordered or approved their actions. CU president at the time of the attack on Rozek was Arnold Weber, now president of Northwestern University. It can logically be concluded that Weber approved Rozek's persecution. Rozek's memoirs of the period include the following scene involving Weber:

> Shortly after my primary campaign for Regent in 1980, I received word indirectly from a distinguished professor of law that the president of the university Arnold Weber had invited six professors to a dinner at the Red Lion Inn. Among them were well known leftists David Hawkins and Hazel Barnes (a professed Marxist), Hunter Rawlings, and Homer Clark. They had cocktails, a full course dinner with wine and after dinner liqueurs. Then Weber informed them that the reason he had invited them was to ask them which faculty members should be fired. Mine was among the names mentioned. No member of the political science department was present during this strange deliberation of academicians. The only one who did not speak was Homer Clark, who was appalled at Weber's question. A few months later, the vicious investigation of me, in which the university's police and auditors participated, began. Later, at a meeting of faculty that included Hawkins and Rawlings, I confronted them with what had been said on that occasion. They offered no correction or refutation.

Was Edward Rozek the victim of persecution by the legal system and by his academic institution because of his political beliefs? Any reader who remains in doubt should consider the following question: What if, instead of Edward Rozek, the victim of a groundless and humiliating investigation had been a member of the university's favored political left? Would the same abuses have been allowed? Would a Special Prosecutor have been given a free hand by the District Attorney to call down upon an innocent man the forces of three police departments, the IRS, and the FBI? If the target had been a liberal professor, would a Special Prosecutor have been appointed in the first place, in the absence of any formal charges being filed?

Almost without question, in that case, the university would have invoked the Laws of the Regents to justify stepping in to assure that the (liberal/leftist) victim's academic freedom was protected. And in that case, the university assuredly would have successfully resisted the inappropriate use of its auditors, police, and lawyers in an expensive campaign of harassment. For Rozek, however, not even the Bill of Rights, Constitution, and fundamental right to be presumed innocent were sufficient to protect him. His arrest and handcuffing by university police, the sealing of his office, and the search of his home, could have been prevented had he adhered to the liberal/leftist orthodoxy, would have aroused universitywide and then nationwide protests.

On the day in 1984 when all charges against Rozek were dropped, the Boulder courtroom was empty except for Rozek, his attorney (Harold Haddon), the judge, and court stenographers. There were no civil-liberties or affirmative-action advocates, no reporters from the liberal media, no outraged members of "Faculty for Social Responsibility," and no university officials.

As Rozek and Haddon sat waiting for the court proceedings that would clear Rozek of all charges, Haddon expressed his surprise at the virtual silence. "Isn't it ironic," he commented to Rozek, "that when the charges were filed against you, reporters from all the newspapers were here. They smelled the blood on the floor. But when the charges are dismissed, where are they? What irony!" The proceedings were concluded in silence. The silence surrounding the injustice of the Rozek case has prevailed until the present time.

Dr. Donnelly, who now resides in Vancouver, Washington, writes on educational and political issues in addition to persuing her career as a geologist. She holds a B.Sc. in Geology from Stanford, an M.A. in Paleontology from the University of California at Berkeley, and a Ph.D. in Geology from the University of California at Santa Barbara. In 1986, after residing in Colorado for eight years, she became a candidate for a statewide seat on the University of Colorado Board of Regents. Though narrowly defeated in a highly publicized primary election, she brought to public attention the injustice of discrimination against conservatives at the university.

CHAPTER TWENTY

APPEASING THE CENSORS:
A CHRONICLE OF
CAMPUS FREE SPEECH ABUSES
by LES CSORBA, III

Academic freedom was initiated to protect those who held anti-establishment positions. Those who represent the government have more than ample access to the media so that anyone seriously interested can easily find out their position. If opponents choose to disrupt government representatives, it reflects a protest against government policies and not an abridgment of freedom of speech.

- Professor Robert Cherry, Brooklyn College

FREE SPEECH. IT comes, it stays, but sometimes it vanishes for a moment, a generation or indefinitely. It is treasured and it is destroyed. The Hungarian people who rose up against the Soviet puppet regime in Budapest in October of 1956 briefly experienced free speech. It lasted for five wonderful days. Newspapers, some seven or eight new publications, were freely distributed in the streets and on the campuses. Magyar men and women were arguing and debating about how the new government should be structured. There were rallies. And there was much talk of free elections and pulling out of the Warsaw Pact. Free speech was a blessing from God, many thought. And so they fought gallantly for the right, and defended it to the death, as Soviet guns and bullets shot it down. Freedom was gone, again.

Like any other right in a democratic society, freedom of speech is always threatened. History illustrates that the greatest threat to any right or liberty is the man who abuses it — King George III, Hitler, Mussolini, Amin, Castro, Ortega. So how can freedom loving people continue to enjoy this sacred right so that when it has triumphed, it can perpetuate and be maximized for others?

"Those who expect to reap the blessings of freedom must, like men, undergo the fatigue of supporting it," wrote Tom Paine, the radical philosopher in his work *The American Crisis IV*. Yet in the academy, where free speech should be most actively exercised, there is a question that should be more frequently asked: "Do intellectuals and their students, and the university which governs their campus behavior, undergo the fatigue of supporting the rights of those with whom they disagree?" There is much evidence that shows that they do not. There is much evidence that free speech is only free for those who subscribe to a particular orthodoxy or groupthink on college campuses; specifically, a hostility toward the West, America and its allies, its free institutions and its liberties.

Adolfo Calero, a Nicaraguan who is leading men and women, boys and girls, in a fight for precisely this sacred right and other liberties, has experienced the lack of fatigue exhibited by university officials when he has chosen to present his case to the intellectuals of the American academy. And like the Pharisees, whose tolerance for the teachings and message of Jesus Christ became intolerant, the academics have forced Calero away from the podium and away from an opportunity to speak freely time and time again.

On October 2, 1987, Mr. Calero, educated at Notre Dame, traveled to Harvard at the invitation of the Law School's College Republicans to offer his comments on the Arias Peace Plan, the future of the Nicaraguan democratic resistance and the future of freedom and democracy in Central America. A wounded but brave man, Calero had been attacked by radicals at Northwestern University in 1985. His jacket was doused with blood and a Marxist English professor took over the microphone, yelling: "He has no right to speak. He should feel lucky to get out of here alive."

Again, Calero was behind the microphone at an American institution of higher education. As Joseph McNabb, a writer for the *Boston College Observer* put it, "I went to see him. I was going to write about what he had to say. Now I cannot."

As Mr. Calero began to address the packed hall of students and faculty members, a Tufts University senior named Joshua Laub ran down the aisle yelling "Death to the Contras!" He vaulted the podium and attempted to grab Mr. Calero by the throat. The podium and microphone were thrown to the side as Mr. Laub continued to yell and as security officers attempted to restrain him. He was swiftly thrown back, his head hitting the floor, his face bloodied. He was removed, but the damage was already done. Campus officers ushered Calero out of the hall — never to return. Laub was released from police custody on $15 bail.

Calero told me that he insisted that he be allowed to continue. "I was ready to go," he said a week later. But Harvard officials would not permit Mr. Calero to continue his speech. A university offical explained that the audience was to disperse after the Harvard police had informed her that Mr. Calero left the building. But Mr. Calero was just outside the room, waiting to return. "By the time Calero wanted to return, the security at the doors was gone and a speech to a solidly conservative audience," said the Harvard spokeswoman, "would feed off the poor ticket distribution, fostering the idea that the Republicans were trying to exclude liberals." Joesph A. Anderson, president of the Republican group, complained: "She forbade us to return to the podium because she said so many liberals had left." And so Mr. Calero could not return. Freedom of speech again on a college campus was trodden upon.

A courageous Calero told me that he would like to go back to Harvard and to other college campuses to present his point of view. And surely he will be invited to speak. But what will prevent closed minded students and faculty members from attacking Mr. Calero and other conservatives again? Certainly justice will not, especially if those assailants and free speech abusers are punished with minor fines and slapped on the wrist. The fact of the matter is that university administrators, who more frequently today must deal with scenarios such as these, are *appeasing the censors*, fearful of further violence and disruption, but ultimately encouraging, rather than discouraging, the radicals to strike again and again.

Allan Bloom has written that the universal acceptance of "moral relativism" on college campuses has closed the minds of many young Americans. Indeed, the narrowness, the intolerance of these academic philistines and deep thinkers, has closed the minds of many intellectuals on a number of issues, especially with respect to their opposition to U.S. foreign policy in the 1980s. Their minds are made up. They are right, and President Reagan is wrong. Calero is a murderer; Ortega, the people's revolutionary hero. The Sandinistas are the morally legitimate representative of the Nicaraguan people ("we have no business intervening in their affairs") and the "contras" are the immoral, illegitimate voice of the Nicaraguan people. And so, as expected, when Mr.

Calero bravely walks up to the microphone, he is frequently disrupted, and at times, physically attacked.

And while most liberal and conservative academics condemn such behavior, there are some in academia, even well-respected voices, who have difficulty chiming in to show their distaste. Herein lies part of this crisis: dissent about the type of dissent that should be tolerated on college campuses — even though the question is distinctly between non-violent and violent forms of dissent.

In May, 1987, Randall Kennedy, an assistant professor at the Harvard Law School, played Robespierre to campus Jacobins, as columnist Don Feder put it, with an address titled "In Defense of Disrupting Speech by South African Government Officials." The flyer promoting the lecture read, "Hey, Hey...Ho, Ho...Free Speech Has Got To Go." After applauding the blockade of a Harvard talk (such things have a tendency to occur at this leading university these days) by the vice consul of the South African Embassy, Professor Kennedy defended the prevention of the speech on the grounds that "toleration has its limits," the limits being defined, of course, by some logic of his own choosing. When a student asked if the professor would abridge the rights of say, a contra spokesman or a Reagan or Republican secretary of defense, Mr. Kennedy argued that he would not condemn the silencing of them. Certain cabinet officials? Again, he would not condemn the silencing of their talks.

Don Feder asks: "To what lengths can this totalitarian principle be carried? How would he respond if a lecturer in his open session category was beaten or killed during a protest, another questioner asked? 'It's a close call, something I'd have to think deeply about,' the law instructor replied, thereby raising the possibility that he'd countenance murder." Mr. Kennedy is a board member of the Massachusetts Civil Liberties Union.

Other scholarly types such as Professor Robert Cherry of Brooklyn College have let their views be known. Mr. Cherry, who heads the violent International Committee Against Racism on campus, wrote in a letter defending such disruptive campus behavior:

> Academic freedom was initiated to protect those who held anti-establishment positions. Those who represent the government have more than ample access to the media so that anyone seriously interested can easily find out their positions. If opponents choose to disrupt government representatives, it reflects a protest against government policies and not an abridgment of freedom of speech.

One of Mr. Cherry's colleagues at San Diego State University, Tom Weston, a professor of philosophy and also the leader of InCAR on campus, confronted me at a campus lecture I gave in San Diego in 1986 titled the "Dishonesty of the Campus Left." Weston applauded the effort of a professor at Northwestern University who, along with others, prevented Calero from speaking. Weston pledged to do the same at San Diego State University if Calero was invited. But he was not.*

In the fall of 1985, philosopher Sidney Hook of the Hoover Institution at Stanford University said there is no freedom of speech on college campuses for anyone who expresses a point of view disapproved of by a militant minority, especially for speakers who defend American foreign policy. Although Dr. Hook was primarily focusing on such institutions as the University of California, Berkeley, his assertion made in the 40th anniversary of *Commentary* magazine may exaggerate the case — but only slightly. Right-thinking speakers do in fact speak freely on many college campuses. There is civil behavior during these events. But there is certainly no freedom of speech for conservative spokesmen on the large campuses, the Harvards, the Berkeleys, the Northwesterns, etc, where radical groups are actively opposing American foreign policy.

As one who has written extensively on this subject, specifically offering formal and prudent recommendations on the problems of student disorder during testimony before the Scranton Commission on Campus Unrest in July of 1970, and as one who has dedicated much of his academic life to offering solutions to many of the campus threats to academic freedom and free speech, Dr. Hook's point is a compelling one that ought to be addressed by top educators across the country. But it's ignored.

America's top educator, Education Secretary William J. Bennett, recently addressed this question. In return, Mr. Bennett was heavily criticized by other leaders in the academy who tend to play down the problem of campus hooliganism, or ignore it entirely. In a speech before the American Jewish Committee on May 15, 1986, Secretary Bennett pointed out that "instead of promoting tolerance, freedom of inquiry and the acquisition of knowledge, campus radicals nowadays tend to see the university as a kind of fortress at war with society, an arsenal whose principal task

---

*Incidently, in front of me and hundreds of students, Weston explicitly defended the torturous practise known as "necklacing," whereby radical South African blacks fill tires with diesel fuel, drape them around the necks of moderate South African blacks and set them ablaze.

is to raise 'revolutionary consciousness,' frustrate the government, discredit authority and promote a radical transformation of society." Secretary Bennett noted that in recent years a "significant body of opinion on the campuses...openly rejects the democratic ethic."

Irving Kristol of New York University wrote in the *Wall Street Journal* two days later: "When one dares to mention this fact, it always provokes a storm of protest." And it had. Kristol noted that "a gaggle of liberal columnists, journalists, and editorialists ridiculed [Bennett's] assertion..." Others, most notably those educators closest to the academic fortresses and blind to this disturbing development accused the Secretary of Education of "exaggerating." Dr. Ernst Benjamin, General Secretary of the American Association of University Professors (AAUP), said that "radicalism has declined" on the college campuses and has been replaced by a more "conservative ethos." And *New York Times'* education columnist Fred Hechinger wrote on June 17, 1986, "Today's protesters so far are not guilty of the 1960s radicals' often obscene and totalitarian assaults...If there has been some occasional heckling of speakers, why, in a democratic setting, where applause is permitted, should disapproval be outlawed? Only the silencing of speakers should cause alarm." Mr. Hechinger and Dr. Benjamin are ignorant of the reality of academic intolerance, which includes not only the silencing of lecturers but, as we have discussed, physical abuse.

The Secretary of Education pointed to the two famous incidents in 1983 when Ambassador Jeane Kirkpatrick and Defense Secretary Caspar Weinberger were effectively prevented from expressing themselves freely on campuses. At the University of California, Berkeley, where Ambassador Kirkpatrick was invited to deliver the prestigious Jefferson Lecture, members of the pro-Marxist Committee in Solidarity with the People of El Salvador (CISPES) wore black and white death masks and shrieked: "Genocide!" "Imperialism!" and "40,000 dead!" Ambassador Kirkpatrick was forced to leave when protesters began throwing eggs and other foreign objects at her. Ambassador Kirkpatrick's talks have also been disrupted at the University of Washington, the University of Wisconsin and other campuses.

When Secretary Weinberger was invited to give an address to his alma mater, Harvard University, members of the violent Spartacus Youth League, a Trotskyite organization, yelled and screamed, filled water ballons with red dye, and hurled them at the Secretary of Defense, hitting the stage and barely missing the target.

These incidents are certainly not exceptions. They have happened before and continue to happen on college campuses today. In fact, tolerance is a one-way street on many campuses today where fat fees and courteous receptions are offered for leftist speakers such as Angela Davis, Archbishop Desmond Tutu, cartoonist Garry Trudeau, and members of the Communist Sandinista government of Nicaragua and the Communist-led African National Congress. When Yale School Dean Guido Calabresi posted a notice reminding students and faculty members of the right of dissenting voices to be heard on campus, it was ripped down.

Professor Kristol writes that "there is — there always is — a minority of leftwing activists amongst the students. But they would not be nearly as influential as they are if they did not have such substantial faculty support, overt or tacit. And today they are influential. They have, in effect, banished prominent conservative spokesmen from our major university campuses. They accomplish this in the simplest way: by disrupting the meetings where such spokesmen dare to appear."

The key word in professor Kristol's statement is "prominent," especially conservatives who have been influential in the formulation, management and execution of American foreign policy (e.g. Ambassador Jeane Kirkpatrick, Secretary of Defense Caspar Weinberger and former Secretary of State Alexander Haig) and prominent conservative spokesmen on controversial social issues such as pro-life activist Joseph Scheidler. "These students are able to disrupt campus appearances by a Caspar Weinberger or a Henry Kissinger because the faculty refuses to punish their behavior," writes Professor Kristol. As a result, he adds, "prominent conservatives simply decline the occasional invitation that may reach their desks, preferring to avoid a probably humiliating experience.

Why have we witnessed this recent rise of campus censorship from students and faculty members who paradoxically during the sixties allegedly championed the cause of tolerance as they held banners of free speech high in the air at Berkeley, Harvard, Columbia and other such institutions of learning? David Horowitz, a former Marxist who edited *Ramparts* magazine, provides some insight into this question in a June 1986 interview with *The California Review:*

> The history of the left shows that it is committed to dishonest politics. Many of the organizers and hard core activists in these move-

ments have a total — and ultimately totalitarian — agenda." He adds that the New Left "seeks out issues that will appeal to moderates and liberals, but its real strategic intent is to involve large numbers on a single issue and to push them towards a confrontation with the legal system.

In other words, many campus liberals, some undoubtedly sincere, are being duped by the committed radicals into supporting radical causes within the context of a liberal campus agenda. In many cases campus liberals betray the tradition of intellectual tolerance necessary for the proper functioning of a university. Consequently, violent and illiberal tactics are utilized by many young idealists, who reject the democratic ethic while retaining the full support of the liberal community.

One of the top organizers of the anti-apartheid divestiture movement in the University of California system was recently convicted of issuing a bomb threat designed to disrupt a speech by UC President David Gardner. Student-activist Jim Burns revealed to *Campus Report:* "I have been involved in the anti-apartheid protests for the last two years, and out of frustration, due to lack of progress, I took part in this act." Burns, a leading liberal activist who studied at the University of California, Davis, initially denied making the threat, but later admitted to it after police obtained eyewitness reports and fingerprints from the phone Burns used to call in the threat. Burns, who was forced to relinquish his student council seat and who was put on two months' probation (escaping a one-year jail sentence), refused to name his accomplices "out of fear" for his life. Burns and other anti-apartheid activists had reportedly discussed different methods of protest such as damaging the university president's automobile and/or kidnapping the president's daughter, a student at UC Davis. Burns admitted to the possibility that some of the more radical factions on campus might have taken such actions, while others at UC Davis said that such threats were actually issued.

Burns claimed that the bomb threat is "a borderline violent act." He conceded to *Campus Report:* "I have long advocated non-violence...I'm sorry the anti-apartheid movement has come to this point."

In 1985, at the University of California, Davis, after Archbishop Desmond Tutu spoke to an estimated 12,000 students, it was suggested by this writer that the university invite Zulu Chief Gatsha Buthelezi, an apartheid opponent who does not support divestment, to the Davis campus. Although the Zulu chief, who represents some 6 million South African blacks, was in the area at the time, such an invitation was not extended because, as one student government official put it, "there would surely be violence and disruptions." Indeed, when Mr. Buthelizi attempted to speak at Boston University there were disruptions as some students called the Zulu leader a "traitor" and a number of others walked out of the hall chanting "Go home, Gatsha."

Professor Kristol believes that the intolerance of those leftist students, supported by an even more radical faculty, stems from the fact that "universities are living in a time warp, in a kind of self-imposed exile from American realities. A case can be made that many of those students and faculty members who call themselves "liberals" and who participate in the uncivilized behavior noted by Professor Kristol and Mr. Horowitz have divorced themselves from the notion of true classical liberalism, which has historically respected diversity and tolerated dissent.

A liberal education should offer a student a diversity of viewpoints and afford the student the freedom to search for knowledge and truth without disruption — this is the student's right of academic freedom, the freedom to speak and to listen. Unfortunately on many campuses, freedom of speech is nothing more than mere rhetoric, selectively defended by the campus Left for those with whom they agree, while offended for those whose opinions do not mirror their own. This is the popular campus ethos that Sidney Hook described in 1985. (See Appendix A for a partial listing of documented cases of efforts made to silence speakers on college campuses; some successful, others unsuccessful.)

SELF-CENSORSHIP AND THE IMBALANCE OF SPEAKING INVITATIONS

Besides the outright disruption of speeches and the silencing of campus guest lecturers, many conservative speakers are reluctant to accept speaking invitations because of potential violence and the lack of security provided. Dr. Hook has said: "A host of speakers think twice about accepting invitations to speak...and every successful disruption increases the likelihood of the self-censorship on the part of the faculty — not inviting those who may be objectionable to the fascist left." (e.g. It took three years after the incident at UC, Berkeley when Ambassador Kirkpatrick was shouted down for another prominent conservative to be invited to speak on campus.) Professor Kristol argues that disruptions are now relatively uncommon. On the whole, this may be true. Liberal commentators have, as Kristol writes, used "the absence of such episodes as evidence that all is quiet on the campus front." Indeed, Ambassador Kirkpatrick, who has received probably some of the worst treatment from campus radicals, has been able to speak freely on many college campuses in recent years. In 1986, for example, Ambassador Kirkpatrick addressed students at Southern Methodist University, Trinity College, and the College of William and Mary. There isn't, however, much freedom of speech for prominent conservatives on the larger campuses where radical groups such as InCAR, CISPES and the Spartacus Youth League are active in opposing American foreign policy. If Ambassador Kirkpatrick were to speak today, say, at Columbia, Northwestern, Berkeley, Harvard or U.Mass., Amherst, more than likely there would be disruptions and campus disorder. Granted, the chances of such disorder and violence are less than they were in 1983 when Ambassador Kirkpatrick was a more visible player in American foreign policy, but the fact that she remains an influential voice and defender of U.S. foreign policy makes her a target for disruptions on the larger, more volatile campuses. Mr. Jim Keppler of Keppler and Associates, a Washington based firm that represents such speakers as William F. Buckley, John Kenneth Galbraith, Jimmy Carter, Phyllis Schlafly and Charlton Heston, believes that the problem of free speech occurs without regard to ideology. Mr. Keppler blames student governments and university administrations for trying to silence speakers with whom they disagree. Keppler believes that many speakers today, as a result of disruptions, will not accept invitations simply because of the self-censorship that surfaces from having to deal with disruptive campus groups. Self-censorship indeed is a major difficulty that often goes unnoticed. But more significant is the imbalance of invitations that are given out to various speakers on the major college campuses.

At the University of Colorado, Boulder in 1980, Students for a Better America, discovered that 78% of those speakers invited by the student government were of the liberal-left, while only 12% were of the conservative-right. A study by John Carson, a recent law graduate from the University of Colorado and former director of Students for a Better America, analyzed the "balance" of invited speakers during the past five years (1981-1986). The results paralleled those in 1980. During the period between 1980 and 1985, 82% of the speakers hosted by the Cultural Events Board, the service responsible for inviting and hosting speakers at the University of Colorado and which is supported by students' fees and state subsidies, were of the liberal-left. Only six speakers were of the conservative-right, one being former Secretary of State Alexander Haig, whose 1984 speech at the University was violently disrupted. Another, pro-life activist Joseph Scheidler, was shouted down in October of 1985.

The SBA report was sent to the regents and a thousand supporters and alumni, charging the university and the Cultural Events Board with "an ongoing and pervasive bias toward the left end of the political spectrum." As a result, the regents passed a bill creating an oversight committee that will withhold money from the Cultural Events Board until a better balance of speakers is presented at the University of Colorado. If there is no significant change in the balance of speakers, the regents have promised to offer students a check-off system during class registration which would allow the students the option of not paying fees to support CEB programs.

Professor Kristol's point about the lack of commencement invitations to prominent conservatives to "truly major universities" in 1986 is especially significant. In a special ABC Nightline segment on June 27, 1986 on commencement addresses, ABC reported that the top two requested speakers from universities were New York Governor Mario Cuomo with 160 invitations and Lee Iaccoca with 150. Other top invitees included New York Senator Daniel Patrick Moynihan, Rep. William Gray (D-PA), cartoonist Garry Trudeau, comedian Bill Cosby, Faye Wattleton of Planned Parenthood, ABC Nightline host Ted Koppel and William F. Buckley, Jr.

The dearth of conservatives being invited to address graduates is somewhat ironic considering that college students, according to the American Council on Education, are more than ever before identifying themselves as conservatives. And according to Gallup, 61% of students voted Reagan-Bush in 1984. Undoubtedly, Professor Kristol's earlier point about the influence of liberal college faculties has something to do with the imbalance of speakers on the major college campuses — coupled with the influence and energy of the most active politicos on campuses, the student left.

There is no way to measure the effect that these factors have had on the diversity of opinion and academic freedom on the campuses with any sort of precision. One might reasonably say, however, that the radical left, with the help of liberal student governments, the liberal campus press and liberal professors, has effectively succeeded in monopolizing debate on the large college campuses by providing an imbalance of speakers, while issuing threats and using brown-shirt tactics to prevent those with whom they disagree from speaking.

CAMPUS GROUPS REJECTING THE "DEMOCRATIC ETHIC"

Many campus organizations themselves are responsible for the type of violence witnessed on the campuses in recent years. Some student hooligans simply act independently without direction. Others, however, act collectively in deliberate attempts to attract attention to themselves while disrupting speakers. None are more intent on rejecting the democratic ethic of freedom of speech than three organizations active on college campuses nationwide: The International Committee Against Racism (InCAR), the Spartacus Youth League (SYL) and the Committee in Solidarity with the People of El Salvador (CISPES).

InCAR

The International Committee Against Racism, active on the larger campuses across America has openly admitted to advocating violence to prevent appearances by "extremist," "racist" or "imperialistic" speakers. In one flyer distributed on California campuses, InCAR threatened a local conservative organization, stating that it "must be stopped from spreading its racist filth on campus." The organization of conservative and moderate students called CAMPUS (Conservative and Moderate Students at the University of California, Santa Cruz), InCAR writes, "provides forum (sic) for fascist groups like Accuracy in Media and Accuracy in Academia. These groups have links with death squads in Latin America and CIA...We in InCAR say that these are Fascist groups and they must be violently stopped...Fascism cannot be ignored. It cannot be stopped by peaceful picket lines, singing or praying. It must be crushed violently by building multi-racial unity of workers and students. We openly unite with the Communists in the Revolutionary Communist Progressive Labor Party...Join InCAR."

Another InCAR flyer, "NO FREEDOM OF SPEECH FOR FASCISTS," was distributed during the scheduled appearance of J. Michael Waller and a Nicaraguan freedom fighter representative at Wellesley College. It advocated violence to prevent Waller and the freedom fighter from speaking. This flyer boasts of its "successful" effort which "drove Adolfo Calero off the speaking platform" at Northwestern University a year before.

In the spring of 1986, InCAR in Los Angeles issued threats against conservative organizations on campuses in the area. One conservative organization called NEMESIS has received death threats on its telephone answering service, and is offering a reward for any information leading to the arrest and conviction of those responsible. One message called NEMISIS members "Mother F — — - Zionist Jews." In May, UCLA's Associate Dean Robert A. Ringler wrote InCAR about a leaflet which states that "violence" is appropriate when applied towards campus organizations that don't share InCAR's point of view. In the letter, Dean Ringler requested that InCAR representatives meet with him regarding the flyer and alleged death threats against other campus groups.

Besides having students and members of the general public who belong to the organization, InCAR has many faculty participants across the country who lead its activities. At Northwestern University, a self-avowed Marxist English professor, Barbara Foley, responsible for preventing a speech by Calero and yelling that "he'll be lucky to get out of here alive," was disciplined. More recently, because of unruly behavior "unbecoming of a member of a Northwestern University faculty," the administration denied Professor Foley tenure. InCAR held demonstrations during the spring of 1986, demanding that Foley be re-hired.

The San Diego State Chapter of InCAR is led by Professor of Philosophy Tom Weston who explicitly defended the torturous practice known as "necklacing" in South Africa. At Brooklyn College, Professor Robert Cherry heads InCAR.

"SPARTS"

When Secretary of Education William Bennett pointed out in a speech in May of 1986 that some radical campus groups openly reject the democratic ethic of freedom of speech, he may have been referring to the Spartacus Youth League, a Marxist, pro-Soviet organization, which is active on a number of college campuses. Known as the "Sparts," the members of the group have been especially active in recent years denying the right of free speech to anti-Communists invited to speak on campuses across America.

The Spartacus Youth League (SYL) received national attention in November 1983, when the Sparts were blamed by Harvard President Derek Bok for disrupting a Cambridge speech by Secretary of Defense Caspar Weinberger, himself a Harvard graduate. Weinberger was interrupted after every sentence by heckling. According to Elizabeth Green of the *Chronicle of Higher Education,* radical students draped an American flag upside down near signs reading "U.S. Get Your Bloody Hands off the World — Spartacus Youth League" and "Weinberger Equals War Criminal." Also in 1983, the Sparts at the University of California, Berkeley shouted down former UN Ambassador Jeane Kirkpatrick. Again at Berkeley in January 1985, the Sparts encircled a ROTC recruitment table and chanted slogans such as "Recruiters lie, Marines die." According to a *Policy Review* (Spring, 1985) article by David Brock, one SYL member said the group intended to "drive the Marines off campus." The SYL has also opposed CIA recruitment; campus police were called on at the University of Michigan in October 1985 to ensure that Spartacus anti-CIA rallies would not get out of hand. At Ohio State University, the Sparts even heckled a pro-nuclear freeze speaker for not being pro-freeze enough. And in March of 1984, a Spartacus publication, *The Young Spartacus,* ran a headline which read "Drive War Criminals Off Campus!," referring to El Salvadoran ambassador Ernesto Rivas-Gallont, who was about to deliver a speech at the University of California, Los Angeles.

Bob Zirgulis, a U.C.L.A. campus activist with the Young Americans for Freedom, told *Campus Report* that the "Sparts are violent." Zirgulis added, "They've tried to incite violence at our events and have threatened some of our members' lives."

The Spartacus Youth League is an arm of the Spartacist League, which began as a small group of dissidents who broke away from the Socialists Workers Party in 1960, according to Congressional hearings on "Subversive Influences in Riots, Looting, and Burning." Under the leadership of James Robertson, who still leads the "Sparts" today, the League published the first issue of its official publication, *The Sparaticist*, in March 1964. The League grew out of the Revolutionary Marxist Caucus of the Students for a Democratic Society (SDS), according to the *Chronicle of Higher Education.*

The "Sparts" are especially active on larger campuses such as the University of California, Berkeley, Harvard University and Columbia. And although it is the youth branch of the Trotskyite Communist Spartacist League, the League is pro-Soviet. One League flyer states: "We are socialists who stand for defense of the U.S.S.R. against imperialism...We believe that the Red Army is on the right side in Afghanistan. We collected $25,000 to defend the Nicaraguan revolution, and we think Nicaragua should get MIGs to mop up the contra filth.... And we stand with the Cuban troops defending Angola against the South African army and the CIA."

The SYL has hailed the victory of the Vietnamese revolution and has called for a "military victory" for the Communist guerrillas in El Salvador. The parent Spartacist League claims in a flyer to be the only "left tendency which openly supports a victory on the battlefield for the heroic insurgents in El Salvador...The line is drawn in El Salvador. Which side are you on? Down with the Junta, workers to power. Military victory to the Salvadoran Leftists. Defense of Cuba/U.S.S.R begins in El Salvador."

In a flyer distributed at New York University in 1983, the Spartacist League writes: "The only road to peace is through workers' revolution to disarm the capitalists and establish a workers' government as the Bolsheviks did in Russia in 1917."

In the *Workers Vanguard*, another publication of the Spartacist League, an April 27, 1984 headline reads: "Hang Margaret Thatcher" for being an "outright war criminal."

Many of the views of the "Sparts" do not differ from those of a number of other radical campus organizations, such as the Progressive Student Network or the Democratic Socialists of America. Members of these groups, however, object to the League's tactics of expounding on the urgency of a workers' revolution. In the February 12, 1986 issue of the *Chronicle of Higher Education*, the SYL's "disruptive tactics" were described as annoying and frustrating to other student leftists, particularly those involved in the anti-apartheid movement on the campuses.

Kevin Brown, an Oberlin College senior, told the *Chronicle of Higher Education* that "whenever there's a demonstration, [Sparts'] tactics will always be alienating. They have a bull horn and big cardboard signs and speak rhetoric that is inhibiting and alienating to the general campus left."

Elizabeth Greene of the *Chronicle of Higher Education* reported that many campus activists "say the dogmatic nature of Spartacus tactics helps to give the campus left, which is already threatened by a growing conservative trend, a bad name." University of Wisconsin student Kris Pennistan noted that the "Sparts" offered to rally with her group, the Progressive Student Network, against CIA recruiting on campus. But the offer was rejected, said Pennistan, after the League insisted on promoting a pro-Soviet platform. The League's members attended the demonstration anyway, displaying a large sign which read: "Support the Soviet Union."

At Harvard on October 2, 1987, the "Sparts" were reportedly actively disrupting the proceedings before Adolfo Calero was attacked. According to Joseph McNabb, a student at Boston College who attended the event, members of the League gathered outside to protest the event. While some members chanted outside, said McNabb, other "members of its ranks scaled the walls to scream in the windows and disrupt the proceedings in any manner they could."

They began their chants with "Protect the Soviet Workers' State," and later chanted "Hey, Hey, One, Two, Three. Overthrow the bourgeoisie."

CISPES

The Committee in Solidarity with the People of El Salvador is probably the most well-organized and well-financed of the radical campus groups on the left. Although supporters do not openly admit to advocating violence and disruptions on campuses as InCAR does, many have stormed administration offices, urinating in office plants, turning over filing cabinets and ripping telephone jacks out of the walls, according to J.Michael Waller who has written a report on CISPES. Many have been arrested for disrupting campus speakers, including former Secretary of State Henry Kissinger at the University of Texas and Ambassador Kirkpatrick at Berkeley.

CISPES has provoked fights at places such as American University, where CISPES supporters screamed at and threatened a Catholic priest, a U.S. Congressman and the Salvadoran Ambassador to the United States. At the University of Colorado, Boulder, CISPES radicals attempted to assault former Secretary of State Alexander Haig by throwing a container of blood at him. Founded in 1980 with the assistance of Cuban Intelligence officers and Communist Party members, CISPES is the nation's largest "US out of El Salvador" organization. It claims between 350 and 400 local chapters, mostly on college campuses. CISPES was founded and now functions as a propaganda support apparatus for the FMLN-FDR guerrillas in El Salvador. Its stated goal is to "defend the Sandinista revolution." The FMLN claimed responsiblity for the killing of four American Marines at a sidewalk cafe in San Salvador in the summer of 1985. And the FMLN expressed "happiness" over the space shuttle Challenger disaster because two of the astronauts were "war criminals."*

---

*A report on CISPES by J. Michael Waller of the Council for Inter-American Security, which reveals that CISPES was established by the founder of the El Salvadoran Communist Party, has been used as evidence by the Attorney General's office to decide whether or not CISPES should be forced to register as an agent for a foreign government. CISPES was also the subject of testimony before the Senate Subcommittee on Security and Terrorism, and some CISPES activists have been reportedly questioned by the FBI for the

Sadly, in almost every free speech abuse that takes place on the campuses today, weak-kneed administrators have been reluctant to enforce campus regulations against disruptions and punish those responsible. Some administrators argue that it is almost impossible to identify those who are responsible for the disruptions, and that to arrest hundreds of protesters would infringe on the rights to "disagree" with the speaker. There is little merit to this argument, since a number of institutions have shown that disruptions can be controlled or prevented by providing adequate security and dealing firmly with the ringleaders, whether they be students or faculty members.

A large part of the problem is that many of the demonstrators and disrupters of the sixties and seventies have become college professors and administrators in the eighties. They are in some cases openly sympathetic with the disrupters. They may encourage or condone their activities. President David Adamany of Wayne State University said in a recent speech before the American Association of University Professors that it was shameful that those who don't condone such activities did not strongly condemn them.

President Adamany said: "The whole nation knows that faculty members, students, academic administrators and some governing boards have in recent years silenced unpopular speakers — especially those on the right. The shame for those of us who are active liberals is that we do not join in a chorus of condemnation of our colleagues when right-leaning speakers are kept off our campuses by threats or silenced by disorder."

organization's alleged involvement in illegal activities, including questioning in relation to the November 1983 bombing in the U.S. Capitol building.

According to the *Dallas Morning News* (April 6, 1986, pg. 1), CISPES was infiltrated by an FBI agent who subsequently described CISPES plans to commit acts of violence against Republican activists, including the President of the United States during the 1984 Republican National Convention in Dallas, Texas.

Four different CISPES officials in Washington were asked about Mr. Waller's report, but no one would discuss the charges leveled against the organization. One spokeswomen did state that she remembered the disruptive incidents cited in this report, but she refused to comment any further.

Although all the groups discussed are active on the larger campuses across the country, it is hard to estimate the membership of these groups. However, the so-called "non-violent" pledge of resistance, a nationwide movement which attempts to involve Americans in pledges to resist further "U.S. intervention in Central America," recently boasted of 80,000 signatures. Signers pledge themselves to engage in civil disobedience activities on the campuses.

Dr. Sidney Hook has similarly criticized the failure of faculty and students who disapprove of this undemocratic and often disruptive behavior to take a public stand against it. He warned that "the most serious threat to the integrity of teaching and learning comes not from the criminal violence of the extremists but from measures of appeasement, of capitulation, adopted in the vain hope of curbing their frenzy."

There is a danger if this situation is not remedied — our institutions of higher learning will graduate a large number of bright students who will be vulnerable to the totalitarian temptation. The spirit of tolerance that has kept this land a bastion of liberty in the face of an impressive expansion of totalitarian power and influence will be seriously undermined. The sad fact is that in the countries that have succumbed to the totalitarian tide since World War II, those who must bear most of the blame are not the unlettered proletariat, but the privileged intelligentsia. This was recognized by the Marxist philosopher, Herbert Marcuse, who concluded that students would have to be the spearhead of any Marxist revolution in the United States, since the workers were too satisfied with the status quo.

Fortunately, the public is slowly recognizing the hypocrisy of those in academia who proclaim their undying devotion to academic freedom and then fall silent when freedom of speech is denied to those with whom they disagree. Accuracy in Academia, through its monthly publication *Campus Report*, is helping to mobilize public sentiment to back freedom of speech for everyone on our college campuses. Public exposure can galvanize public concern. Hopefully, public concern can be turned into public action towards institutions that fail miserably in upholding the free speech rights of its off-campus guests.

Appendices

APPENDIX A

CAMPUS FREE SPEECH ABUSES:
A CASE STUDY
by LES CSORBA, III

WHAT FOLLOWS IS just a partial listing of the attempts made by radical students and professors to silence campus guests on college campuses in recent years. Some of the victims have been either disrupted, disinvited, prevented from finishing their lectures, silenced completely or physically assaulted. Many of these cases listed here were reported in *Appeasing the Censors,* published by Accuracy in Academia in August, 1986.

• According to David Brock in *Policy Review* (Spring, 1985), Duane T. Gish, a proponent of creationism, was shouted down by students and faculty members at the University of California, Berkeley in April of 1982.

• On December 1, 1982, the Harvard Republican Club sponsored a lecture by Major General Thomas K. Turnage, the director of the selective service system. But as General Turnage prepared to speak, according to the *Harvard Salient* (October, 1986), an audience member yelled, "No free speech for fascists!" General Turnage was heckled throughout his lecture, preventing many of the students in the audience from hearing his speech.

• The late Representative Larry MacDonald of Georgia was prevented from making a presentation at American University in Washington D.C in November of 1982, according to the campus paper, *The Eagle* (November 12, 1982). Congressman MacDonald pointed out, amidst the yelling in the room, that "This is an illustration of what would happen if this segment of the population took power."

• Former Black Panther leader Eldridge Cleaver was prevented from delivering a speech at UC Berkeley in May of 1982 according to *Policy Review*. In March, 1983, he was repeatedly disrupted at the University of Minnesota. At the University of Wisconsin, radicals heckled and screamed, drowning him out. Cleaver wrote on the blackboard behind him: "I regret that the totalitarians have deprived us of our constitutional rights to free assembly and free speech. Down with Communism. Long live democracy!"

• Phyllis Schlafly of Eagle Forum, according to *Policy Review*, was jeered and disrupted at an appearence at the University of Iowa in March of 1983. Mrs. Schlafly has received similar treatment on other campuses in recent years.

• According to the *Harvard Salient* (October, 1986), during the Rev. Jerry Falwell's April 25, 1983 speech, audience members burst into chants in an effort to drown out his words. Two hecklers reportedly jumped up in the middle of the lecture and made a determined effort to shout Falwell down. Caleb Nelson of the *Salient* reported that "despite the fact that two protesters physically assaulted police officers, and despite the fact that they and many of their fellows prevented Falwell from effectively expressing his views, neither one was arrested. The administration did nothing to discipline them."

• At Columbia University in November of 1985, *Policy Review* reported that former Nicaraguan freedom fighter Eden Pastora was "systematically disrupted with whistles and shouts. He had to scream to be heard," said one of the Young Social Democrats who sponsored the event.

• In the spring of 1980, the *FPI news service* reported that William F. Buckley, Jr. was scheduled to deliver the Vassar College commencement address, but declined the invitation after he was warned that a large number of students and faculty members did not support his invitation and that he would be shouted down and would risk personal injury.

• In the winter of 1984, *Policy Review* reported that former Secretary of State Alexander Haig was invited to speak at the University of Colorado, Boulder. After a few minutes, General Haig was disrupted by screaming leftist members of the Committee in Solidarity with the People of El Salvador (CISPES) who, during the course of the event, threw a container of blood at him.

• In 1984, UCLA's Center of Latin American Studies Department invited Colonel John Waghelstein to lecture on El Salvador. According to the *FPI news service*, a group of militant students jumped up and down yelling "murderer" and "assassin." Some students apparently yelled that Col. Waghelstein deserved to die like his colleague Commander Albert Shaufelberger had. Cmdr. Shuafelberger was murdered by the Marxist FMLN guerrillas in El Salvador in 1983.

• In October of 1984, several of the American medical students rescued in Grenada were harassed during campus appearances across the country. At UC Davis, *The California*

Aggie (October 26, 1984) reported that medical student and Russian emigre Misha Lanzat was heckled throughout his speech. At Ithaca College, rescued student Ruth Brandau was heckled as she appeared on stage with New York State Assemblyman H. Sam McNeill.

• In March of 1984 at Georgetown University, a speech by Roberto D'Aubuisson, leader of the conservative ARENA party of El Salvador, was cancelled when the university could not provide sufficient security to quell campus disrupters, reported David Brock in *Policy Review*. In December of 1984, when Robert D'Aubuisson did speak at Georgetown, the audience could hardly hear him as protesters shouted and threw themselves in front of television cameras to prevent reporting of the event.

• In April of 1984, according to the National Center for Public Policy Research, speeches of two Central American students, Alvaro Montalvan and Alvaro Baldizon, were disrupted at the University of Massachusetts by a group of some 60 demonstrators who staged a mock guerrilla war with plastic guns. At Amherst College the following day, scheduled talks by Montalvan and Baldizon were canceled due to the violence at the University of Massachusetts. At the State University of New York, Albany, they had not yet reached the auditorium when militants chased them away, yelling "there is a CIA agent, let's hang him...We have guns, do you?"

• In May of 1984, Dr. Henry Kissinger's speech at the University of Texas, Austin, was disrupted by radicals who waved banners and chanted slogans, according to the *Daily Texan* (March 23, 1984). After one radical student who kept interrupting Dr. Kissinger with questions was dragged out of the room, the audience gave Kissinger a standing ovation. Fifty-three persons were arrested and charged with disruptive activity — one of the few examples of campus security acting prudently against campus hooligans.

• Also in the spring of 1984, two spokesman from the Nicaraguan Democratic Resistance (FDN) were violently disrupted at the University of Massachusetts, Amherst, according to *The Minuteman* (June 22, 1986). One member of InCAR threw red pennies at the speakers, while others yelled throughout the presentation. Some of the InCAR protesters toted plastic guns and engaged in war games while the speech continued. When one organizer of the event tried to use the lecture hall's telephone to call security, InCAR members pushed the organizer away from the telephone.

• In December of 1984, student radicals at Brown University repeatedly interrupted a program presented by two CIA representatives, according to *Policy Review*. Students held a "citizen's arrest" and read a list of charges. Similar incidents occured at Tufts University, the University of Massachusetts and the University of Michigan.

• In January of 1985 at UC Berkeley, a large group of radicals encircled a ROTC recruitment table, chanting slogans such as "Recruiters lie, Marines die." According to a member of the Spartacus Youth, the group intended to "drive the Marines off campus," reported *Policy Review*.

• On May 2, 1985, South African Counsel General Abe Hoppenstein was scheduled to speak at Harvard. In the report published by Harvard Commission of Inquiry that subsequently investigated the incident, Director of Police Paul Johnson offered his version. "[The protesters) began to physically prevent [the Hoppenstein party] from entering Lowell House by pushing, shoving, grabbing, and striking at members of the party and the Counsel General himself. It was only with the utmost effort that the police present, together with Conservative Club members, were able to get the party into the antechamber to the Junior Common Room. During the speech, the protesters, according to police officers, "continued to poke, shove, scratch and kick." Even the Dean of Students agreed that some students "sought to shout at close range and to strike the counsel."

• In the spring of 1985, campus preacher Jed Smock, who held a banner supporting President Botha's reforms in South Africa, was tackled, kicked, and beaten by pro-divestment students at the University of California, San Diego. Mr. Smock has been confronted by disrupters on practically all campuses on which he has spoken. He has had eggs thrown at him and has been punched on occasion. Most recently he suffered ·a broken leg after students tackled him at the University of Michigan.

• At Northwestern University in the spring of 1985, Nicaraguan freedom fighter leader Adolfo Calero attempted to speak, but was unable to deliver his presentation when protesters managed to disrupt the meeting. As the widely reported speech was about to begin, students and faculty members rushed the stage and threw a red liquid on Mr. Calero. Others chanted slogans and yelled threats. The microphone was seized by English professor Barbara Foley, a self-described Marxist, who yelled: "He has no right to speak...He should feel lucky to get out of here alive."

• In the fall of 1985, nationally syndicated columnist Allan Brownfeld visited the campus of the University of Wisconsin, Madison, to speak on problems concerning the media. He was met with abusive students who yelled "racist" and "fascist" and who accused him of defending governments which murder children and torture women. Later, it was discovered that the disrupters had held a meeting prior to Mr. Brownfeld's arrival to determine whether or not they would permit him to speak. This time they allowed him to speak, but not without hurling threats and insults.

• In the fall of 1985, anti-AIDS activist Paul Cameron was invited to speak at the University of Massachusetts, Amherst, where angry demonstrators disrupted his speech and threw eggs, according to *The Minuteman*. During the speech, Cameron wore a bullet-proof vest because of earlier threats. Some members of the gay and lesbian community reportedly yelled: Cameron shouldn't be allowed to speak." During the event, 200 out of 600 or so members of the audience turned their backs on Cameron. Many of the demonstrators circled Cameron and attempted to touch him in some sort of symbolic meditation. Each time he tried to speak, the disrupters yelled louder. Cameron attempted to speak over the noise, but many of the disrupters kept unplugging the audio equipment.

• In October of 1985, according to Peter Moons of *The California Review*, Nicaraguan opposition leader Arturo Cruz attempted to speak at the University of California, San Diego, but was drowned out by student radicals who chanted slogans and pounded drums.

• In the winter of 1985 at UC Berkeley, Maranatha Christian ministries reported that they were showing the anti-abortion film, "Silent Scream" when campus hooligans stormed the hall, disrupted the meeting and attempted to destroy the tape.

• In the spring of 1985, Education Secretary William Bennett was scheduled to deliver the commencement address at the University of the Pacific in California. According to a University spokesman, Bennett was disinvited, however, after the university buckled under the threats of student and faculty radicals.

• In October of 1985, Joseph Scheidler of the National Pro-Life Action League was invited to speak at the University of Colorado where he was met with 300 or so protesters who yelled and screamed profanities as he attempted to speak, reported John Carson, the author of a report on the lack of balance of campus speakers at the university. The protesters, mostly feminists, lesbians and members of the CISPES, blamed the conservative group Students for a Better America for the disturbances and accused them of "provoking violence" by inviting this "controversial" speaker. By raising his voice above the yells and chants from the crowd, Mr. Scheidler was able to finish his presentation. Mr. Scheidler's speeches have also been disrupted at the University of Iowa, the University of California, San Francisco and the University of Illinois, Champaign-Urbana.

• At Northwestern University in January of 1986, Accuracy in Media Chairman Reed Irvine addressed a gathering of students and faculty members. After a female student repeatedly interrupted his talk, Mr. Irvine invited her to take the microphone to say what was on her mind. When she demonstrated that she had nothing constructive to say, but refused to surrender the microphone, campus security physically ejected her, permitting Mr. Irvine to finish his talk. The student, a member of InCAR, was later cleared by the university. When conservative students pressed charges against her off campus before a local county court, she was fined and placed on probation.

• In April of 1986, J. Michael Waller of the Council for Inter-American security, and Jorge Rosales, a spokesman for the Nicaraguan Democratic Resistance (FDN), attempted to speak on three Massachusetts campuses. According to a report by the National Center for Public Policy and Research in Washington D.C., they were met with fierce disruption and harassment. At the University of Massachusetts, Amherst, several dozen protesters jeered: "No freedom of speech for fascists." Security was forced to end the event after hundreds of students inside and outside of the hall began getting restless and increased their heckling.

• At Harvard, Waller and Rosales were hustled out of the hall just after arriving, as disrupters stormed the podium, shouting: "Death, death, death to fascists." Rosales was hit in the eye by an egg and knocked to the ground. Waller was hit in the neck with an unknown object. At Wellesley College, outside of Boston, Waller and Rosales were met by disrupters who threw eggs and pig's blood at them. After five minutes of attempting to speak over the loud chants and yells, Waller and Rosales were forced to leave. At Wellesley, campus officials later tried to play down the incident, claiming that Waller and Rosales could have stayed and spoken. According to one Wellesley official, the "level of disruption was reasonable."

• Attorney General Edwin Meese was supposed to deliver a speech at Harvard University in early May 1986, but students and faculty members threatened to present the administration with petitions signed by over half the student body who disapproved of Meese's invitation and planned award, according to the University Professors for Academic Order. The university canceled the original date, but rescheduled the speech.

• In May of 1986, *The Daily Northwestern* (Jan 10, 1986) reported that fourteen members of InCAR at Northwestern University were escorted out of a forum after continously heckling and interrupting a spokesman for the Nicaraguan freedom fighters. Throughout the speech, InCAR members hissed, screamed questions and shouted "Fascists have no right to speak."

• In early November of 1986, *The Richmond Times-Dispatch* (Oct 6, 1986) reported that a Reagan administration official in charge of humanitarian assistance was booed throughout his speech at Duquesne University in Pittsburgh, Pennslyvania. One faculty member was so angered by the decision to allow the official to speak that he quit his job. The political scientist, Rev. Michael Drohan, resigned because, "I took objection to this man who is sponsoring murder in Nicaragua being invited to a Christian institution."

• On November 14, 1986, according to the *Massachusetts Daily Collegian* (Nov 18, 1986), a CIA recruiter was prevented from speaking at an information center by members of the Radical Student Union and other campus activists.

• On November 18, 1986, a number of divestiture activists at Boston University interrupted Zulu Chief Gathsa Buthelezi's address, according to *The Collegian* (Nov 18, 1986). About ten students filed out of the auditorium yelling "go home." Another heckler who shouted "traitor" was ushered out of the room. Buthelezi received a standing ovation when he finished.

• On October 29, 1986, Republican Senatorial candidate Ed Zschau tried to speak at UCLA, but a band of left-wing students shouted him down, according to Young Americans for Freedom. Zschau was forced to cancel his speech.

• In February 1987, according to *The Wall Street Journal*, demonstrators hit former President Gerald Ford with an egg at the University of Michigan, his alma mater.

• On March 3, 1987, about 40 members of Cornell University's Marxist-Leninist Institute and the Committee on U.S Latin American Relations, viciously heckled Jorge Rosales Nicaraguan Democratic Resistance, according to *The Cornell Review* (March, 1987). Rosales could only speak for five minutes. "Cornell Administrators at the event did nothing to maintain order," according to *The Review*. The editorial concluded: "Free speech is fiction at Cornell; it does not exist here. Communists and other left-wing extremists disrupt speech whenever they want to."

• In March of 1987, 14 students at Harvard were arrested after they disrupted the speech of the vice-counsel of the South African embassy, Duke Kent-Brown, according to *The Harvard Crimson* (May 18, 1987). In a letter to the editor, Harvard Mathematics professor Vishwambhar Pati defended the silencing of Duke Kent-Brown, "...there is no provision under U.S. law that guarantees Mr. Brown uninterrupted free speech...Mr. Brown's privilege to air his views from a Harvard podium is hardly a 'right.'"

• On April 16, 1987, Education Secretary William Bennett was continuously interrupted by jeers, hisses and laughter at Smith College, according to the *Collegian* (April 17, 1987).

• In early May of 1987, police at the University of Minnesota arrested three demonstrators who attempted to block an aisle in an auditorium where Vice-President George Bush was speaking, according to the *Chronicle of Higher Education* (May 6, 1987). Despite the continuous heckling and chants of "murderer" and "stop the lies," Bush was able to complete his speech. The disruptions were organized by the Progressive Student Organization and Women Against Military Madness.

APPENDIX B

AMY: A LEFT-WING MICROCOSM
by LES CSORBA,III.

AMY CARTER, THE innocent, freckle-faced little girl who stood at her father's knee when he was President of the United States, is now a self-described "feminist-socialist" torpedo in the arsenal of the America-hating campus left.

Even then, however, we knew that Amy had potential. President Carter himself had spoken of little Amy's concerns about a nuclear holocaust. Now the CIA is the immediate danger.

Amy, 19, is now under the tutelage of Abbie Hoffman, a half-century old relic from the 1960s counter-culture who believes that the CIA must be stopped at all costs. Newspapers around the country recently carried a photograph of Amy staring blankly into a microphone during a court proceeding in which she was charged with illegally protesting CIA recruitment on the campus of the University of Massachusetts at Amherst. Amy was quoted as saying she occupied a university building and blocked police buses trying to take arrested demonstrators away because she "had to."

Amy, who objects to CIA involvement with the Nicaraguan freedom fighters, added: "It's flat wrong to fund the contras." Our involvement, she huffed, "is corrupt from start to finish."

How could it happen? Jimmy and Rosalyn Carter certainly bear blame. But the American academy, which has come under harsh criticism during recent years, must also accept responsibility for how Brown University sophomore Amy Carter is turning out.

After Amy traveled north to this prestigious Ivy League school, she decided that she was not going to become a scholar but an activist. "Graduation is not important to me," she pronounced proudly. So at Brown, where students not too long ago voted to urge the university to store cyanide pills in the event of a nuclear war, Amy was placed on probation for disrupting a board of trustees meeting.

She travelled to Washington and was arrested for her march on the South African embassy. At the anti-CIA protest at

Amherst, Amy joined with the assorted lefties in singing "No Pasaran," a song from the Comintern (Third Communist International) which means "they shall not pass" in Spanish. Then she threw herself in front of buses and, like a banshee, she shrieked, kicked and yelled at police officers who hauled her off for obstruction of justice and disorderly conduct.

Amy Carter typifies the student activist on the left today. While self-righteous politically, Amy and her ilk are terribly misinformed, hypocritical and intellectually lazy. Her type condemn the human rights violations of the racist regime in South Africa, but hardly mention anything about the torture and mass murder in neighboring Marxist Zimbabwe.

There is silence from Amy and the student/faculty divestiture crowd, not only with respect to the huge black opposition to sanctions in South Africa, but also regarding the use of "necklacing" as a means for the Communist-led African National Congress to win power in South Africa. While Amy and the student left condemn "contra atrocities" in Nicaragua, they ignore the Communist Sandinistas' crackdown on the Catholic Church, the persecution of Miskito Indians and the muzzling of *La Prensa*, which was Nicaragua's only opposition paper at the time.

Nobody is suggesting that the CIA does not engage in highly sensitive controversial activities. One of those activities is taking place in the mountains of Afghanistan, where the CIA has been instrumental in helping the Mujaheddin rebels fight against their Soviet invaders who, among other atrocities, drop little toys that blow up in the hands of Afghani children. But Amy argues that the agency is riddled with criminals, the same sort of libel that is printed by Moscow's *Izvestia* or Nicaragua's *La Barricada*.

Amy contends that the CIA and the Reagan administration are the criminals, not her. And so like many campus unintellectuals, Amy has joined the Communist Party USA in calling for the impeachment of the President and the elimination of the CIA from the campuses.

"The worst part of it is that Reagan doesn't even know what's going on and can't get the facts straight. Has there ever been a president this bad? I don't know," she answers for herself. "It's only the second president I remember." The first president, of course, was her father, who helped bring the Communist Sandinistas to power in Nicaragua and who said he didn't know what Soviet Communism was all about until the Soviets invaded Afghanistan.

A court in Massachusetts cleared Amy and her gang of charges of disorderly conduct, sending a destructive message to college students today: If one disagrees with controversial organizations or agencies on the college campuses, one needs only to engage in illegal, disruptive activity to prevent others from pursuing their career choices and exercising their academic freedom.

This article appeared in the San Diego Union *on May 15, 1987 and is reprinted here with permission.*

MARXIST SCHOLARS CONFER
by LES CSORBA, III

EVERY FEW MONTHS or so, Marxist scholars congregate on various American campuses to discuss the status of their progressive academic movement. Last summer (1985), they met at the University of Minnesota, and last fall (1985), they joined together at Central Florida State University. I caught up with these professors at their spring gathering held at the University of Washington in Seattle.

Sponsored by something called the Marxist Educational Press (MEP), these joyous occasions have to represent one of the strangest ironies taking place under the Ivory Tower today. Peering out over the tranquility of American college campuses, these happy Marxist scholars are seldom troubled by images of barbed wire, mass graves, Soviet toys of terror, watchtowers or food lines. Almost nothing can shake them of their cherished assumptions.

In greater numbers than ever before, Marxists, neo-Marxists, quasi-Marxists, and other assorted revolutionaries have crept onto the college campuses — some even into the classrooms. Not too long ago, these advanced thinkers were heard muttering on street corners as they passed out their leaflets and manifestos. As students, many were active in the "make love, not war" movement of the 1960s. Now in the 1980s, they have become college professors.

Joseph Epstein, editor of *American Scholar*, has written recently of this political/academic phenomenon: "It sometimes seems to me quite bizarre the extent to which left-wing ideas, put to rout in electoral politics for the moment, remain entrenched in the university. Marxism, a doctrine discredited among economists around the world, and one that has brought more misery to mankind than any other modern body of ideas, is very much a going concern in American universities."

While many liberal and conservative academics have played down this bizarre development (many for fear of being branded "McCarthyites"), other scholars and literates such Thomas Sowell, Arnold Beichman, Jeffrey Hart, and Irving

Kristol have also reflected upon the ironies of it all. Others, not surprisingly, regard this scholarly miracle as a potential philosophical triumph.

In his report to the 22nd National Convention of the Communist Party, U.S.A. in 1979, party chief Gus Hall saw a bright future on the college campuses where "Marxism-Leninism has emerged as a much greater influence." But the party, he admonished, has not been diligent enough in its efforts. Comrade Hall concluded: "The new central committee must make some decisions and plans that will correct this weakness in our work. If we do not, we are missing an historic opportunity."

Alas, the Marxist academicians have not disappointed their visionary leader. Back in 1934, Joseph Stalin also reminded his party that "education is a weapon, whose effect depends on who holds it in their hands and at whom it is aimed. It is unlikely that the Marxists would ever hold American education entirely in their hands. But to downplay and ignore their campus activities and proposed adventures would be foolish — a form of academic appeasement.

So, this spring, I attended their spring get-together in Seattle. The hosts, the MEP, boasted that some 500 to 600 Marxist professors, peaceniks and members of the Communist Party attended. In one of the seminars on the "cancer" of "Anti-Communism, Anti-Sovietism," one professor shared his experiences as a lecturer in the U.S.S.R., praising the "scholarly freedom in the Soviet Union." Another professor, a Canadian, presented a paper on "Afghanistan as a Linked Issue. Afganistan is better off" since the Soviets sent troops into the country in 1979, said the older professor, praising the Soviets for paving the streets of Kabul.

Another comrade told participants that the "Soviet Union has never exported revolution. It is a beacon of peace." A hand from the crowd shot up in the air. "Did I hear you correctly? The Soviet Union has never exported revolution? " The Marxist scholar replied: "As Communists, we know that the Soviet Union has made mistakes. But basically, we know that the Soviet Union has the correct policies. This notion of oppression in the Soviet Union is nonsense."

Herbert Aptheker, chief theoretician of the Communist Party, U.S.A., and law professor at the University of California, Berkeley, addressed the conference in a "Special Session on Peace," denouncing the United States as the "leading force for war today." Its goal, he huffed, "is to eliminate all socialist nations." He called for the victory of socialism worldwide against the "imperialist forces" through a new era of peaceful

317

coexistence. Mr. Aptheker contended correctly that "Marxism is different from pacificism" and that "there are just wars" that must be fought. He reminded his audience that the "Soviet Union maintains the theory of peaceful coexistence...it is written in their constitution."

In a seminar on "Teaching Marxism," the Marxist participants advocated the use of the classroom to "move the students toward a Marxist direction." University of Washington philosophy professor Ken Clatterbaugh said "If they want the other side, they should watch TV or read the newspapers."

Mr. Clatterbaugh pointed out that in the classroom, "You are sometimes dealing with working students who are being exploited by the bourgeoisie." He added, "I try to encourage students to identify their exploitation."

Mr. Clatterbaugh then excited his fellow travelers when he said: "As a result of the University of Washington hosting this conference, a local alumnus wrote the University out of her will to the tune of $9 million."

Other scholarly workshops included "AIDS: A Marxist perspective," "Marxism and Feminism, A Marxist Approach to Literature," and another on "A Marxist Analysis of the AIDS Hysteria."

The main attraction, however, was Angela Davis, who teaches at San Francisco State and remains a member of the Central Committee of the Communist Party, U.S.A.

Miss Davis urged some 700 listeners to "inject as a constant theme" in the struggle, "a need to bring a swift end to the arms race." She concluded, "if we are committed to the revolutionary transformation of Socialism — the promise of emancipation — then, certainly we can safeguard our planning for future victories."

This column originally appeared in The Washington Times *on July 16, 1986 and is reprinted here with permission.*

CAMPUS BATTLEFIELDS
by THOMAS SOWELL

ACADEMICS ARE IN an uproar over a newly formed organization called Accuracy in Academia. It is a classic case of becoming alarmed about symptoms, after years of ignoring the disease.

The past generation has seen a growing prostitution of the classroom to political crusades — environmentalism, the anti-nuclear movement, the endless other "causes" that engage academics. Almost all these causes are of the political left, just as most academics are of the liberal-left.

It is perfectly legitimate for anyone to believe in any of these causes, but that is very different from saying that a course which appears in the college catalogue as a history of social theories should be turned into a propaganda barrage for nuclear disarmament. As the head of the Accuracy in Academia says: "If you ordered steak in a restaurant and were served liver, you would have a justifiable complaint." Reporting on these and other dishonest practices in colleges is the stated objective of Accuracy in Academia.

The issue is not the philosophy of professors, but whether they behave dishonestly — propagandizing ideas instead of teaching what they claim to be teaching. It there were more diversity of opinion in the "social sciences," perhaps the off-setting biases of different professors would present students with sufficiently varied viewpoints to form their own opinions. Unfortunately, in many "social science" departments, the only diversity is between the moderate left and the far left.

Some leftist professors have even admitted they give students lower grades for disagreeing with Marxism or other leftist visions, because that only shows that the students don't really "understand" these doctrines. Still others say publicly that they see their classrooms as recruiting grounds for ideological disciples and activists.

None of this has aroused serious interest — much less protest — from the faculty, from college presidents, or from media editorialists. What has aroused their anger are efforts to do something about it.

Parents who protest against textbooks undermining the values they have tried to teach their children are accused of "censorship." In many of these books, all the sins that have plagued the human race for thousands of years are depicted as the special depravities of American society. If Americans hold land as a result of the armed conquest of the Indians, that is pictured as something extraordinary in its wickedness — though the sad fact is that this is how most land has been acquired by most nations and most peoples, including the Indians themselves. Yet everything from racism to the horrors of war are treated in some books as if they had been invented in America.

People who believe these ideas have every right to do so, no matter how mistaken they are. But we cannot become so fascinated by one set of rights that we let them override the rights of others. Parents, students, and taxpayers have a right to know what's going on. Accuracy in Academia has no power to do anything more than tell them.

Nothing dire is going to happen to tenured professors, no matter how much they abuse the students' trust and academic standards. But students may learn whose courses are not even about the subjects listed in the catalogue, whose lectures are propaganda, and which teachers grade you according to whether you agree with their political visions.

There is nothing new about published student evaluations of professors and courses. What is new is the need to confront an ever more audacious betrayal of trust and standards. Deep thinkers are worried about the confrontation — not about the cancerous problem that requires it.

HIDING IN THE CAMPUS IVY

A recent story in the *Texas Review*, a student newspaper at the University of Texas, reported the antics of a history professor whose language seemed to come from the sewer — and his politics from *Pravda*.

Although the course was on American history before the Civil War, he devoted a large part of one lecture to denouncing the Star Wars defense system, according to the *Texas Review*. Apparently, this is an ongoing pattern.

The professor's opinions are his own business, but turning his course into an indoctrination center and a stage for juvenile vulgarity is a betrayal of trust. Unfortunately, stories like this are all too common on campuses across the country. Usually the "responsible" college officials see no evil and hear no evil.

Even professors who participate in violent disruptions of campus speakers don't like to do so with impunity, in most cases. Some college presidents or deans may work up the courage to "deplore" such behavior, but if asked what they are going to do about it, they will usually mumble something about the professor's "academic freedom." (Other people's freedom doesn't count.)

Since nothing serious is being done about the continuing degeneration of education into propaganda, what can students and their parents do?

After all, a college education is supposed to develop the student's ability to think and to weigh opposing arguments, not change some party line or be recruited for "causes" by faculty guerrillas and gurus.

Once a student is enrolled in a college where indoctrination has become an accepted norm, his options are limited. But they are not zero. This kind of irresponsible faculty behavior flourishes in the dark. Turn some light on it.

Parents should be told about it. Newspapers should be told about it. If it's a state university, the legislators should know what the taxpayer's money is paying for. Write some letters.

If it is a private college, the alumni whose money supports it should be told. Many of these alumni may still think of the college in terms of their fond memories of a time when the philosophy was: "We're here to teach you how to think, now what to think."

Let them know that those days are long gone. The alumni association needs to understand that Mr. Chips has often been replaced by little propaganda ministers who bring their soapboxes to the classroom.

What good will it do? Well, overnight miracles are unlikely. But the near-hysteria among academics when the organization Accuracy in Academia was formed a couple of years ago is one indication of how much they fear being exposed to the public. This organization has no power to do anything other than publish reports of faculty misconduct.

You, too, can turn over a few rocks and let the public see what is crawling underneath.

An even more effective approach is for students and their parents to look into such things before choosing a college in the first place. That is not as hard as it might seem. You may not be able to pick up subtle biases from reading a college catalogue or from a campus visit. But we are talking about things that are gross.

For example, something like a hundred colleges and universities across the country use a textbook called *A People's History of the United States* by Howard Zinn. It makes no pretense of balance and the crudeness of its anti-American propaganda would embarrass *Pravda*.

If you go to a college bookstore during your campus visit and find this is the textbook used in their history course, that tells you all you need to know. If you can't visit the campus, ask the college to mail you the reading list for American History — and for other courses, such as introductory political science or courses in "women's studies" or various ethnic "studies."

Again, you won't be able to tell subtle biases, but what you are looking for is blatant propaganda. If there is one main textbook and it hammers away with one ideology, then you know the course is a loser. And if most of the "social science" courses are like that, the college is probably a loser.

It's all right if a political science list includes the *Communist Manifesto* — if it also includes *The Federalist Papers* or other viewpoints. But if its a steady diet of Marx, Lenin, Mao, Franz Fanon and the like, then they are not interested in education but in getting followers for some Pied Piper.

If a women's studies course presents the views of Gloria Steinem and Betty Frieden on one side with Midge Decter and Phyllis Schlafly on the other, then they are probably trying to educate students to confront opposing arguments. But if it's all one party line, then it's propaganda time.

Parents, high school teachers and librarians may be able to help students by taking a look at some of the reading lists they collect from the colleges they are considering. It's not necessary to spend a lot of time trying to puzzle out what a course is about. All you are looking for is whether it is gross propaganda.

All too often it is.

Comparison shopping among colleges can make the difference between getting a good education — something that enlarges and enriches our whole understanding of the world — and wasting a lot of time and money on something shallow and dishonest. It can also help to make colleges start to clean up their acts.

STANFORD'S IDEOLOGICAL HOSTILITY

The Hoover Institution has been under siege from the surrounding academic community at Stanford University for longer than the eight years that I have been at Hoover. The first time I saw the Hoover Institution, back in 1972, its shattered plate glass windows were a visible sign of the hostility on campus.

That hostility has taken many other forms over the years. It has now reached a climax with Stanford's recently announced intention to oust the Hoover Institution's director, W. Glenn Campbell, when he turns 65.

This is more than one of those academic tempests in a teapot that does not affect anyone outside the ivy walls. To understand the larger stakes, it is necessary to understand something about the Hoover Institution — and about the growing academic intolerance that Professor Allan Bloom of the University of Chicago has so aptly called "the closing of the American mind."

The Hoover Institution is a think tank with a variety of thinkers in a variety of fields, some on one-year appointment of less, and others who have remained for decades. Among those affiliated with the Hoover Institution in one way or another are four Nobel Prize winners, and perhaps one or two others who should be.

Although a number of Hoover Institution scholars are also professors at leading universities, or have been, there are other Hoover scholars who have never been professors in universities at levels comparable to their own scholarly achievements.

At least one long time Hoover scholar has never been a professor anywhere, despite an international reputation in his field, based on books that have been acclaimed in scholarly journals in the United States and overseas.

Likewise, a very intelligent woman scholar at Hoover has had a terrible time getting her academic career under way elsewhere, despite having a Ph.D., publications and glowing letters of recommendation from professors who are giants in her field. Similar stories could be told of a number of other able Hoover scholars in a number of fields.

Scholars like this, for whom the Hoover Institution has long been a haven, are almost invariable out of step with the liberal-left ideology that increasingly dominates the so-called "social sciences" at most leading universities.

While conservative scholars certainly find a refuge at Hoover that they cannot find at many other places, not all Hoover scholars are conservative. The ideological diversity at Hoover far exceeds that in most academic social science departments which usually range only from the moderate left to the extreme left.

Like Americans in general, Hoover scholars are about evenly divided politically between Democrats and Republicans, except for people like me who hate politics in general.

While not too different in overall political orientation from the country at large, the Hoover Institution stands out like a sore thumb in the left-leaning atmosphere of the Stanford campus, and in the academic world in general. Hence, it is often labeled a "conservative think tank."

The issue is not conservatism, however, the issue is whether the intolerant left, having driven many fine scholars out of the professional ranks to seek refuge at Hoover, shall also be able to destroy that refuge as well.

Two factors have been crucial to the Hoover Institution's ability to achieve national recognition while serving as a sort of intellectual community in exile.

One key factor has been the autonomy that it has had within the Stanford administrative apparatus, so that leftist professors at Stanford cannot block the appointment of people whose ideas threaten their ideological predominance on campus. But what makes this autonomy effective is the Hoover director's willingness to use it, even in the face of the campus hostility around him. That is also why there have been attempts to force him out, long before this latest effort based on his approaching 65th birthday.

For example, although W. Glenn Campbell put the Hoover Institution on the map as a think tank, he has been paid far less than the heads of other think tanks who merely administer organizations that were already well-known before they arrived. That has not forced him out, however, or even inhibited his efforts.

No small part of Mr. Campbell's success has been due to his remarkable ability to raise money. The Hoover Institution's endowment is now about $300 million. While leftists on campus attack Hoover for ideological reasons, pragmatists in the Stanford administration want to get their hands on that money.

They don't need any change in administrative procedures. They need a Hoover director who will cave in and cooperate by handing out more goodies to Stanford professors, as well as giving outsiders more say in Hoover appointments. From long years of experience, they know that Glenn Campbell is not their man.

What is at stake here is not whether one man can be forced to retire. What is at stake is whether we will see another chapter in the sad story of the closing of the American mind.

Thomas Sowell, author of numerous books, including Marxism, Knowledge and Decision, *and* Compassion Versus Guilt, *is a Senior Fellow at the Hoover Institution on War, Revolution and Peace. These columns are reprinted with permission from the Scripps-Howard News Service.*

Index